Paradise of Snakes

. . . A DEMONIC EDEN,
THIS PARADISE OF SNAKES
—*Nostromo*

Paradise of Snakes

AN ARCHETYPAL ANALYSIS
OF CONRAD'S POLITICAL NOVELS

by Claire Rosenfield

THE UNIVERSITY OF CHICAGO PRESS
CHICAGO AND LONDON

The quotations from Conrad's works are reprinted by
permission of J. M. Dent and Sons, Ltd., and of the
trustees of the Conrad estate. The lines by Robert Graves
quoted on page 11 are reprinted by permission of the
poet and of Collins-Knowlton-Wing, Inc.

Library of Congress Catalog Card Number: 67-25522

THE UNIVERSITY OF CHICAGO PRESS, CHICAGO & LONDON
The University of Toronto Press, Toronto 5, Canada

FOR MY MOTHER AND FOR ALMA

Preface

When confronted by the pleasurable task of acknowledging intellectual debts, one often feels that not thanks but apologies are due. Having made the work of others her own, the critic begins to hesitate before the fact that she has shamelessly manipulated the ideas of men she obviously admires. Within the context of our modern world, to distort by practice the concepts of the dead is easier than to reinterpret those of the living; the former presences can merely haunt her dreams. Perhaps Sigmund Freud and Otto Rank would ignore the way their theories sometimes merge with those of C. G. Jung; and Jung, were he alive, would understand why many of his ideas are more palatable to me when filtered through the unifying intelligence of Joseph Campbell.

When I begin to think of my debt to Northrop Frye, confusion overwhelms me. Like all innovators, Frye has been so unjustly and unreasonably abused by critics and scholars alike, that I hesitate to add to his burden by placing in print some analyses that might be used against him. Yet I like to think that I have done exactly what he recommends—absorbed those relevant parts from his inexhaustible suggestiveness into the structure of my discussion, rather than debased his ideas. One of the threads pervading the labyrinths of this book—that myth, when used to order the literature concerned with our level of experience, usually takes an ironic form—is, as all will recognize, his. That his kindness is no less wide than the range of his ideas does, finally, encourage me.

When I attempt to mark precisely my greatest debt—to Albert J. Guerard—I can no longer determine exactly where the debt begins, only that it never ends. Anyone who aspires to publish, secretly covets some manner of critical excellence—though, of course, to admit this is immoderate. Anyone writing a book about Joseph Conrad's novels must approach the task with frustration, since he realizes that the best study of that author's works has already been written. It was in Albert Guerard's classes at Harvard that I first joined the Conradian fellowship; I became "one of us," part of an apparently amorphous group temporally spanning several graduate-student generations but actually encompassed within an invisible circle because of our devotion to Conrad and to Guerard. Often the latter must have shuddered before our innocent errors of taste and fact, our blatant egotism, and our fumbling quests for Truth. But his support never wavered; his willingness to admit divergent points of view never faltered. And since the demands of graduate study have been left behind, I have had no reason to modify the judgments of the past: the man who was—and is—the most conscientious of teachers is still the most tolerant of critics and the most generous of friends.

A much shorter version of my chapter on *Nostromo* appeared in *Texas Studies in Literature and Language*; I am grateful to be allowed to reprint it here. The Rutgers Research Council provided funds for typing part of the manuscript, and I am happy to acknowledge their support. Although most of this book was written before I received a grant from the American Council of Learned Societies to study at the Center for Advanced Study in the Behavioral Sciences, my year there enabled me to correct my littérateur's-eye view of anthropology and, hence, saved me from many egregious assumptions about myth. Ralph Tyler, the Center's director, and Preston Cutler and Jane Kielsmeier deserve endless tributes (and endless books) for making that "magic mountain" as much like a Platonic ideal of the community of scholars as is possible in this imperfect world. To Miriam Gallagher and Joan Warmbrunn, also of the Center, go my thanks for extensive, competent, and sensitive criticism and efficient typing, respectively. Helen Tierney of Pittsfield, Massachusetts, also performed effortlessly when sent pages of manuscript for typing, with absurd deadlines.

To over-fastidious readers, my expressing gratitude to an identical twin may sound like self-praise: not only did we share the same personal environment and the same educational background, but we still share the same ideas. Having so often as a child let her bear the responsibility for my actions, I wish I could now say that all this book's virtues are my own; all its faults, hers. Perhaps I have put her name on a separate page to indicate her special "authorship."

Princeton, New Jersey

Contents

Introduction

Emotionally committed to the community of all mankind, Joseph
Conrad dramatized in his work the complete loneliness which an
emphasis upon the private world and the interior journey toward
personal understanding can cause. Cut off from his Polish past by
choice, yet always a foreigner within the country whose literature
his novels enhanced, he could look both with ironic detachment
and with sympathy upon those of his artistic creations that reflected
the insecurity, rootlessness, and anonymity of modern life. But Conrad's Polish heritage and his personal anxieties do not concern me
here. What my methodological study of *Nostromo, The Secret
Agent,* and *Under Western Eyes* attempts to analyze is Conrad's
use of recurrent images, archetypal patterns, in his efforts to communicate. My main interest is how Conrad employed these traditional motifs, specifically how he used the myth of the hero to uni-
versalize a particular vision of reality. Ultimately the question of
authorial intention presents its dragon head to slay, or be slain. An
author's intention becomes as fluid as myth itself during the process
of creation—as countless statements by authors reveal. No matter
what the intention, no matter how firm the conscious purpose, the
creation of a work of art also manifests the unconscious life. It requires the whole man, the irrational as well as the reasonable.

Statements by authors and critics alike reveal how little the
finished product may resemble the author's initial plan and how

much of the actual "planning" takes place within the very moment of creation—or of creative inactivity. One diary of the process of composition is Gide's *Journal of "The Counterfeiters,"* begun on June 17, 1919, and finished on June 9, 1925, with the novel itself. Though unreliable, as Guerard tells us,[1] because intermittently kept and because too brief in its final form, it does reveal a significant truth about intention. As writing proceeded, some "intentions" weakened; major incidents became minor ones; Gide's central subject—originally a devil figure derived from Dostoevsky's *The Possessed*—all but disappeared. As we have Gide's journal, it might be random notes kept by a Hollywood writer for a movie script based on a novel rather than what it is—a presentation of a working novelist's genuine anguish during creation, a revelation of the force of the irrational in rational man.

Moreover, reliable observers have confronted authors with statements of meaning which these same authors have seen "there" only in the final text. Sigmund Freud, who wrote very little literary criticism, and who admitted that analysis must lay down its arms "before the problem of the creative artist,"[2] once presented his friend Stefan Zweig with an interpretation of one of the latter's stories "Four-and-Twenty Hours in a Woman's Life." About this incident Freud says:

> This little masterpiece ostensibly sets out only to show what an irresponsible creature woman is, and to what excesses, surprising even to herself, an unexpected experience may drive her. But the story tells far more than this. If it is subjected to an analytical interpretation, it will be found to represent (without any apologetic intent) something quite different, something universally human, or rather something masculine. And such an interpretation is so extremely obvious that it cannot be resisted. It is characteristic of the nature of artistic creation that the author, who is a personal friend of mine, was able to assure me, when I asked him, that the interpretation which I put to him had been completely strange to his knowledge and intention, although some of the details woven into the narrative seemed expressly designed to give a clue to the hidden secret.[3]

---

[1] Albert J. Guerard, *André Gide* (Cambridge, Mass., 1951), pp. 149–50.

[2] Sigmund Freud, "Dostoevsky and Parricide," *Collected Papers*, ed. James Strachey, International Psycho-Analytical Library, No. 37 (5 vols.; New York, 1959), V, 222.

[3] *Ibid.*, p. 239.

Zweig's story is about a young man's mania for gambling and an older woman's unsuccessful attempt to save him from self-destruction. Ironically, its author, well-aware of the intellectual currents of his place and day, had previously written a study of Dostoevsky and that genius's own neuroticism and self-destructive tendencies as they were particularly manifested in compulsive gambling.

Possessing a mastery of formal techniques, enormous learning, and an almost over-rational concern for the irrational, Thomas Mann perhaps too readily admits the possibility of any number of interpretations which the author has not planned. In an essay concerning his writing of *The Magic Mountain*,[4] he tells how he read a manuscript by a then unknown young student at Harvard University, Howard Nemerov, a dissertation called "The Quester Hero. Myth and Universal Symbol in the Works of Thomas Mann." In this archetypal study Nemerov places Hans Castorp in a tradition which is "not only German but universal."[5] After two paragraphs summarizing the dissertation, Mann writes, "Young Nemerov's is a most able and charming commentary. I have used it to help me instruct you—and myself—about my novel, this late, complicated, conscious and yet unconscious link in a great tradition."[6] If Mann wrote this with tongue in cheek, the final irony is that his then condescending statements are more than half-true.

Moreover, the artist does not write in a vacuum but as part of a social order within historical time. He must communicate to other men, or he has no valid existence as an individual creator. It is because the artist employs typical images and forms derived from his reading, from his experience both as a man and as a recipient of cultural patterns and values, that he can make artifice viable. So in its structures as well as its substance "all art is equally conventionalized."[7] As Northrop Frye points out, "Poetry can only be made out of other poems; novels out of other novels. Literature shapes itself,

---

[4] Thomas Mann, "The Making of *The Magic Mountain*," *Atlantic Monthly*, January, 1953, pp. 41–45.

[5] *Ibid.*, p. 45.

[6] *Ibid.*

[7] Northrop Frye, "Ethical Criticism: Theory of Symbols," *Anatomy of Criticism* (Princeton, N.J., 1957), p. 96.

and is not shaped externally: The *forms* of literature can no more exist outside literature than the forms of sonata and fugue and rondo can exist outside music."[8] Surely Conrad's allusions to common Hebraic-Christian motifs were consciously employed—the Bible being a part of his cultural heritage. Surely, if only on the fringes of his consciousness, he was aware of the patterns of classical story, that there were similarities in the narratives of traditional heroes. How he manipulated these facts that he had inherited constitutes his originality, his independent genius.

The harder task is to justify the critic's method—to show how these archetypes, these "primordial images," these "associative clusters . . . which are communicable because a large number of people in a given culture happen to be familiar with them,"[9] function in a work of fiction. Certainly the archetypal critic approaching an epic like the *Iliad* or *Paradise Lost* will meet with less objection than one approaching a more contemporary author, for both Homer and Milton could not, even if they would, conceal their debts to the past of myth and revelation. In the works of both we have "undisplaced myth, generally concerned with gods or demons, and which take the form of two contrasting worlds of total metaphorical identification, one desirable and the other undesirable. These two worlds are often identified with the existential heavens and hells of the religions contemporary with such literature."[10] In its abstractly mythical worlds, worlds predicated upon a belief in absolute orders having nothing to do with the ways things of the phenomenal world are, the supernatural requires no literary justification. But Joseph Conrad is using a mode, the novel, which results from man's new reliance upon immediate sense experience as opposed to Platonic abstractions or metaphysical speculations. He has moved from a cosmos in which "all meaning was in the group, in the great anonymous forms, none in the self-expressive individual,"[11] to one where the individual has replaced the group as the center of concern. Within the plausible world of Conrad's heroes, gods and demons have lost their privileged roles; what is divine and demonic within human endeavor has be-

---

8 *Ibid.*, p. 97.   9 *Ibid.*, p. 102.   10 *Ibid.*, p. 139.

11 Joseph Campbell, *The Hero with a Thousand Faces* (New York, 1956), p. 388.

come the emphasis for authorial conjecture; reality is endless opposition between morality and desire.

The problem for the archetypal critic is, then, to show how the novel is related to the rest of literature and to the culture in which it participates; to dissect, to analyze, to evaluate, and, ultimately, to unify. In dealing with the specific work he must show how both mythical structures and patterns enable the author to communicate his vision of reality, which is essentially timeless. How do they affect organization, characterization, tone? By what intricate techniques does the novelist subordinate the facts of "undisplaced myth" to his narrative to make them not only plausible but also aesthetically valid? If these patterns can function variously and enrich a text, if they can reveal the novel's relationship to literature as a total construct, then the critic is justified in seeking them.

But these comments have been predicated upon the assumption that the archetypal critic is, indeed, a critic—that his task is to evaluate a work of art as well as to justify artistically the function of typical motifs and mythical movement. This role most critics of criticism wish to deny him. They regard the archetypal critic merely as a collector of images, much as a man may be a collector of butterflies. They see him as a leveller, and they quote Susanne Langer to damn him: "Mrs. Langer points out that the peculiar weakness of Freud's theory as applied to poetics is that it tends to 'put good and bad art on a par, making all art a natural self-expressive function like a dream and "make-believe." ' "[12] They fear that he is flagrantly anarchistic, that he wishes to destroy all previous critical techniques and provide a new dispensation—though he uses the past both of literature and of criticism, though he insists upon the suggestiveness of his insights. Northrop Frye presents *Anatomy of Criticism* "as an interconnected group of suggestions which it is hoped will be of some practical use to critics and students of literature."[13] Even as perceptive, as sympathetic and as recent a critic as Angus Fletcher, wishing to defend the complexity of allegory, accuses the "myth critic" of searching "for certain recurrent archetypal patterns (e.g.,

---

12 William K. Wimsatt, Jr., and Cleanth Brooks, "Myth and Archetype," *Literary Criticism: A Short History* (New York, 1962), p. 714.

13 "Polemical Introduction," *Anatomy of Criticism*, p. 3.

the dragon-slaying myth) at the heart of stories which would present a more complex appearance to another critic who did not think
in terms of archetypes."[14] Thus, books like Joseph Campbell's *The
Hero with a Thousand Faces* are said by Fletcher to "collapse literary distinctions."[15] So antipathetic are some voices that they
"prove" their platitudes by regarding as criticism books that have
nothing to do with that particular genre. In *The Hero with a
Thousand Faces* Joseph Campbell is not claiming the mantle of
critical competence; Jung was a psychologist and, though he was
often extravagant in his utterances, did not claim that the collective
unconscious should measure artistry. Nor is archetypal criticism
synonymous with motif index. If certain novels yield abundant bou-
quets for the study of traditional motifs and ritualized designs while
other novels yield only crab grass, so it is also true that certain poets
(the metaphysicals) are more susceptible than others to the blan-
dishments of the purveyors of paradox. The critic who does not
recognize that he too is eclectic in choosing his evidence, is, at best,
self-deceptive.

What some critics also choose to ignore is that the recognition or
designation of a work of art often depends upon the fashion of the
particular age. General acceptance makes a value judgment "look
objective."[16] By stressing this, by maintaining that "value-judgments
are founded in the study of literature; the study of literature can
never be founded on value-judgments,"[17] Frye has been exposed to
the charge that he believes the critic should not make any value
judgments. What, in fact, he does assert is that "comparative esti-
mates of value are really inferences . . . from critical practice, not
expressed principles guiding its practice."[18] Good taste results from
the "study of literature; its precision results from knowledge but
does not produce knowledge."[19]

---

[14] Angus Fletcher, *Allegory: The Theory of a Symbolic Mode* (Ithaca, N.Y., 1964),
p. 14. Fortunately Mr. Fletcher often means by "allegorical" what I mean by "mythic"
—hardly a coincidence when one considers how much we both owe to the intellectual
achievement of Northrop Frye.

[15] *Ibid.*

[16] Frye, "Polemical Introduction," *Anatomy of Criticism*, p. 20.

[17] *Ibid.*   [18] *Ibid.*, p. 25.   [19] *Ibid.*, p. 27.

Fortunately, the merit of a work of art transcends the vagaries of taste. Shakespeare's plays survived the literary pronouncements of a Rymer because other critics evaluated Shakespeare's works from their experience of all of literature, rather than from the confined perspectives of French neoclassicism. Nor have initiates into the mysteries of criticism failed to marvel at the fact that we praise the metaphysicals for those same ingenuities for which Dr. Johnson damned them. Were I analyzing the separate novels of several authors in a hypothetical study called *The Great Archetypal Tradition*, I would probably seize upon Dickens' *Great Expectations* as a fitting artistic companion for Conrad's *Nostromo*—and in that choice would probably have the wide support of the critical community no matter what persuasion the individual man might espouse. My "taste," if not my methodology, would be vindicated. Yet F. R. Leavis, whose critical stance has a deservedly wide acceptance, has "proved" that *Hard Times* is superior to *Great Expectations*—or, at least, more satisfactory.[20] In each case, analysis is preceded by a prior assumption of aesthetic worth based upon our experiences with literature. But then, having analyzed the particular text of our choice, would either of us really believe that our analytical method alone had established for all time the "superiority" of either one of the Dickens' novels over the other?

Like the writer-in-residence who stresses his own formal and substantive preoccupations in a class of creative writers, so too the critic who views other practitioners through the lenses of his own method. He will insist that the archetypal critic, unlike the New Critic, for example, imposes an artificial meaning upon the text, sees mythic figures behind every fictional tree but ignores the structure of language that builds the novel; that, in other words, the critic who pursues conventional images substitutes his own work for the author's. But that which is true of the scientist is no less true of the critic. As Thomas S. Kuhn reminds us, "What a man sees depends both upon what he looks at and also upon what his previous visual-conceptual experience has taught him to see."[21] Concerned with noting only

---

20 F. R. Leavis, *The Great Tradition* (London, 1948).

21 *The Structure of Scientific Revolutions* (Chicago & London, 1962), p. 112.

what is *there*, the critic forgets that his experience in Western culture, the very language he uses, the books he covets, the precise details he selects to order his "close reading" impose a meaning upon the text he is examining. Enamored of "the Truth" to the point of believing that his one method is infallible, he denies the complexity of the work of art as well as its social existence within a world of real men; he forgets that it is "most pleasing" when it is "embraced and open to most" critics.

Writing about the structure of scientific revolutions, Kuhn points out that Aristotle and Galileo, looking at swinging stones, saw different things: "the first saw constrained fall, the second a pendulum."[22] He continues: "The world does not change with a change of paradigm," but "the scientist afterward works in a different world."[23] Though environment remains the same, new conceptual categories—once accepted—inevitably cause a shift in vision. The literary product is fixed in space; the creation of a new paradigm, a new critical method (though archetypal criticism is new only in the sense that it still provokes passions), must make us, the audience, look at fictional worlds with a reawakened awareness.[24] Unlike the scientist, however, we do not have to substitute one frame of reference for another; two, or three, or four conceptual schemes can exist side by side, mutually operative, mutually enriching. So, too, a radical change in artistic form, as T. S. Eliot implies in his critical writings, especially " 'Ulysses,' Order, and Myth," forces us to read all previous novels with new expectations, not because the novels have changed but because our visions have.

Before attempting to detect the persistent images and structures by which Joseph Conrad expressed his unique reality, to analyze the associative clusters derived from man's experience in a time-obsessed world, I devote chapter 1 of this book to myth, its definition, its ties to the Sacred, its effect upon thought and behavior, its relationship

---

[22] *Ibid.*, p. 120.

[23] *Ibid.*, p. x. For Kuhn paradigms are "universally recognized scientific achievements that for a time provide model problems and solutions to a community of practitioners."

[24] An interesting speculation, perhaps illumined by Kuhn's brilliant book, might be whether archetypal criticism could have antedated the writing of Joyce's *Ulysses*.

to literature, its ultimate subordination as metaphor and structural component in the world of the Profane. The value of such a discussion—or my rationalization of its value—is precisely in its recognition of the fact of historical change and the continuity of human experience. In Conrad's novels, the tone of which is so consonant with our contemporary despair and insecurity, the recurrence of past motifs, their effect upon design, intensify the irony; belief, after all, no longer accompanies the stories that now echo exploits in godless worlds by unheroic mediocrities.

It is important to try to understand what has been lost in the shift from myth to literature; and what gained. By adapting pure myth to the demands of the possible, by making the artist the only visible creator of new worlds, have we unwittingly proclaimed the substitution of art for religion? Have we provided in fiction the only timelessness sufficiently meaningful in a phenomenal world to replace reliance upon an unknowable eternity? While chapter 1 does not begin to answer these questions, it at least sets up the frame of reference within which the intricacies of Conrad's ironic visions can be judged; and it endeavors to show that he belongs not to Poland but to Western culture and the world; that his novels partake of the total experience of literature.

From Myth to Literature, from Sacred to Profane

There is one story and one story only
That will prove worth your telling
Whether as learned bard or gifted child.
ROBERT GRAVES, "To Juan at the Win-
ter-Solstice"

To some students of literature and of comparative mythology, all myths are phases of one composite myth; there is literally "one story and one story only" to which every culture has collectively contributed the products of its imagination. Even the Christian myth does not take precedence at the Round Table constructed by modern scholarship. Christ is no King Arthur here. Rather, Christ and King Arthur sit as equals, each a hero and a dying god.

But if scholars in comparative mythology seek to establish unity where diversity was thought to exist, scholars of other disciplines have reaffirmed diversity almost to the point of chaos. All myths may be one; all definitions of myth, all investigations of origin, are not one. From loose usage in colloquial discourse, the word "myth" has acquired connotations which are, at best, misleading. False "myths" may be created by a state, foisted upon populations who "need" to believe them, and flourish briefly—as did Hitler's, based upon a belief in the reality of Aryan superiority—but myths are not "false." Moreover, literary critics and scholars have contributed to the Babel by translating Aristotle's word for the arrangement of incidents, mythos—in the Greek poets, the "word uttered" —into the jargon of modern literary criticism. So mythos may be the narrative or plot of a work of fiction; hence, literally false.

11

While such transference is valid, it obscures the fact that to Aristotle's contemporaries, though they no longer believed in the Homeric gods, the plots of tragedy were based upon narratives at one time presumed to be true.

For centuries the word "myth" suggested one dominant vision to the mind of the reader, a vision embodied by the beautiful gods of the Homeric poems—perhaps enjoying nectar and ambrosia on the slopes of Mount Olympus or human revelry on landscapes patently Italian. During the Middle Ages, the Renaissance and the eighteenth century, references to Greek mythology flourished in art and literature—especially on the continent of Europe. But allusions flourished both because of and in spite of an antagonistic Church. Because they had to be subordinated to the religion of the present, they could not exist in their own dress. First, following the practice of a pagan named Euhemerus, the apologists and Christian Fathers had taken the gods from a timeless Olympus and made them into human heroes, "earthly rulers, whom the gratitude or adulation of their subjects had raised to a place in heaven."[1] In written sources Alexander the Great and Caesar may appear under those names or the more prestigious Mercury and Prometheus. Because of their royal origins and godly status, many mythological heroes became the "ancestors" of particular kings or dukes. So Hercules may have been the progenitor of peoples in number exceeding that of his labors. Or the gods survived because within an alien culture they were literally relegated to the heavens; they were identified with heavenly bodies as celestial or cosmic symbols, part of an astrological tradition. As exemplar, they pointed to theological truths and moral allegories. The Diana who represented theology had as little in common with the earlier classical figure as with the later court ladies who loved to play the role. As the virgin goddess supervising her flock, she even penetrated the enclosed world of nuns to "teach"—with a silent beauty reminiscent of Keats's Grecian Urn—the virtues of their lot. When

---

[1] Jean Seznec, *The Survival of the Pagan Gods*, trans. Barbara F. Sessions (New York, 1953), p. 12.

taught in Jesuit colleges, mythology became "a body of moral precepts, cunningly hidden under the mask of fiction."[2]

While Catholic Europe transformed classical myth into something it was not, England afforded it an even less happy position. Since parliamentary law proclaimed it blasphemy to use the label God in stage dialogue, often—as in Shakespeare's *King Lear*—"the gods" made an acceptable substitute because it was "mere classical allusion."[3] In the Age of Reason myths were often reduced to the role of amusement alone and used to appease the licentious eyes of the voyeur-gallant and his lady. Ladies of fashion everywhere posed for portraits in which they assumed the dress, or undress, of Greek goddesses, Diana the Huntress being a particular favorite.

What had once dominated the art of the classical world now affronted because it had become "fictional" or because it was only ornament or decoration. Dr. Johnson's criticism of Milton's "Lycidas" must be placed within this context: "Passion plucks no berries from the myrtle and ivy, nor calls upon Arethuse and Mincius, nor tells of rough *satyrs* and *fauns with cloven heel*. Where there is leisure for fiction there is little grief."[4] Such a statement reflects the attitude which did much to popularize the pejorative connotation of "myth" until this connotation became the primary denotation: "Myths are untrue stories." So the editors of the New English Dictionary could with a certain justice give the definition of the word as "a purely fictitious narrative usually involving supernatural persons, actions, or events, and embodying some popular idea concerning natural or historical phenomena."[5] Students of literature and the arts not only perpetrated this definition, but also tended to regard only classical myths as significant. Moreover, the word "myth" could not be applied to biblical history be-

---

[2] *Ibid.*, p. 276.

[3] Alfred Harbage, "Introduction" to *The Tragedy of King Lear* (Baltimore, Md., 1958), p. 19.

[4] Samuel Johnson, "Milton," *Lives of the English Poets*, ed. George Birkbeck Hill (3 vols.; Oxford, 1905), I, 163.

[5] *New English Dictionary on Historical Principles*, ed. James A. H. Murray (10 vols.; Oxford, 1888), VI, 818, under the word "myth."

cause of the implications of falsehood. Doctor Johnson, in the same essay on Milton, proceeds to criticize the author of "Lycidas" for including sacred (that is, Christian) allusions with pagan (classical) ones. Nor did the poets whose works exploited the myths of civilization willingly recognize the existence of primitive cultures whose sacred stories had not yet been collected.

Ironically, what the polished surface of the eighteenth century reduced to fiction, decoration, or pornography, became among serious philosophers part of the long debate concerning the nature of reason and the ideas of human progress. Frank E. Manuel[6] explores the way Pierre Bayle and Bernard Fontenelle level Greek sacred story as it reflects a living religion, savage practices as they are recounted in travel literature, and the superstitious eruptions of the Christian populace. An analysis of Greek myths—that, for instance, celebrating Orpheus—proved that the Greeks had once been as barbarous as the American Indians. These perceptions, however, did not lead to optimism. Rather, these men bemoaned the spontaneity of error and the ultimate failure of reason, though Vico, who "had little recognition or influence in his own century,"[7] used pagan myth to show how even the most licentious and vulgar were "man's first striving toward divine truth . . . necessary stages in the attainment of rational justice."[8] Whatever the conclusions about myth and its origins among thinkers as diverse as Newton, Vico, Bayle, Hume, Fontenelle, myth served continually to sanction revealed religion or to proclaim the primacy of man's reasoning faculties. In using it to posit a theory about the primitive mentality, in making the pagan— whether early Greek or contemporaneous American Indian—a "foil for the man of reason, the official posture of the age,"[9] the later thinkers were able to turn myth against itself and, finally, to banish it from a discourse largely lost in mathematical abstractions.

The desire to define myth became a lust for order in the late nineteenth and early twentieth century, primarily because of the work of the classicist Sir James Frazer. Each mythographer tenaciously

---

[6] *The Eighteenth Century Confronts the Gods* (Cambridge, Mass., 1959).

[7] René Wellek, *A History of Modern Criticism* (New Haven, 1955), I, 135.

[8] Manuel, *The Eighteenth Century Confronts the Gods*, p. 154.

[9] *Ibid.*, p. 11.

perpetuated the fallacy that there was one myth and one myth only —and that one, *his* myth; and each suffered the eclipse that such simplistic assertion deserves. That school which regarded all myth as allegorized history—as actual events that somehow in the course of collective retelling acquired supernatural sanctions that universalized and obscured facts that had been unique—became discredited. Nor was myth the savage's attempt to comprehend and explain natural phenomena. No linguistic evidence could support Max Müller's generalization that all myths have their genesis in poetic speculations concerning cosmic bodies. To envisage gods as symbols of nature endowed "primitive man with a sort of scientific impulse and desire for knowledge"[10] that the hard practicalities of existence would not let him enjoy. No shaggy-headed Phaedrus confronted an equally shaggy Socrates in primitive cultures and attempted to tease the latter into interpretations of the landscape. Where to live requires daily struggle; there is little leisure for speculative dialogue.

Yet while myth defies any reduction to what is universally applicable, the components of an adequate definition can be gathered from the writings of twentieth-century scholars. Whatever the merits of his linguistic argument, Erich Kahler indicates the intimate relationship between myth and religion when he asserts that myth and mystery, meaning "secret rites and teachings,"[11] go back to the same verbal root. The initial word *mü, mu* imitated

> . . . an elementary sound such as the lowing of cattle, the growl of beasts or of thunder, and originally meant in articulate sounding of all kinds: bellowing, booming, roaring (Lat. *mugire*, Fr. *mugir*), murmuring, humming, rumbling, groaning, muttering, or, in humans, non-verbal utterance with closed lips—and, by derivation, the closing of the mouth; muteness (Lat. *mutus*). . . .
>
> By the linguistic process that so often turns a word into its opposite—as in the case of the Latin *muttire*, to mutter, and *mutus*, mute, becoming the French *mot*, word—the Greek *mu*, signifying inarticulate voicing with closed mouth, evolved into *mythos*, word.[12]

---

[10] Bronislaw Malinowski, "Myth in Primitive Psychology," *Magic, Science and Religion* (Garden City, N.Y., 1948), p. 98.

[11] Erich Kahler, "The Persistence of Myth," *Chimera*, IV, 3 (Spring, 1946), p. 2.

[12] *Ibid.*

Only after its use by the early Greek poets did *mythos* take on the specific meaning which was once again to relate it to its original root; it became "the word as the most ancient, the most original account of the origins of the world, in divine revelation or sacred tradition, of gods and demi-gods."[13] *Logos*, for the Sophists the "word as rational construction,"[14] became particularly associated with the concept of the Word of God in Christian theology "through which the Creator by an act of mind and will brought into being and shaped the world, and which in itself contains all Creation."[16] Together *mythos* and *logos* form the English word "mythology." By reviewing its etymology, then, the critic is better able to recognize the more sacred extensions of the word: myth requires belief.

Many anthropologists and sociological theorists have added a second functional dimension to any consideration of the meaning of myth: the religious cannot divorce itself from the social. Indeed, Emile Durkheim attempts to show that the most elementary religions—as well as the most complex—result from the eminently "collective consciousness" of man and reflect social rather than natural causes. And since myths are an essential part of religion, are necessary to reaffirm the individual's relationship to the group, they too depend upon and reflect social forces.

> But the mythology of a group is the system of beliefs common to this group. The traditions whose memory it perpetuates express the way in which society represents man and the world; it is a moral system and a cosmology as well as a history. So the rite serves and can serve only to sustain the vitality of these beliefs, to keep them from being effaced from memory and, in sum, to revivify the most essential elements of the collective consciousness.[16]

The pattern of behavior accompanying myth serves to reinforce a group's sense of its communal nature. But often a myth must account for a ritual practice, must explain why the rite is relevant to the existing social order. Moreover, sacred tradition may transform

---

[13] *Ibid.*, pp. 2–3.   [14] *Ibid.*, p. 3.   [15] *Ibid.*

[16] Emile Durkheim, *The Elementary Forms of the Religious Life*, trans. by Joseph Ward Swain (Glencoe, Ill., n.d.), p. 375.

the facts of the society until they are expressed only symbolically or metaphorically. Because belief does not require literal truth, however, does not mean that myth is untrue to the society that created it.

> Between society as it is objectively and the sacred things which express it symbolically, the distance is considerable. It has been necessary that the impressions really felt by men, which served as the original matter of this construction, should be interpreted, elaborated and transformed until they become unrecognizable. So the world of religious things is a partially imaginary world, though only in its *outward form*, and one which therefore lends itself more readily to the free creations of the mind.[17]

So myths are also symbolic and may be so regarded by various cultures. Modern emphasis upon primitive societies combined with erroneous suppositions concerning a "primitive mentality" have obscured this point. Lucien Lévy-Bruhl, in maintaining that there is a way of thinking peculiar to natives,[18] has caused some philosophers to deny that symbols exist as such to the primitive mind. (Rather, it might be more accurate to say that they simply have no theory of symbolism.) Thus the native, incapable of abstraction, governed by the "participation mystique" instead of the laws of logical thought, makes no distinction between the symbol and its meaning; between the mask that represents the god and the god himself. A kind of "prelogical mystic," he is no slave to the analytical reason which separates and categorizes; he experiences life as a unity; he "sees life steadily, and sees it whole." Having fallen victim to the same intellectual fallacy, Susanne K. Langer —and Ernst Cassirer before her—writes that the mind that can "apprehend *both* a literal and a 'poetic' formulation of an idea is in a position to distinguish the figure from its meaning."[19]

Nor can any critic in formulating an adequate definition separate myth from the cultural facts upon which it depends. Malinowski reacts to the limitations of scholars who merely record the myths from classical or Eastern sources without leaving their libraries.

---

[17] *Ibid.*, p. 381. Emphasis added.

[18] Lucien Lévy-Bruhl, *How Natives Think* (London, 1926).

[19] *Philosophy in a New Key* (Cambridge, 1942), p. 149.

Separated from the vitality of a living faith, they have forgotten that the myths of civilization were once believed, regarded as fact, just as the myths of primitives are still believed.

> This myth is to the savage what, to a fully believing Christian, is the Biblical story of creation, of the Fall, of the Redemption by Christ's Sacrifice on the Cross. As our sacred story lives in our ritual, in our morality, as it governs our faith and controls our conduct, even so does his myth for the savage. . . . Studied alive, myth, as we shall see, is not symbolic, but a direct expression of its subject matter; it is not an explanation in satisfaction of a scientific interest, but a narrative resurrection of a primeval reality, told in satisfaction of deep religious wants, moral cravings, social submissions, assertions, even practical requirement. Myth fulfills in primitive culture an indispensable function: it expresses, enhances, and codifies belief; it safeguards and enforces morality; it vouches for the efficiency of ritual and contains practical rules for the guidance of man. Myth is thus a vital ingredient of human civilization; it is not an idle tale, but a hard-worked active force; it is not an intellectual explanation or an artistic imagery, but a pragmatic charter of primitive faith and moral wisdom.[20]

These narratives, because they are functional, because they form the "dogmatic backbone of primitive civilization,"[21] are often intimately connected to the society by means of formalized behavior. Indeed, the proper rites are recurring symbolic acts by which men reaffirm their relationship to the group or "communicate an *idea* of the feelings that begot their prototypes."[22] The simplest religious feelings create rituals; the movement of images creates narrative. Sometimes these images tell the story of sacred persons whose past reality influences and determines the present actions of men, providing the impetus for all ritual, all moral action, all social stratification; then we have a myth. In Lord Raglan's theory the rites are believed to

---

[20] Malinowski, "Myth in Primitive Psychology," *Magic, Science and Religion,* pp. 100–101. While Malinowski here insists that "myth is not symbolic," everything he tells us about it suggests that it is. What one assumes is that for Malinowski "symbolic" is somehow synonymous with "fabulous" or "unreal" or "artistic." Or else "symbolic" has a Freudian connotation that Malinowski, with his vigorous attack on the universality of the Oedipus complex, wishes to deny.

[21] *Ibid.,* p. 108.

[22] Susanne K. Langer, *Philosophy in a New Key,* p. 152.

have been sanctioned by sacred persons who, according to tradition, performed the initial actions which became the ritual. "The stories of their activities, the myths, then perform the dual function of sanctifying and of standardizing the ritual."[23] Because these actiological myths were created to explain the ritual whose origin is lost or forgotten, the proponents of this school believe that all myths *must* have a relevant rite. So ritual is given a chronological primacy over myth by Lord Raglan, a privilege that present-day anthropology finds suspect.

Ritual, however, is not necessary to myth nor myth to ritual.[24] Among the Mojave Indians, where myths are sometimes the results of dreams, there is a complex mythology, but a "poverty of ritual."[25] The Toda, on the other hand, emphasize ceremonial behavior that does not seem to parallel any relevant narrative. The anthropologist's joy and the classicist's despair are the Papago, whose sacred tales and rites embrace every possibility. Myths and the ceremonial behavior that may or may not accompany them tend, finally, to be symbolic expressions to gratify "culturally recognized needs."[26] Because they are believed, they help men to adjust to their societies; because they are habitual and persistent, they mitigate man's insecurities in a world of change and caprice.

No matter how fabulous these myths may seem to us, then, the society which created or evolved each one believed in its truth, regarded it as a "statement of primeval reality," which sanctioned the very substance of society. Even when the critical mind of modern scholarship denies factual truth, it must still admit symbolic truth, the validity of actions, values or emotions. Even when armchair anthropologists and littérateurs concern themselves with stories alone, the modern reason must recognize the possibility of

---

[23] Fitzroy Richard Somerset, Fourth Baron Raglan, *The Hero* (New York, 1956), p. 128. In Durkheim's attempt to distinguish between myths that were believed and mere stories (between the Sacred and the Profane), he too erroneously perpetuates the generalization that myths must have accompanying rites. (What differentiates the religious myth from the fable is "its relation to the cult": Durkheim, *The Elementary Forms of the Religious Life*, p. 83.)

[24] Clyde Kluckhohn, "Myths and Rituals: A General Theory," *The Harvard Theological Review*, XXXV (January, 1942), 45–79.

[25] *Ibid.*, p. 48.   [26] *Ibid.*, p. 79.

a cultural context, or else fall victim to the disease of hypertrophied fact, that disease which regards all myths or the one myth as false, as fable, as fiction.

Another discipline, psychology, moves the emphasis in myth from the social sphere to the individual mind, from the outer realm of activity and social organization to the interior world of dreams and fantasy. Man, not society, becomes the cynosure in this interpretation. Sigmund Freud in his *Psychopathology of Everyday Life* wrote, "I believe in fact that a great part of the mythological view of the world, which reaches far into the most modern religions, is *nothing other than psychological processes projected into the outer world.*"[27] Metaphysics does, indeed, become, as Freud points out, metapsychology. These daydreams of the race possess the same characteristics as individual dreams do—"condensation, displacement, symbolism."[28] Even the distortions apparent in personal neurosis, distortions which manifest themselves in dreams, exist on a phylogenetic scale in the larger patterns of myth. Myths, however, are expressed in a coherent, although apparently fabulous, narrative possessing causal sequence, as opposed to the images which run riot in the mind of the dreamer. "Dream is the personalized myth, myth the depersonalized dream; both myth and dream are symbolic in the same general way of the dynamics of the psyche."[29] Where myth is lived, it is the effect of the narrative upon behavior rather than the sacred story itself that takes precedence. In the psychological interpretation, the narrative events are also secondary; what is important is the reading derived from the images, the symbols of the inner experience. The primary difference in the two points of view rests in the shift of emphasis; we have moved from an explanation that is socially oriented to one that is personally, or psychically, oriented, from a view that recognized spiritual factors to one that emphasizes the human unconscious apart from any metaphysical, hence external, force. The two interpretations are not, however, mutually exclusive.

---

[27] Sigmund Freud, *Psychopathology of Everyday Life*, as quoted in Ernest Jones, *The Life and Work of Sigmund Freud* (3 vols.; New York, 1957), III, 353.

[28] Ernest Jones, *The Life and Work of Sigmund Freud*, III, 320.

[29] Joseph Campbell, *The Hero with a Thousand Faces*, p. 18.

In the dreams of individuals, the infantile fantasies which have been repressed reveal themselves in a disguised form. Therefore, an interpretation of dreams—as well as the analysis of the fantasies of children and the delusions of psychotics—can provide us with the method for understanding myths, what Karl Abraham calls the "fragment of the repressed life of the infantile psyche of the race."[30] In order to justify its own existence, every race, according to Abraham, evolves a creation myth. In these myths humanity has descended from some divine source. Such an illusion satisfied early man's egocentricity by allowing him to project his wishes into a world he could not experience by means of his own sense impressions.

The same egotistical elements pervade the various episodes of the composite hero myth as it is elucidated by Otto Rank.

> The hero is the child of most distinguished parents, usually the son of a king. His origin is preceded by difficulties, such as continence, or prolonged barrenness, or secret intercourse of the parents due to external prohibition or obstacles. During or before the pregnancy, there is a prophecy, in the form of a dream or oracle, cautioning against his birth, and usually threatening danger to the father (or his representative). As a rule, he is surrendered to the water, in a box. He is then saved by animals, or by lowly people (shepherds), and is suckled by a female animal or a humble woman. After he is grown up, he finds his distinguished parents, in a highly versatile fashion. He takes revenge on his father, on the one hand, and is acknowledged, on the other. Finally he achieves rank and honors.[31]

To understand the formation of the idea of the hero, which slowly evolved from the prehistory of the race, one may proceed by making an analogy to the prehistory of the individual life—childhood. So the high-born parents reveal the *"child's longing for the vanished happy time, when his father still appeared to be the strongest and greatest man, and the mother seemed the dearest and most beautiful woman."*[32] In a slight variation of the composite myth, the hero

---

[30] *Dreams and Myths*, trans. William A. White, Nervous and Mental Disease Monograph Series, No. 15 (New York, 1913), p. 36.

[31] Otto Rank, "The Myth of the Birth of the Hero," *The Myth of the Birth of the Hero and other Writings* (New York, 1959), p. 65.

[32] *Ibid.*, p. 71.

may be born of a virgin with the suggestion that the real father is a divine being. The virgin afterward may take a mortal husband. This emphasis upon the mother as virgin symbolizes the child's hostility to the father, his repudiation of the male role in the child's birth. Indeed, in all myths the high-born and low-born parents are in reality one—the father figure combining the additional roles of tyrant or god—echoing in the collective form the ambivalent feelings of the child for the male parent and the incestuous or exaggerated love for the mother. Godhead itself, then, is no more than the mass representation of the child's awe before what he considers the "magnitude, power, and perfection of the father."[33]

Finally, Jung has provided us with a name, derived from classical sources as early as Cicero and Pliny, for the elemental symbols or images "of a collective nature which occur practically all over the earth as constituents of myths and at the same time as autochthonous individual products of unconscious origin."[34] They are archetypes, called "imagos" in Jung's earlier works. The mind produces the images not as a result of "inherited ideas,"[35] but because of a "functional disposition."[36] It is not simply a question of the inheritance of ideas acquired by one's ancestors but of the actual physiology of the brain. "The primary image is a memory deposit, an engram derived from a condensation of innumerable similar experiences—the psychic expression of an anatomically, physiologically determined natural tendency."[37]

Some readers might consider more important to this study than Jung's application of the name "archetypes" to the primary images which form the narratives of myths his concept of the source of

---

[33] *Ibid.*, p. 81.

[34] C. G. Jung, *Psychology and Religion* (1938), as quoted in Joseph Campbell, *The Hero with a Thousand Faces*, p. 18 n.

[35] Jung, "Part One: The Song of the Moth," *Symbols of Transformation*, trans. R. F. C. Hull, Bollingen XX (New York, 1959), 102.

[36] *Ibid.*

[37] Jung, *Psychologische Typen* (1921), as quoted in Joseph Campbell, *The Masks of God: Primitive Mythology* (New York, 1959), p. 32.

these images in the collective unconscious. Each psyche contains a personal unconscious where reside the repressed or forgotten memories, instincts, and emotions acquired as a result of a man's confrontation with life. Below this—topographically—is the collective unconscious, the contents of which are not related to the specific experience of the individual. Rather, they are a racial inheritance, a biological structure which is innate, which no amount of personal experience can change. The motifs of all mythologies are the spontaneous creations of the pyche unaffected by personal psychotic or neurotic distortions. The wisdom of the prehistory of the race as it manifests itself from the collective unconscious does not reflect the egotistical or sexual nature which Abraham or Rank, using Freud's theories, emphasized. Myth is divested of any relationship to a mass "obsessional neurosis."[38]

The concept of the collective unconcious is, however, a dubious one, one which critics of Jung immediately seize upon in order to demolish his entire system. Jung himself cannot provide empirical evidence for the existence of inherited memory imprints, though the animal world does seem to give support to certain similar situations.[39] The chick, for example, newly emerged from his protecting shell, will seek cover at the sight of a hawk or the created image of a hawk even if no other bird of the same species is present to instil fear or sanction such behavior. Yet the immediate sight of a flying pigeon or heron does not invoke such a ruffled response. E. H. Gombrich uses the findings of animal psychology to depreciate the artistic achievement of the painter Zeuxis, whose grapes were said to have deceived birds. So certain young fishes will instinctively rush to the shelter of the mother's mouth at the sight of her eyes or "two simple dots arranged horizontally."[40]

The experiments of biologists prove "that in the central nervous system of all animals there exist innate structures that are somehow

---

[38] Freud, *Moses and Monotheism*, trans. Katherine Jones (New York, 1955), p. 177.

[39] See Joseph Campbell, *The Masks of God: Primitive Mythology* (New York, 1959), pp. 21–131.

[40] E. H. Gombrich, *Meditations on a Hobby Horse and Other Essays on the Theory of Art* (London, 1963), p. 6.

counterparts of the proper environment of the species."[41] But the human child develops slowly; by the time he is able to walk or communicate, he has already been strongly influenced not only by the trauma of birth but also by the environment into which he has been so rashly thrust. Whatever is innate in his psyche has long since been subject to the conditioning of his environment.

That there is no objective evidence for the existence of the collective unconscious is true; equally true is that there is no objective evidence which proves that a racial memory cannot exist. But in order to explain the similarity in mythical motifs, the sociologist, psychologist, or social anthropologist need resort neither to Jung's theory of archetypes nor to the neutral sentence which introduces this paragraph. As E. H. Gombrich points out, "Ours is a structured universe whose main lines of force are still bent by our biological and psychological needs, however much they may be overlaid by cultural influences."[42] Every man born is confronted by certain experiences which result from what Joseph Campbell calls the "structuring force of life on earth."[43] Although primitive man may not understand the solar system—as indeed many civilized men do not —he does know that night follows the light of day and he projects into the unknown darkness his equally unexplainable fears, his inchoate sense of the existence of strong or evil beings. At night he sleeps and dreams. And the world which is presented to him in his dreams has no correspondence to his day world. Objects which have no visible life during the day may acquire it in the illogical logic of dreams. Stones as well as animals may chase him; brooks and animals may talk; individual human organs may parade before his eyes without the support of a body structure; everything may confound the knowledge he has acquired in the sphere of daily activity.

---

[41] Campbell, *The Hero with a Thousand Faces*, p. 35. I am aware of the real dangers of saying that any behavior pattern in animals is innate, inherited, unlearned. Probably the only safe assertion is that the late maturation of the human animal makes it impossible to determine what behavior—if any—is independent of its environment. See Daniel S. Lehrman, "Problems Raised by Instinct Theories," *Quarterly Review of Biology*, Vol. 28 (1953), 337–65.

[42] Gombrich, *Meditations on a Hobby Horse*, p. 6.

[43] Campbell, *The Hero with a Thousand Faces*, p. 57.

Fortunately he wakes and his waking experience becomes associated with sunrise. As Joseph Campbell writes:

The night fears and night charms are dispelled by light, which has always been experienced as coming from above and as furnishing guidance and orientation. Darkness, then, and weight, the pull of gravity and the dark interior of the earth, of the jungle, or of the deep sea, as well as certain extremely poignant fears and delights, must for millenniums have constituted a firm syndrome of human experience in contrast to the luminous flight of the world-awakening solar sphere into and through immeasurable heights. Hence a polarity of light and dark, above and below, guidance and loss of bearings, confidence and fears (a polarity that we all know from our own tradition of thought and feeling and can find matched in many parts of the world) must be reckoned as inevitable in the way of a structuring principle of human thought.[44]

But the orderly rhythms of the solar system are no more mysterious than the equally strange rhythms of earth. In areas subject to seasonal change, the plants which decay during one season may reappear again in similar abundance within a specified space of time. Even lands which have perpetual vegetation have periods of more abundant growth after rainy seasons, or their peoples plant according to a cycle based on repetitive experience. What happens to vegetation below the dark surface of the ground may be systematized by modern scientists, but it is the subject for the creative imaginings of primitives, children, and uneducated Westerners.

All men are born. Once born, they are subject to natural laws which enable them to be children, grow to manhood, mature, and decline to death. There has as yet been no human who was exempt from the physical facts of biology. In every society symbolic acts called rites of passage accompany the difficult transitions from one stage of development to the next. This ceremonial behavior helps us across the critical periods to which we are all subject. Why, then, should the scholar marvel that the hero's quest in most mythologies follows "the formula represented by the rites of passage: separation

---

[44] *Ibid.*

—initiation—return"?[45] Nor has there been a man yet who, in spite of the tortured rationalizations of Macbeth, was not born of woman. The whole phenomenon of human birth, so near to death in the simplest societies, provides innumerable possibilities for mythopeic thinking. Man moves from the darkness of the womb to the light of day and descends again into the darkness of earth which becomes equated with the first darkness from which he was born. The waters of the womb in which the fetus floats may become identified with those which insure fertility of the soil; they may become associated with both life and death. Earth, from whose fertile darkness we receive food, offers the obvious analogy in the whole process of human gestation and birth and death.

Every human being as he grows becomes aware of some principle of authority, whether that principle be the father, as in Western culture, or, as in some matrilineal societies, the mother's brother, or the clan head or king or god. Love and rebellion may go hand in hand. Whether we call the manifestation of hostility and ambivalence an Oedipus complex or an avuncular complex, or see in disobedience the political revolutionary or the incipient atheist, makes little difference. What is important is the impression which the presence of a male authoritative principle makes on the psyche and the influence of that impression upon the imaginative and emotional life of the human animal.

Finally, Joseph Campbell cites the early work of Adolf Bastian who, before Jung, noted that certain ideas occur in slightly varying form again and again throughout mankind.[46] But the fundamental concepts—the "elementary ideas"—could nowhere be divested of their local, particular, unique—"ethnic"—manifestations. Whatever composite myth the scholar wishes to regard as the *one myth*, therefore, he will never find it articulated in its pure form. Rather, he will find the particular mythic motifs modified by the environment

---

45 *Ibid.*, p. 30. Arnold Van Gennep, who gave to anthropology and to the theory of religion the term *les rites de passage*, originates this three-part schema, but he uses the terms "separation-transition-incorporation." See Arnold Van Gennep, *The Rites of Passage*, trans. Monika B. Vizedom and Gabrielle L. Caffee, intro. Solen T. Kimball (London, 1960), p. 11.

46 Campbell, *The Masks of God: Primitive Mythology*, p. 32.

which evolved the sacred story. The elementary, or psychological, and ethnic, or culturally conditioned, unite in any consideration of myth. But, as we have noted, the imprints of experience possess a uniformity which external natural order and human biology demand.

But myth is not literature, although the artistic impulse may be a causal one in the creation of myth as it is in the creation of literature. Durkheim admits that the artistic impulse is behind myth, and myth is essential to religion. Moreover, the "principal forms of art seem to have been born of religion and . . . for a long time they retained a religious character."[47] With a sociological emphasis upon the factual and functional, Durkheim regards myth as true because it "works" in the social structure and art, as "a system of fictions."[48] The former belongs to the realm of the Sacred; the latter, to that of the Profane. Kluckhohn gives myth a role similar to literature in cultures which are illiterate: the Navaho recite myths "around the fire on winter nights."[49] And while bemoaning the fact that scholars have given too much weight to the literary aspects of myth, even Malinowski concedes that myth "contains germs of the future epic, romance, and tragedy; and it has been used in them by the creative genius of peoples and by the conscious art of civilization."[50] A scholar like Jane Harrison, whose area of specialization was the classical world, does not immediately establish a hierarchy of values in stating a relationship between myth and literature:

> This primary sense of *mythos* as simply the thing uttered, expressed by speech rather than action, can never, so long as he reads his Homer, be forgotten by the literary student. But when we come to myth in relation to religion, myth contrasted with ritual, we are apt to forget this primary and persistent meaning, and much confused

---

[47] Durkheim, *The Elementary Forms of the Religious Life*, p. 381.

[48] *Ibid.*

[49] Kluckhohn, "Myth and Ritual: A General Theory," *The Harvard Theological Review*, XXXV (January, 1942), 64.

[50] Malinowski, "Myth in Primitive Psychology," *Magic, Science and Religion*, p. 143.

thinking is the result. The primary meaning in religion is just the same as in early literature; it is the spoken correlative of the actual rite, the thing done. . . .[51]

Myth is not literature. Nor are mythologies created by the formal arrangement of language into literature. A. H. Krappe's statement that myths were wholly aesthetic phenomena,[52] that without the epic poets myth could not exist, "confuses the myth-making stage of thought with the literal stage."[53] The former stage does not question: the latter stage does not believe. The former is the gift of feeling; the latter, the curse of thought. But Krappe's statement *does* possess more than a half-truth, for the epic poets ordered and formalized into poetry those myths which the myth-making mind created but could not save from oblivion or from the constant fluidity of oral transmission. And Mrs. Langer's statement that the "highest development of which myth is capable is the exhibition of human life and cosmic order that epic poetry reveals"[54] does recognize the role of myth in the advancement of human thought and culture. Myth may be a necessary step *toward* a literature—indeed, toward art in general. And though the primary impulses behind myth are social and psychological, the artistic impulse is always present.

Krappe bases his position upon the evidence of the "myths of civilization"—particularly Greek mythology—rather than primitive myths, myths studied in their cultural context. Accustomed as we are to the stereotyped belief that the Greeks possessed a religion dominated by beauty and reason, we tend to forget that Greek religion and mythology reached its apogee in the anthropomorphic gods of the *Iliad*, the *Odyssey*, and Hesiod, and that very near the surface of this civilization the more primitive forms of ritual worship still manifested themselves. And though the Greek gods existed before Homer, the particular conception of the Olympian or heav-

---

[51] Jane Ellen Harrison, *Themis: A Study of the Social Origins of Greek Religion* (Cambridge, England, 1912), p. 328.

[52] Krappe, *La Genèse des mythes* (1938), as quoted in Susanne Langer, *Philosophy in a New Key* (New York, 1948), p. 159.

[53] Langer, *Philosophy in a New Key*, p. 159.

[54] *Ibid.*, p. 164.

enly deities was, in truth, the creation of the Homeric poems. W. K. C. Guthrie asserts that the Olympians arose to serve the political and social needs of the city-state, whose leaders demanded submission to a higher power, and could not satisfy the deepest religious needs of the entire populace.

> Their relations with men are purely external, and approximate to those between two levels of aristocracy in a society with a basis of strictly observed caste. Each knows its place and keeps to it, and there is little more to be said about the duty of man to god.[55]

On the other hand, the older, more barbaric deities, the *chthonici* or gods of fertility and the realm of the dead, satisfied man's irrational desire for some sort of significant immortality. Once Homer had given the Olympians their marked personalities in an art form, they became "the common property of the whole of Greece"[56] as the primitive chthonians never could. That mythology "was historically the mother of the arts"[57] is made very clear by Jane Harrison:

> Our minds are imbued with current classical mythology, our imagination peopled with the vivid personalities, the clear-cut outlines of the Olympian gods; it is only by a somewhat severe mental effort that we realize the fact essential to our study that *there were no gods at all*, that what we have to investigate is not so many actual facts and existences but only conceptions of the human mind, shifting and changing colour with every human mind that conceived them. Art which makes the image, literature which crystallizes attributes and functions, arrest and fix this shifting kaleidoscope; but, until the coming of art and literature and to some extent after, the formulary of theology is "all things are in flux."[58]

Although belief in the Olympians declined with the political decline of the city-state, the universal fascination of the gods of Homer still dominated the minds of the people, revealing to us

---

[55] W. K. C. Guthrie, *The Greeks and Their Gods* (Boston, 1955), p. 214.

[56] *Ibid.*, 219.

[57] Campbell, *The Masks of God: Primitive Mythology*, p. 42.

[58] Jane Ellen Harrison, *Prolegomena to the Study of Greek Religion* (New York, 1957), pp. 163–64.

the stability and essential oneness of a people who could accept dethroned gods with equanimity and still incorporate them into dynamic artistic creation. Dominated by a common sense of identity, their myth had once performed a social and religious function —as it still does in primitive societies. It attempted to give a validity to that communal experience which shared a unified pattern of beliefs. So the literature created by "mythologically charged"[59] societies, including the Greek society, was motivated by the wish to shape artistically the cultured inheritance of a group. In other words, social and religious reasons still motivated the audience's attendance and the artist's creation. But the artistic impulse was also revealed in the individual's work of art and the audience's enjoyment of form. The rituals involving active participation were replaced by the rituals associated with certain techniques of communication. But we no longer live in a homogeneous and "mythologically charged" community. Rather, the individual has become the center of the cosmos in the world of values, though not in the world of fact. Humanity is not as important as the single life. Not Man but a man. The desirable goal seems to be, first, the unified personality; then, the well-ordered society. The narrative aspects of myth are seen as figures of speech, metaphors, for the reality of an interior landscape—or dreamscape. Myth as it is used in the "realistic" narratives of an individually oriented society has become, as Northrop Frye says, the union of "ritual and dream in pattern of verbal communication."[60] Whether the world presented in the art forms of modern society approximates dream or nightmare depends upon the separate author's vision of the nature to which he has adjusted his myth.

Everything about life on earth reminds us that we live in a world of inevitable flux and change, a world dominated by the concept of time. The fact of birth makes each of us an event in the chain of events running in a straight line from the distant past and proceed-

---

[59] Campbell, *The Hero with a Thousand Faces*, p. 387.

[60] Frye, "Ethical Criticism: Theory of Symbols," *Anatomy of Criticism* (Princeton, N.J., 1957), p. 106.

1

ing into the mistier future. History begins once we are able to assign a particular moment in this continuous flow to a particular reference. Lord Raglan defines history as "the recital in chronological sequence of events that are known to have occurred."[61] Myth, on the other hand, is timeless. It belongs to the remote past, the prehistory of tribes and races; yet in its presence it makes time timeless. The rites often associated with myths do, indeed, "render visible the mythological age itself,"[62] and are attempts to reassure corruptible man that some form of eternity does exist beyond the single events of history, establish a community between the living and the dead, or reconcile him to the world of change by the enactment of what has been performed before and will be performed again. In Lord Raglan's *The Hero*, ritual can be explained by aetiological myths attributing the initial symbolic actions to superhuman beings of the distant past. Though very vague memories may be said to exist concerning the "originator of the ritual,"[63] these memories are devoid of any historical sense, for

> . . . the idea of history is meaningless to the ritualist. History is what happens once, but things that happen once only are nothing to the ritualist, who is concerned only with things that are done again and again. Myth is ritual projected back into the past, not a historical past of time, but a ritual past of eternity.[64]

The rituals associated with explanatory myths, therefore, are designed to establish a sense of continuity with the bottomless past, a "renewal of the past in the present."[65] Even those myths pro-

---

[61] Raglan, *The Hero*, p. 4. Lord Raglan's definition of history has as one of its virtues the denial of the idea of historical time as it appears in Christian writing. Since Augustine in *The City of God* assumes that historical time is linear and that it extends from the beginning of the world to the Apocalypse, he includes as "sacred history" accounts that my analysis assigns to myth. Precisely because Augustine perceives history as sacred and includes events derived from the literature of revelation rather than from evidence of the senses, his view requires the commitment of faith as Lord Raglan's does not. See Saint Augustine, *The City of God*, trans. Marcus Dods, D.D. (New York, 1950).

[62] Campbell, *The Masks of God: Primitive Mythology*, p. 179.

[63] Raglan, *The Hero*, p. 147.

[64] *Ibid.*

[65] Thomas Mann, "Freud and the Future," *Essays by Thomas Mann*, trans. H. T. Lowe-Porter (New York, 1957), p. 320.

viding a code of behavior, a system of values, political organization, or social stratification but based upon events believed once to have happened—even those myths, which order the cultural life of the present, attempt to give that present time sanction by associating it with timeless tradition. Malinowski describes as the function of myth the necessity to "strengthen tradition and endow it with a greater value and prestige by tracing it back to a higher, better, more supernatural reality of initial events."[66] Finally, that ritual phrase of folk and fairy tale—"once upon a time"—fixes a frame of mind in the listener which accepts no-time as all-time and now.

Myth, then, annihilates momentarily our obsessive awareness of time. In its lack of concern for temporal processes it can be compared to the unconscious. And so it should be if we remember that, defined in psychological terms, myth becomes the outward manifestation of inner events raised to phylogenetic proportions. Thomas Mann reminds us of the intimacy between the two in his essay ironically titled "Freud and the Future." Myth is the "timeless schema, the pious formula into which life flows when it reproduces its traits out of the unconscious."[67] And Freud himself revealed the true nature of the unconscious with its ignorance of the symbolic or the actual ticking of clocks:

> There is nothing in the id which can be compared to negation, and we are astonished to find in it an exception to the philosophers' assertion that space and time are necessary forms of our mental acts. In the id there is nothing corresponding to the idea of time, no recognition of the passage of time, and . . . no alteration of mental processes by the passage of time. Conative impulses which have never got beyond the id, and even impressions which have been pushed down into the id, are virtually immortal and are preserved for whole decades as though they had only recently occurred . . . the repressed remains unaltered by the passage of time.[68]

---

[66] Malinowski, "Myth in Primitive Psychology," *Magic, Science and Religion*, p. 146.

[67] Mann, "Freud and the Future," *Essays by Thomas Mann*, p. 317.

[68] Freud, *New Introductory Lectures on Psycho-Analysis*, trans. W. J. H. Sprott (New York, 1933), p. 104.

Manifestations of the unconscious life which we know as dreaming may occur in a few minutes of our sleeping life; but the images which render these dreams so absurd can be symbols of repressions or emotions taking place in one moment or in the passage of 50 years. And these images, though they may be reflections of the distant past in the waking life, are outlined with a clarity which suggests that they are part of the action of the preceding day.

Myth in literature presents the reader with a special problem, for art is itself an event in time which happens once. Like the myths of civilization which now appear in sacred literature, art lacks the fluidity of pure myth. Its timelessness, however, is derived from the formalized structure which is itself a kind of ritual and from the changeless values which it mirrors in its content. Each performance, each rereading is a re-creation of the initial event. In a lucid and suggestive study, Hans Meyeroff[69] develops three views of eternity found in literature which are relevant to human thought in general. As he points out, there is no real evidence in the objective order of nature for the concept of a timeless realm; no reliance upon empirical data and sense experience can prove to us that eternity exists. But most religions promise us the equivalent of what Christianity posits as a "City of God 'unchangeable from all eternity' and holding the promise of 'eternal life' ";[70] the timelessness of philosophy is that of "eternal verities and values";[71] and, finally, politics anticipates a timelessness within history, a time of "apparently permanent, fixed social and political structures (as in the feudal period)."[72] All visions of a utopia can fall within this last view of eternity since the concept of a classless society postulates "an eventual suspension of the dialectics of history, thus hinting at a dimension of 'timelessness,' i.e., a cessation of the dialectical march of time, even within the context of human history and society."[73] Psychological theory adds another eternity: the realm of the unconscious that is subject to mental processes which ignore both

---

[69] See Hans Meyerhoff, *Time in Literature* (Berkeley, Calif., 1955).

[70] *Ibid.*, p. 89.

[71] *Ibid.*, p. 90.

[72] *Ibid.*

[73] *Ibid.*, p. 98.

temporal and spatial problems and which we place arbitrarily and metaphysically in the lower stratum of the brain.

In literature possessing mythic themes, traditional frameworks of eternity become subordinated to the larger theory of time as cycle. This concept applies the orderly movements of the solar system to human history. As the sun sets in the evening only to rise again, so everything returns. There is "nothing new under the sun."[74] As life in myth, "life as a sacred repetition, is a historical form of life,"[75] so the recognition of the cyclic theory of time attempts to assure us that certain situations will recur, that there is a real continuity between the past and the present.

This belief in the continuity of all human experience—the realization that time may annihilate but only for a moment, that some rebirth is inevitable—enables us to read the literature of the homogeneous periods of human history, aware that life and death are part of one community and that the individual hero and his society have shared aims. But modern society no longer presents us with certitude. And the modern novel—the genre of the individual-oriented society—with its vision of twentieth-century man's anguish and failure of identity, is obsessed with historical time. Time, which Thomas Mann calls the "medium of narration, as it is the medium of life,"[76] becomes often one of the main subjects of the novel (as it does in *The Magic Mountain* or *The Secret Agent*). Not content alone but form may be visibly affected. Often the structural devices an author employs are those which destroy the calendar assumption and the Christian one of time as continuous duration, as linear sequence; we become obsessed with a new subjectivity reflected in historical events, as we do in *Nostromo*. The stream-of-consciousness novel purports to approximate the no-time of the unconscious by means of techniques of association.

What mythic themes do to an art form which results in part from man's concern for things, in part from his new awareness of his entanglement in time, is to reveal the fundamental estrangement

---

[74] *Ibid.*, p. 79.

[75] Mann, "Freud and the Future," *Essays by Thomas Mann*, p. 318.

[76] Thomas Mann, *The Magic Mountain*, trans. H. T. Lowe-Porter (New York, 1953), p. 541.

of life and death. The constant cycle within nature, demonic in its rotation, as Frye reminds us,[77] guarantees only generic rebirth; the individual rebirth promised by religion is denied by reason and analysis. Life itself may be a form of death. But the greater estrangement is that which exists between man and his society. Essentially isolated, fragmented, unable to communicate, the hero of the novel is forced into the timelessness of the interior life where he may grapple with a despair that can reach heroic proportions or where he may sink into his complete indolence as a result of his inadequacy.

In its origin the novel,[78] as the art form of modern society, seemed a negation of all the characteristics which had dominated literature *before* the eighteenth century, seemed, in truth, a denial of the mythopeic past. Because the eighteenth-century philosopher was an empiricist, his "reality" was the concrete, physical world available to his senses, not the whole system of abstractions or Platonic ideas which had pervaded thinking from the classical world through the scholastic tradition. The first novelists, too, emphasized the immediacy of sense impressions. Plots based upon traditional and legendary material were abandoned for particular situations which purported to be either wholly new or to be authentic contemporary history. The so-called hero of the novel was not superior in degree or in background to the ordinary middle-class inhabitant of London. Neither godlike nor better than life, he lived an unidealized existence among trivia recognizable to his readers. Like Prufrock he "measured out . . . life in coffee spoons." The hero's flaws were not epic in proportion or tragic in scope; rather, they revealed the weaknesses and mediocrity expected by the canons of plausibility.

Myth and legend had provided timeless stories for writers of epic and tragedy wherein the temporal dimension was either ignored or fixed by Aristotelian tradition. But realism demanded a minute emphasis upon day to day events, detailed records precisely dated,

---

[77] Frye, "Archetypal Criticism: Theory of Myths," *Anatomy of Criticism,* p. 162.

[78] For an analysis of the rise of the novel and its relationship to Protestantism, see Ian Watt, *The Rise of the Novel* (London, 1957). I have relied sporadically upon this excellent book for my discussion of the origins of the novel.

lives lived by clock and calendar. Although individuals within the novel possessed pasts, these pasts were important because they indicated causes of present action. The letters of Richardson's *Pamela* and *Clarissa*, the journals of Defoe's *Robinson Crusoe*, Smollett's epistolary novels, Sterne's experiments with Lockian formulas—all these depend for verisimilitude upon an acute awareness of time. Odysseus might roam the known or the unknown world without the credulity of the audience being strained by too great an accumulation of precise detail, settings in Shakespeare's plays might be Troy or Egypt but were always so vaguely evoked that audiences willingly suspended disbelief; but the characters of the novel were placed within a minutely described landscape where the particularized environment assured recognition. Even when heroes travelled as freely as Robinson Crusoe, vividness of detail recalled an unidealized and familiar world. Prospero's island cannot easily be accepted as part of our own globe; Crusoe's, can. Every-time and every-place, no-time and no-place became this-time and this-place. Everything about the novel, then, postulated that this new form was not concerned with primeval reality or collective experience. Indeed, as Ian Watt reminds us, "from the Renaissance onwards, there was a growing tendency for individual experience to replace collective tradition as the ultimate arbiter of reality."[79]

Historically, the religious phenomenon called Protestantism had helped to wean the individual from the corporate tradition which had preceded it. Men were suddenly confronted by a cosmos in which salvation was not based on faith or good works. Rather, God had determined his elect at the creation of the world. Neither priest nor Savior could intervene to save the damned; neither devil nor the self could cause the saved to lose grace. Max Weber emphasizes the unutterable personal isolation and "unprecedented inner loneliness of the simple individual"[80] that such doctrine could precipitate. Each man, unable to have any certainty concerning his membership in the elect, scrutinized the most unobtrusive detail of his external

---

[79] *Ibid.*, p. 14.

[80] Max Weber, *The Protestant Ethic and the Spirit of Capitalism*, trans. Talcott Parsons (London, 1956), p. 104.

and interior life for some hint of divine purpose. The journals of the early Puritans and Quakers reveal this increased concern for spiritual processes. Bunyan's allegory, *Pilgrim's Progress*, anticipating the narrative techniques used in the novel, reveals a man so obsessed by his own desire for salvation that he ignores the existence of his family in order to seek the celestial city. In what is regarded as the first English novel written in journal form, *Robinson Crusoe*, the hero's actual enforced solitude is symbolic of his spiritual isolation.

But if Protestantism, especially in its Calvinistic phase, resulted in a growing concern for the inner life, it also created a society of men each dedicated to his own economic gain. Denied knowledge of the next world by the limitations of his senses, each concentrated all his activity in this one as a means of forgetting his very real fears of damnation. Men garnered vast fortunes not for the sake of wealth but for the greater glory of God. Moreover, accumulation of wealth itself was not a sin—only idleness or the pleasures of the body which wealth fostered. And since work was predicated upon an assumption of religious devotion, waste of time became the deadliest sin. Time was gold, having commodity value as well as spiritual value. This deification of activity simultaneous with this denigration of what wealth could purchase led at once to capitalism and to personal asceticism within the world.

Perhaps that genre, long regarded as frivolous, which mirrored both the staunch individualism of the new class and its concern with wealth, provided the least sinful of pleasures. The treasures which were the rewards of traditional heroes—treasures which might be material ones but which were often much less substantial—became very simply, in the novel, money. The deity who presided over the ritual practices of the counting house and the novels it produced was John Ruskin's Goddess of Getting-On. And marriages were made, like money, in this world; the most desirable heroine always gave her hand to the largest fortune. After each successive matrimonial venture Moll Flanders counts her shillings and pounds nor ever lets love interfere with economic gain. Foundlings like Tom Jones and Humphrey Clinker acquire both respectable parentage and some real measure of financial security before marriage.

Here most obviously the ageless motif of the hero of unknown parentage suddenly found itself wrenched to fit the demands of a different kind of reader. Even in the more limited and more moral universe of Jane Austen the successful suitor must first prove he is a successful man. Where previously the hero's accomplished quest redounded to the public benefit, now the quest for personal gain had equally personal ends. And when a fictional character was to be excluded from the benefits conferred by this materialistic world which he might scorn but with which he nevertheless desired to reconcile himself, he first of all lost his means of support. To be poor was the mark of Cain which, ironically, profitable work could erase.

The novel articulated the values of this new social class as the Homeric epic had once given validity to the political structure of the Greek city-state. Moreover, the novel's hero reflected the changing status and gradual democratization within the social structure, a diminishing of class lines itself stemming from Protestantism. The elect, which formed the aristocracy of the next world, could not be known. Wealth was no guarantee of salvation in that realm beyond our immediate physical perception. But in this world all were equal before God; and wealth consequent to ability and built upon individual effort could, and did, tend to obliterate hierarchical class-structures. Godlike heroes or heroic gods belonged to a past tradition in which action rarely took place on the ordinary level of experience. Birth made the hero of epic or tragedy; ability made the hero of the novel. The human hero of Sophocles or Shakespeare still existed on a plane too remote from everyday life. No one tied him to the possessions and necessities of daily existence; no one asked who was to pay his debt at the inn, provide oats for his horse, or sharpen his sword for battle. The human—all-too-human—hero of the novel is one of us; nothing makes him superior to his fellows—except, perhaps, his wealth which, after all, each of us as autonomous individuals may acquire. Princes and princesses now live happily ever after only in fairy tales or are confined to past literature or to the fantasy world of the unconscious.

Paradoxically, it was the development of a new religion which led to the decline of the belief in an eternal order, a greater secularization, and an inner isolation. Society's emphasis upon the pursuit of wealth made man merely "a productive unit along the assembly lines of society, or a commodity to be used for further production. He is worth what he is worth here and now; and this value of the present moment . . . is determined largely by what he can do or has just done."[81] His isolation and "worldly asceticism,"[82] to use Weber's phrase, were augmented by the realization that the self was cut off from the past which gave it continuity and identity.

The development of Freudianism was, theoretically at least, a logical extension of Protestantism. Emphasizing the unconscious of the individual, it increased man's sensitivity to his interior life and to his essential loneliness. The self, spiritually bankrupted by the struggle for wealth which had reduced it to a material fact, was further torn by the instincts which Freud forced it to recognize, and society—and Protestantism—forced it to repress. The final movement toward secularization occurred when the timelessness of the unconscious substituted itself for the timelessness of a celestial city of God.

The declaration of personal freedom and social mobility, the struggle to succeed with its resultant economic insecurity, the desire to escape the authority of the past whether that past be symbolized by home and parents, by country, or by church—one or all of these led to lack of stability, fragmentation of the self, and unprecedented loneliness. And all this found adequate expression in the novel. *Fathers and Sons* and *Portrait of the Artist as a Young Man*, separated as they are in place and time, both reveal an attempt to declare the autonomy of the self by denying the authority of the father and the values of the country. The expatriated Americans of Hemingway and Fitzgerald are physically free, emotionally lost, spiritually isolated. The anonymity and dehumanization forced upon man by the pressures of his civilization are too well evoked by Gregor Samsa and by K., both of whom represent in a Kafkaesque world the final degradation of the mediocre.

Aware of the forces causing social as well as self-estrangement,

---

[81] Meyerhoff, *Time in Literature*, p. 115.

[82] Weber, *The Protestant Ethic and the Spirit of Capitalism*, p. 95.

many novelists wished to portray what they considered a valid vision of this reality and yet wished to reaffirm man's essential oneness within himself and with his society. Hans Meyerhoff stresses the myth as a symbol of the "typical form of human identity. The quest for mythical roots may not be a quest for personal identity but for an identification with mankind in general."[83] So Stephen Dedalus may repudiate present-day Ireland in order to re-establish his relationship with timeless human situations; he may deny Christ to find again the godlike in himself as artist and as man. Ironically, his search for identity and temporal continuity manifests itself in a technique resulting from the recognition of the "fragmentization of time in the consciousness of modern man"[84]—the badly named stream-of-consciousness method. Thomas Mann in *Joseph and His Brothers*, by dramatizing a "timeless scheme" of the past, wanted to show that life in a timed, historical world does have value because it is "sacred repetition." As Joseph again enacts the myth of the dying and resurrected god, so even in our secular world one may rejoice in "a fresh incarnation of the traditional on earth."[85] What we call "imitation" is revitalized by the new connotations which associate it with "identification."

Some of the modern authors who made use of myth were quick to exploit their knowledge of anthropology and psychology. They not only employed the ritualized motifs of coherent narratives, but also recognized the dark irrational forces of the id which, phylogenetically, had led, according to Freud, to the creation of myth in prehistoric times and could still reassert itself in modern society. Gustave von Aschenbach in *Death in Venice* and Michel in *The Immoralist* dramatize where complete submission to primitive instincts can lead men who had placed rationality above all else. Both novels skillfully employ the riotous symbols of the dream life which have their counterparts in the external events of all myths. And each novel is an orderly proof that the irrational within a society and within an individual may be channeled and made meaningful by art.

---

[83] Meyerhoff, *Time in Literature*, p. 82.
[84] *Ibid.*, p. 118.
[85] Mann, "Freud and the Future," *Essays by Thomas Mann*, p. 318.

But another effect of the use of mythic motifs derived from ritual and dream has not always served to reassert what humanists like to call the "essential dignity of man" within a hostile society. Neither Aschenbach nor Michel nor Stephen Dedalus-Leopold Bloom allows us as readers to experience personal exultation. Rather, our despair often approximates the character's inner despair, despair which the narrative events of the story externalize. Indeed, in novels where parallels are not so defined as in the Joseph saga and in *Ulysses* and in novels where archetypal patterns are "there," but accidentally or unconsciously "there"—in such novels, what we experience is the disparity between two visions of reality. The contrast between the homogeneous society in harmony with itself, its gods, and nature, and the secular society of today where the gods and the past are dead, makes our modern world seem a parody, a nightmare, a perversion. Parallels between the lives of heroes and gods and the mediocre or anonymous or weak (because conceivable) modern protagonist augment the irony within the novel and comment upon the phenomenal world as we must experience it. So Aristotle's formula for the audience's response to events on the tragic stage—"fear and pity"[86]—has been replaced by that of Bill Gorton in *The Sun Also Rises*—"Irony and Pity."[87] Nor am I making a pejorative statement about the fictional mode; rather, modern society, lacking both the motive and shoulders of an Atlas, must bear alone the burden of its own evils. Some of the novel's greatness must rest upon the fact that it has successfully portrayed disintegration without succumbing to it.

Because it presents a world close to our experience and because it reflects the individualism of the class which produced it, the novel stresses the dream aspects of myth more than the ritual or social aspects. The pure mythic structures of written revelation or of a literature articulating traditional stories—the *Iliad*, the Norse sagas, *Paradise Lost*—are no longer possible. What the mind finds desirable and projects into the world has always been, according to Freud, the subject of myth and fairy tale. But now the world, which

---

[86] Aristotle, *On the Art of Poetry*, trans. S. H. Butcher, Library of Liberal Arts, No. 6 (New York, 1948), 17.

[87] Ernest Hemingway, *The Sun Also Rises* (New York, 1926), p. 114.

condones the activity of the free man who makes the world his battleground, no longer understands the dreams of individuals or denies the individual's desires to project his wishes into the cosmos. The mind, forced back upon itself, knows a despair which may at times be greater than the man who bears it. Ultimately, his heroism may be his despair. The night-sea journey—the hero's tortuous quest into the ambiguous darkness of earth or sea or desert for the elixir to save the world—is the externalization in myth of the excruciating internal search, the exploration of the self-scape of the hero of fiction. And the form and content of the novels of Mann, Faulkner, Conrad, Gide, Joyce, Lawrence, Camus, Dostoevsky—to name only a few—possess this intense and frustrated quest for identity and this equally intense and equally frustrated desire for some community understanding.

Perhaps all we can finally say is that the creation of myth is no longer possible because of the increasing secularization of modern life, the emphasis upon the individual and his unconscious, and the tendency to analyze experience rather than synthesize it. With the passing of traditional societies, myth-making has become a function of advertising and the mass media. Or perhaps my assertions need not assume such negative proportions. Perhaps we can say that the myths of modern society are the dreams of individual minds depersonalized, structured, ritualized, synthesized into works of art. Not literally true, good novels are true to the reality of human experience; they are "narrative resurrections," if not of "primeval reality," at least of modern society. And within them they do possess the timeless components of both myth and dream, the images and symbols present in the collective and the individual life.

CHAPTER TWO

Nostromo: *Within a Paradise of Snakes*

During and after the writing of Nostromo, Joseph Conrad's letters reflect his feelings of frustrated failure caused by too intense and too prolonged effort, too deep introspection. In a letter to William Rothenstein he wrote, "I am not myself and shall not be myself till I am born again after Nostromo is finished";[1] and after his "rebirth" he confessed to having written the novel in "the tenacity of despair."[2] That the completed product made him despair can be seen in similar remarks made in two letters to R. B. Cunninghame Graham: "I feel a great humbug";[3] and, again, "For in regard to that book I feel a great fraud."[4]

This chapter and the next are essentially as they appear in my doctoral dissertation, which went into the archives of the Harvard University Library in the summer of 1960. *Texas Studies in Literature and Language* published a modified version of this chapter in January, 1962. Before that publication, Dorothy Van Ghent published an introduction to Nostromo (Holt, Rinehart & Winston, 1961) in which our insights are similar. Since we each base much of our separate interpretations upon the ideas of Northrop Frye, our arguments are often parallel.

[1] Joseph Conrad to William Rothenstein, June 27, 1904, *Joseph Conrad: Life and Letters*, ed. G. Jean-Aubry (New York, 1927), I, 330.

[2] Conrad to Rothenstein, September 3, 1904, *ibid.*, p. 336.

[3] Conrad to R. B. Cunninghame Graham, October 7, 1904, *ibid.*, p. 337.

[4] Conrad to Cunninghame Graham, October 31, 1904, *ibid.*, p. 338.

Almost eight years after the publication of *Nostromo*, in *A Personal Record* Conrad recalls the intensity of his authorial involvement and, in a typical Conradian parenthesis, the very conscious creation required by such an edifice: "All I know, is that, for twenty months, neglecting the common joys of life that fall to the lot of the humblest on this earth, I had, like the prophet of old, 'wrestled with the Lord' for my creation, . . . (there was not a single brick, stone or grain of sand of its soil I had not placed in position with my own hands)."[5] And he records that the novel "is still mentioned now and again, and indeed kindly, sometimes in connection with the word 'failure' and sometimes in conjunction with the word 'astonishing.' "[6] Indeed, both these words describe this novel's unique greatness: It is an astonishing failure.

Nostromo is essentially two imperfectly integrated stories, each with its particular hero, each with a felt life of its own. And the author has separated the life of each hero into the rituals, the recurrent symbolic acts, that unite him to the community, and the dreams by which he idealizes his individual existence as a man. Authorial detachment provides irony; authorial sympathy, tragedy. At many points the two never fuse with the characters of the men who assume the burdens of the symbolic quests.

The obvious critical statement about *Nostromo* is that it is a political novel. It is "political" because of its "vision of our historical moment and our human lot."[7] It is "political" in its artistic imitation of man's universal impulse to order social and natural phenomena. Finally, it is "political" in its revelation of the policies, compromises, and partisan roles that dominate man's persistent attempts to govern other men. Conrad deals with no time and no place that we know; and yet the author's imaginative evocation of Sulaco convinces us that it is all time and every place.[8]

The first story is the *historical* one which deals with the Costa-

---

[5] Joseph Conrad, *A Personal Record* (New York, 1925), pp. 98–100.

[6] *Ibid.*, p. 98.

[7] Robert Penn Warren, "Introduction," *Nostromo* (New York, 1951), p. xxxix.

[8] How relevant *Nostromo* is to our own moment in time and to Latin American politics is vividly illustrated by Irving Howe, "Conrad: Order and Anarchy," *Politics and the Novel* (New York, 1957), p. 105.

guana past, the events of the Montero rebellion, and the attempts of the Republic of Sulaco to separate from the rest of Costaguana. Once we accept the fictional world of the Conradian vision, we accept the life within that world as factual; the imaginative re-creation of history becomes more real than the newspaper accounts which deal with actual worlds, but worlds that the reader has never visited. No mere visitor could be confronted by such an abundance of information so dramatically and thoroughly evoked. However, as Lord Raglan says, "All history depends . . . upon chronology, and no real idea of chronology can be obtained except by seeing the facts tabulated in chronological sequence."[9] Within the fictional reality of *Nostromo*, chronology does exist. Or rather the chronology exists within the mind of the author who must have had some coherent story prior to his artistic and temperamental violation of the temporal sequence. Though the disruptions of time are often baffling and though precise events often cannot be measured exactly in days or months or years, an ordered pattern can be reconstructed from the accounts of the characters.[10] And as if the memories of the characters were not sufficient record, Conrad has provided the reader with a written authority for events of the fictional past—an unpublished work by the late Don José Avellanos called "History of Fifty Years of Misrule." Of course this written source, like the events which it records, exists only within the framework of the novel. But its presence helps to support the historical nature of one of the plots; for history, after all, is a form of knowledge which "depends upon written records."[11] And "Fifty Years of Misrule" supplies the exact chronology of Costaguana affairs.

Don José is not the only historian of Sulaco. The unimaginative Captain "Fussy Joe" Mitchell, "having spent a clear thirty years of his life on the high seas before getting what he called a 'shore billet,' was astonished at the importance of transactions (other than relating to shipping) which take place on dry land. Almost every event out of the usual daily course 'marked an epoch' for him or else was

---

[9] Fitzroy Richard Somerset, Fourth Baron Raglan, *The Hero: A Study in Tradition, Myth, and Drama* (New York, 1956), p. 5.

[10] Howe also provides a methodical reconstruction of the facts of Costaguana history.

[11] Raglan, *The Hero*, p. 8.

'history.' "[12] He recalls the "epoch" marked by the days between Nostromo's ride to Cayta and the final separation of Sulaco from the Occidental Province; he is "penetrated by the sense of historical importance of men, events, and buildings."[13] Yet if we use Lord Raglan's standard for the historian, Captain Mitchell is not a true historian because his narrative within the fictional frame is oral. The captive listener, confused by the surfeit of names and events and information, is much like the audience at any factual or complicated fictional narrative. He remembers too little or distorts what he has heard. Were he to relate the events to another he would turn history, the record of facts in a timed world, into tradition or myth, which is timeless. Captain Mitchell, this superintendent of the "Oceanic Steam Navigation Company (the O.S.N. of familiar speech)," is a true historian only because the author has made him one. Conrad has created a written record of the former's oral account of "cosas de Costaguana" as his fictional reality. The storyteller, the novelist, is the only actual historian of Sulaco.

The history of the fictional Sulaco can be reconstructed, though that reconstruction requires an attentive and involved reader. Some time in the recent past a 15-year tyranny of Guzman Bento, the "Citizen Savior of his Country," dominated the political sphere of this recorded world. Both Don José Avellanos and Dr. Monygham experienced the hatred of Bento, the former because he was an aristocrat, a "Blanco," the latter because the old tyrant imagined a conspiracy to overthrow him. After the death of Guzman Bento, the mine was confiscated when the miners "incited to revolt by the emissaries sent out from the capital, had risen upon their English chiefs and murdered them to a man."[14] Then Charles Gould's father was given the perpetual concession of the ruined mine in full

---

[12] Joseph Conrad, *Nostromo* (New York, 1951), p. 124 (112–13). I have used the Modern Library Edition, based upon the text published in 1904 by Doubleday & Co., instead of the Kent Edition, published in 1926 by Doubleday, Page & Co., because certain quotations with which I have supported my argument can only be found in the original text. I have, however, placed the page reference of the same quotation —or of an equivalent quotation with slightly different spelling—occurring in the Kent Edition, within parentheses in each footnote. Where no double citation appears, the quotation has no counterpart in the 1925 edition. Every quotation of more than ten words has been footnoted.

[13] *Ibid.*, p. 531 (475).   [14] *Ibid.*, p. 57 (52).

settlement for forced loans by the fourth Costaguana government in six years. The repeated use of such phrases as "the epoch of civil wars whence had emerged the iron tyranny of Guzman Bento of fearful memory"[15] or "the barbarous ill-usage under Guzman Bento" or a parenthesis assuring us that Guzman Bento was called the "Citizen Savior of the Country"—all these reinforce the narrator's position that he is recording the history of an area which is civilized and corruptible.

As if the abundance of detail provided were not enough, Conrad gives further validity to the "historical" events by juxtaposing the creatures of his imagination with actual historical personages. Giorgio Viola, the Italian innkeeper, is an old companion of and cook for Garibaldi, an "austere republican" whose divinities are "liberty and Garibaldi," and whose personal devil is Cavour, the "arch intriguer." Giorgio combines a high-minded zeal and "devotion to a vast humanitarian idea" with a reverence for the past revolutionary period when men fought with "the spirit of self-forgetfulness." The contempt of this man of the people for the rebellious populace is simply a belief that his present life (a fictional reality) is devoid of the idealism which permeated a particular moment in actual historical time.

The square of Sulaco is dominated by the statue of an actual European ruler, Charles IV, whose marble ineffectuality reminds us of the real Rey of Sulaco, the stony presence of Charles Gould. Nor does this statue of a real emperor possess a greater significance than the plaques celebrating the events of the "third of May" and the Separation of Sulaco from the rest of the Occidental Province, plaques which Captain Mitchell points out to his privileged but captive listener. Indeed, the equestrian statue is removed because, as the historically minded Captain Mitchell tells us, "It was an anachronism." The irony of such a phrase is apparent; yet the word "anachronism" can have no meaning except in a world possessing a sense of the linear progress of time. Pedro Montero, "lackey or inferior scribe, lodged in the garrets of the various Parisian hotels where the Costaguana legation used to shelter its diplomatic dignity,"[16] imagines himself "a sort of Duc de Morny to a sort of

---

[15] *Ibid.*, p. 128 (115).   [16] *Ibid.*, p. 430 (387).

Napoleon"; and so, nurtured by his reading of the history of the Second Empire, he becomes one of the major instigators of the Monterist revolution. Historical fact reinforces fictional fact, which itself pretends to history.

The historical narrative, then, deals with the actual events within a fictional but thoroughly visualized physical setting. It involves activity relating to the formation of a nation, events which are very much a part of a temporal pattern. That the methodical record of actions, time as a "continuous causal chain,"[17] is violated does not mean that a concern with time does not exist. Rather, the violations of the linear progression of time enable us to become more thoroughly involved in the historical events.

Unlike the world of political events, which is within time, there is another world in Nostromo, a traditional one where the motions of the clock have no meaning. The mine's silver—and treasure in general—dominates this second story. Some of the characters do recognize the distinction between history and tradition. Charles Gould confronts Pedro Montero with the fact that he will destroy the San Tomé mine rather than let the Montero government confiscate it:

> But since the San Tomé mine had developed into world-wide fame his threat had enough force and effectiveness to reach the rudimentary intelligence of Pedro Montero, wrapped up as it was in the futilities of historical anecdotes. The Gould Concession was a serious asset in the country's finance, and what was more, in the private budgets of many officials as well. It was traditional. It was known. It was staid.[18]

In spite of the changes of the revolutionary governments, the mine itself is changeless, seeking to be above worldly considerations. Pedro, intellectually nourished on "historical works, light and gossipy in tone," finds himself in Sulaco in a ravaged building. Facing Charles Gould, "that stony fiend," he finds that his imagination is "subdued by a feeling of insecurity and impermanence." The In-

---

17 Georges Poulet, *Studies in Human Time*, trans. Elliott Coleman (New York, 1959), p. 32.

18 Conrad, *Nostromo*, pp. 447–48 (402–3).

tendencia which houses the government can be destroyed; the mind, in any state, is a force, a symbol not only of abstract justice, but also of permanence, of some Absolute.

A dominant characteristic of the world of men is liability to corruption; of the world of immutable values, incorruptibility. Because Nostromo throughout possesses the name and reputation of "Incorruptible," he is entrusted with the saving of the store of silver from the political factions. When the Italian boatswain finally leaves Decoud and the silver upon the Great Isabel, he reminds the latter that there is no necessity for speed or for revealing the hiding place of the silver. " 'And always remember, señor, before you open your lips for a confidence, that this treasure may be left safely here for hundreds of years. Time is on its side, señor. And silver is an incorruptible metal that can be trusted to keep its value forever. . . . An incorruptible metal.' "[19] The final 300 pages of the novel reveal that Nostromo, flesh, is corruptible in every sense of the word, but that the silver, apparently lost forever, does, indeed, have time on its side.

Moreover, time and space have very little meaning to the miners of the Gould Concession and their families. These primitive people, living in their three specially constructed villages, know neither the governmental changes in Sulaco nor the spatial relationships which place Europe and North America in the same universe. Father Roman, ignorant pastor of an almost savage flock, cannot tell his parishioners where Europe is or how history is made.

> But when once an inquisitive spirit desired to know in what direction this Europe was situated, whether up or down the coast, Father Roman, to conceal his perplexity, became very reserved and severe. "No doubt it is extremely far away. But ignorant sinners like you of the San Tomé mine should think earnestly of everlasting punishment instead of inquiring into the magnitude of the earth, with its countries and populations altogether beyond your understanding."[20]

All space is the mine; and all time is simply today and "everlasting punishment." What Lord Raglan states is profoundly true in this fictional reality: "To the folk a thousand years are but yesterday."[21]

---

[19] *Ibid.*, p. 333 (299–300).

[20] *Ibid.*, p. 115 (103–4).   [21] Raglan, *The Hero*, p. 7.

All governmental changes are recorded in the digressions, chrono-logical dislocations, and parentheses so that the very diligent reader can reconstruct a straight line of history. But the unmentioned years which go into the reconstruction of the San Tomé mine can never be calculated with precision.

The mine and the silver, then, present the reader with larger motifs which help to define and control the changing human experi-ence of the Conradian universe. The petty quarrels of the political scene derive an absolute sanction from the mythic world of the silver. Everything which surrounds the treasure—superstitions, guardians, landscape, images used to describe it or to link it with the natural world—reveals figurations which have existed in folklore, fairy tale, myth, and legend. The artist appropriates from the heritage of his cultural life and from the experiences to which all men are subject what approximates a "universal conventional alpha-bet"[22] that can enlarge the most provincial or particular experience. In his fictional presentation of the San Tomé mine and the influ-ence which it exerts over the imagination shaping history, Conrad employs—either consciously or unconsciously—this controlling al-phabet.

To extend this distinction between history and tradition, one need only relate both to the concepts of a perfect and of a fallen world. Sulaco, though its orange groves and isolation suggest Eden, is very different from our conception of paradise. It is inextricably part of the fallen world. Though most of its people are very primi-tive, a decadent Spanish aristocracy exists to remind us that the equality of Eden has long since been forgotten. Or perhaps we might say that this is a microcosm of the fallen world, possessing within its natural barriers all sorts of evil. The Golfo Placido which leads to it grows so dark that it hides from the "eye of God Him-self" the work of man's hand. Although the "luxuriant beauty of the orange gardens bears witness to its [Sulaco's] antiquity,"[23] although it had once found "inviolable sanctuary from the trading world," this paradisiacal state could not continue. It now has access to

[22] See Northrop Frye, "Archetypal Criticism: Theory of Myths," *Anatomy of Criticism* (Princeton, N.J., 1957), pp. 129–239.

[23] Conrad, *Nostromo*, p. 3 (3).

Europe through the steamships of the O.S.N. Company, whose ships "disregard everything but the tyranny of time."

On the other hand, the mine is a "paradise of snakes."[24] When Mrs. Gould reflects upon the influence which the mine exerts after its reconstruction, she speaks of " 'having disturbed a good many snakes in that Paradise.' " And Gould answers, " 'It is no longer a Paradise of snakes. We have brought mankind into it, and we cannot turn our backs upon them to go and begin a new life elsewhere.' "[25] What Conrad presents is a demonic paradise, a parody of the Eden of Genesis wherein the only change was the daily rhythms of darkness and light. This "paradise of snakes" is a prophecy of the future, of the constant threat of corruption over the Conradian universe, of the evil influence of the traditional in the political affairs of the area. The jumbled and tangled natural setting which greets Charles and Mrs. Gould—the Adam and Eve who first yield to the temptations of power—represents the irrational of the individual or the prehistory of the new race born of material interests. Unlike our first parents, who were driven from paradise to found the race of man in time, Charles brings his new race into a demonic Eden.

That early landscape, which in its greenery suggested the Biblical paradise, contained "the thread of a slender waterfall" that "flashed bright and glassy through the dark green of the fronds of tree-ferns."[26] But this waterfall, normally a symbol of regeneration, becomes changed by the activities of the concession:

---

[24] See Frye, *Anatomy of Criticism*, pp. 147–48, 156. This is an example of what Frye calls " 'demonic modulation,' or the deliberate reversal of the customary moral associations of archetypes." That the area containing the mine, a temptation to the Goulds, is described as a "paradise of snakes" increases the irony, since we do not usually associate paradise with the demonic world, the world that "desire totally rejects." The mine, after its rehabilitation, does conform to some of Mr. Frye's criteria for the demonic world. "The demonic divine world largely personifies the vast, menacing, stupid powers of nature as they appear to the technologically underdeveloped society. Symbols of heaven in such a world tend to become associated with the inaccessible sky. . . . The machinery of fate is administered by a set of remote invisible gods, whose freedom and pleasure are ironic because they exclude man, and who intervene in human affairs chiefly to safeguard their own prerogatives. . . . The demonic human world is a society held together by a kind of molecular tension of egos, a loyalty to the group or the leader which diminishes the individual, or, at best, contrasts his pleasure with his duty or honor."

[25] Conrad, *Nostromo*, p. 232 (209).   [26] *Ibid.*, p. 116 (105).

The waterfall existed no longer. The tree-ferns that had luxuriated in its spray had dried around the dried-up pool, and the high ravine was only a big trench half filled up with the refuse of excavations and tailings. The torrent, dammed up above, sent its water rushing along the open flumes of scooped tree-trunks striding on trestle legs to turbines working the stamps on the lower plateau—the *mesa grande* of the San Tomé Mountain. Only the memory of the waterfall, with its amazing fernery, like a hanging garden above the rocks of the gorge, was preserved in Mrs. Gould's water colour sketch.[27]

That the symbol of rebirth has simply been corrupted by mechanization is now apparent. Conrad describes the silver as it descends the mountains as a "stream of silver." The metaphor indicates that the phenomenal world has become charged with a new meaning, because of its association with material interests. By means of the conventional imagery of myth, Conrad reveals how these men who idealize and spiritualize the material give their actions the sanction which Greek or Shakespearean tragedy invested in an orderly but unknown cosmos. After the mine is placed in working order, "Security seemed to flow [emphasis added] upon the land from the mountain gorge."[28] The half-wild Indian miners are like primitive tribes who attribute a human soul to objects of nature and so make little distinction between the human and subhuman and superhuman. Their animism is as much a part of their religious lives as their Catholicism. "They invested it [the mine] with a protecting and invincible virtue as though it were a fetish made by their own hands."[29]

This special world can be seen from Sulaco at night, for it is situated on the side of a mountain. This superior height recalls the tendency of biblical and classical humanity to situate religious shrines in high places. And its lights make it seem outside the spatial considerations of those who are tied to earth; it seems "suspended in the dark night between earth and heaven." Such description contributes to the ambiguity surrounding this traditional force. On the one hand, its paradise is demonic; it destroys the natural. On the other hand, it casts a light in the darkness—whether that darkness be the literal darkness of nature, the darkness representing the in-

---

[27] *Ibid.*, p. 117 (106).   [28] *Ibid.*, p. 122 (110).   [29] *Ibid.*, p. 442 (398).

difference of the universe, the symbolic darkness which is ignorance or the irrational in historical events, or the darkness of a world under a curse. It is nearer heaven than hell. So the question remains: What kind of a force is this mine? Can it order by its very presence the chaotic, disorderly history of Sulaco? Or is the hope it seems to offer simply a parody of divine grace?

Even the human guardians of the silver gain a unique distinction when archetypal patterns attempt to reveal the divine within particular men. The man whose capital helps to finance reconstruction, Mr. Holroyd, is a kind of God figure. (The temptation to point out the similarity of Holroyd to *Holy rōd* is overwhelming.) Or he claims an equal share of divinity because he regards God "as a sort of influential partner." Charles Gould equates the mortal Holroyd and the immortal deity when he speaks of his "trump card," his intention to retain ownership for material interests or to destroy the entire Concession.

> "He—" Charles Gould spoke after a slight pause—"he said something about holding on like grim death and putting our trust in God. I should imagine he must have been rather startled. But then"— pursued the Administrator of the San Tomé mine—"but then, he is very far away, you know, and, as they say in this country, God is very high above."[30]

Like God, dispensing justice to humanity, Holroyd distributes his time with regard to geographical importance. Sulaco receives 20 minutes a month of his undivided attention. But the engineer-in-chief of the railroad reminds us that, where material interests are spiritualized, time is of no consequence:

> "To be a millionaire, and such a millionaire as Holroyd, is like being eternally young. The audacity of youth reckons upon what it fancies as unlimited time at its disposal; but a millionaire has unlimited means in his hand—which is better. One's time on earth is an uncertain quantity, but about the long reach of millions there is no doubt."[31]

This god is, after all, but a self-deceptive idealist who attempts to justify his hopes of absolute power by "a pet dream of a purer form

---

30 *Ibid.*, p. 228 (206).   31 *Ibid.*, p. 352 (317).

of Christianity." But such " 'Food for vanity,' " as Dr. Monygham—
cynic, skeptic, and himself a self-deceptive idealist—reminds us,
" 'makes the world go round.' "

Motifs from fairy tales or Märchen also become associated with
the mine, enhancing its traditional role in the narrative. Unlike a
fairy tale, however, Conrad's story does not divide the characters too
easily into black and white, evil and good. The burden of proof
shifts from one side to the other. Charles's father, a man well read
in "light literature," became so obsessed with the mine that he regarded it as the "Old Man of the Sea fastened upon his shoulders.
He also began to dream of vampires."[32] His correspondence to his
son takes on the "flavor of a gruesome Arabian Night's tale." Unfortunately the son, like the father, has "fallen under the spell of the
San Tomé mine."

Finally, all Charles's actions are dominated by his awareness of
the mine; his idealism takes the form of a "moral romance." As
Decoud explains to Mrs. Gould, he " 'could not believe his own
motives if he did not make them first a part of some fairytale.' "[33]
Decoud, arguing for Separation—Decoud the politician and journalist of Sulaco who both records and shapes historical events—says
again in comparing Charles and himself, " 'Life is not for me a
moral romance derived from the tradition of a pretty fairytale.' "[34]
Even the engineer-in-chief, who claims that the railroad has no practical hobby-horse to ride, and who wishes to establish his neutrality
in the upheavals of Sulaco, claims that Charles is in the position of
the " 'goose with the golden egg.' " The firmness of this position in
the imaginative life of mankind is then emphasized. Decoud's plan
of Separation may fail or may not fail. Ribierism has collapsed because it was "merely rational," based on predictable historical laws.
But the fairy tale has a logic based upon association, which is part of
the imaginative life of the race. " 'The tale of killing the goose with
the golden eggs has not been evolved for nothing out of the wisdom
of mankind. It is a story that will never grow old.' "[35]

To insure success, the world of the mine has its benevolent, protecting feminine presence. Mrs. Gould is described again and again

[32] *Ibid.*, p. 61 (56).   [34] *Ibid.*, p. 241 (218).
[33] *Ibid.*, p. 237 (215).   [35] *Ibid.*, p. 350 (315).

as fairy-like, as resembling "a fairy posed lightly before dainty philtres dispensed out of vessels of silver and porcelain."[36] In one of the reader's last pictures of her she is sitting alone in the "Treasure House of the World." "Small and dainty, as if radiating a light of her own in the deep shade of the interlaced boughs, she resembled a good fairy, weary with a long career of well-doing, touched by the withering suspicion of the uselessness of her labors, the powerlessness of her magic."[37] Many of the affairs of the mine, as well as her good deeds, are conducted in her boudoir, blue and white, approximating the colors assigned by liturgical art to that Christian "good fairy," the Virgin Mary. That she keeps a statue of The Queen of Heaven in a niche in her home reinforces this identification between her benevolence and that of the mother of Christ.

We can imply from the irrationality of the political narrative that history is the story of man's unsuccessful attempts to cope with his fallen state. In the name of security he replaces one imperfection by another equally imperfect. The epoch of civil war is followed by the iron tyranny of Guzman Bento (who at least maintains peace), which is followed by several revolutions and "fatuous imbecility, plenty of cruelty and suffering still," which is followed by the benevolent tyranny of Don Vincente Ribiera, "a man of culture and of unblemished character," which is followed by the revolutions led by men like General Montero, his brother, Pedro, and Colonel Sotillo. Martin Decoud dies in the cause of Separation; in the last few pages of the novel rumors abound of Sulaco's wishing to extend peace to the rest of Costaguana by means of union.

History is, at once, the story of individual men who want to realize or idealize their ambitions—that is, dreamers who delude themselves that they are democrats, that they are concerned with the people—and it is perpetual cycle whereby every human situation will always be repeated. Politics is a constant round of mental and moral failure. The traditional sphere of the mine, the language and iconography derived from myth and fairy tale, must make individual endeavor meaningful within this constant cycle or must give men's actions a moral justification. One of the main clues to the author's own sympathies appears very early in the novel, casually mentioned

36 Ibid., pp. 56–57 (52).   37 Ibid., p. 581 (520).

so that it seems merely a bit of local information which helps to establish the narrator's authority over his material. The author is describing one boundary of Sulaco.

On the other side, what seems to be an isolated patch of blue mist floats lightly on the glare of the horizon. This is the peninsula of Azuera, a wild chaos of sharp rocks and stony levels cut about by vertical ravines. It lies far out to sea like a rough head of stone stretched from a green-clad coast at the end of a slender neck of sand covered with thickets of thorny scrub. Utterly waterless, for the rainfall runs off at once on all sides into the sea, it has not soil enough, it is said, to grow a single blade of grass—as if it were blighted by a curse. The poor, associating by an obscure instinct of consolation the ideas of evil and wealth, will tell you that it is deadly because of its forbidden treasures. The common folk of the neighborhood, peons of the estancias, vaqueros of the seaboard plains, tame Indians coming miles to market with a bundle of sugar-cane or a basket of maize worth about threepence, are well aware that heaps of shining gold lie in the gloom of the deep precipices cleaving the stony levels of Azuera. Tradition has it that many adventurers of olden time had perished in the search. The story goes also that within men's memory two wandering sailors—Americanos, perhaps, but gringos of some sort for certain—talked over a gambling, good-for-nothing mozo, and the three stole a donkey to carry for them a bundle of dry sticks, a water-skin, and provisions enough to last a few days. Thus accompanied, and with revolvers at their belts, they had started to chop their way with machetes through the thorny scrub on the neck of the peninsula. On the second evening an upright spiral of smoke (it could only have been from their camp-fire) was seen for the first time within memory of man standing up faintly upon the sky above a razor-backed ridge on the stony head. The crew of a coasting schooner, lying becalmed three miles off the shore, stared at it with amazement till dark. A negro fisherman, living in a lonely hut in a little bay near by, had seen the start and was on the lookout for some sign. He called to his wife just as the sun was about to set. They had watched the strange portent with envy, incredulity, and awe.

The impious adventurers gave no other sign. The sailors, the Indian, and the stolen burro were never seen again. As to the mozo, a Sulaco man—his wife paid for some masses, and the poor four-footed beast, being without sin, had been probably permitted to die; but the two gringos, spectral and alive, are believed to be dwelling to this day among the rocks, under the fatal spell of their success. Their souls cannot tear themselves away from their bodies mounting guard over the discovered treasure. They are now rich and hungry and thirsty—a strange theory of tenacious gringo ghosts suffering in their starved and parched flesh of defiant heretics, where a Christian would have renounced and been released.[38]

Thus, in order to explain the barrenness of this area, a superstition has gradually evolved. Time has no meaning here; facts are irrelevant (the sailors are *perhaps* Americans); tradition, not history, is at work. Though the events are "within men's memory" and "within the memory of man," no attempt is made to establish a definite chronology, to place it before or after, say, Guzman Bento. The land is simply "blighted by a curse." But so is the world since Eden. Yet the poor "associate ideas of evil and wealth." Evil, as a result of wealth, causes the natural objects to wither, causes the land to reject water, and possesses the souls and bodies of those who succeed. The gringos are under the "fatal spell of their success." Their situation is, indeed, a parody of Christian resurrection. Charles Gould too has succeeded and, as we have seen, is also under an enchantment. The man who came to "redeem" the land by treasure has succumbed to it. But he is unlike the spectral gringos because he deceives himself as to his motives and idealizes the material interests which he serves; he is a victim of his own "moral romance."

Moreover, the area around the mine changes as a result of the endeavors of the Gould Concession. The "slender waterfall" no longer exists in the gorge. "The tree-ferns that had luxuriated in its spray had dried around the dried-up pool, and the high ravine was only a big trench half filled up with the refuse of excavations and tailings."[39] Now the silver coming down the mountain is the only stream; it has replaced natural phenomena. The primitive miners have work and a measure of security; they are, however, herded into three anonymous villages—numbered rather than named. Individual freedom has disappeared.

Not only is the mine's influence over nature destructive, but its influence over its owner is dehumanizing. The relationship between Gould and his wife disintegrates as a result of the enchantment of his opportunity. No children are born to this marriage. If not actually, Emilia is symbolically virginal. She dreads the mine as if it were

---

[38] *Ibid.*, pp. 4–5 (3–5).   [39] *Ibid.*, p. 117 (106).

another woman—" 'Don Carlos' mission is to save him from the effects of that cold and overmastering passion, which she dreads more than if it were an infatuation for another woman.' "[40] Nor can Gould's failure in the realm of love be attributed to the author's own temperamental inability to deal with love between the sexes. As Thomas Moser suggests,[41] Conrad found the subject of love uncongenial; but in Charles Gould he reveals the successful characterization of a man unable to love for reasons which were congenial to Conrad. He is attempting to be faithful to an image of himself; he is a romantic like Lord Jim. Like Lord Jim he allows his egoism to isolate him completely from other human beings. This man who attempts to sentimentalize his actions is simply another portrait of a type which Conrad successfully created again and again—the self-deluded idealist. His role within the novel parallels that of the Fisher King in traditional story, the ruler whose wounds, either actual or symbolic, cause the wasting of his lands; he is the redeemer turned destroyer. In truth, Mrs. Gould is Conrad's only successful characterization of a woman;[42] but this is so because she does not present the usual problems of a woman in love. Although she is young, this fact is hard for the reader to realize because of her good works and because of Monygham's attachment to her. Although she loves, she does not manifest her love in a demonstrative passion; rather, she is simply there—loyal, passive, unobtrusive. Her unhappiness is stressed once—at the end, where it cannot destroy our firm impression of her. Finally, she too is an idealist; she sentimentalizes her husband's actions.

Nor is the mine a stabilizing influence over the affairs of Sulaco. It finances Don Vincente Ribiera, lures Colonel Sotillo's support for the Monterists, and nourishes Pedro Montero's dreams of grandeur. " 'The real objective of the revolted garrison of Esmeralda is the San Tomé mine itself . . . otherwise the Occidental Province would have been, no doubt, left alone for many weeks.' "[43] Dr.

---

[40] Ibid., p. 271 (245).

[41] Thomas Moser, "The Uncongenial Subject," Joseph Conrad: Achievement and Decline (Cambridge, Mass., 1957), pp. 50–130.

[42] Ibid., pp. 81–88.   [43] Conrad, Nostromo, p. 271 (244).

Monygham makes the last pessimistic statement concerning the future of the Concession as a moral and practical force: " 'No!' interrupted the doctor. 'There is no peace and no rest in the development of material interests . . . Mrs. Gould, the time approaches when all that the Gould Concession stands for shall weigh as heavily upon the people as the barbarism, cruelty, and misrule of a few years back.' "[44]

Just as *Nostromo* is two stories—a historical one and a traditional one—so it possesses two heroes who together make the composite hero of the novel. The traditional hero is Nostromo, the Genoese sailor, whose early life is a parody of the characteristics which Otto Rank and, after him, Lord Raglan, assign to the hero myth. His parentage and childhood are unknown. The only cetrain fact about his youth is that he suffered brutalities at the hands of a cruel uncle "who (he firmly believed) had cheated him out of his orphan's inheritance."[45] The exposure myth whereby the elected infant child, born in unusual circumstances, is committed to the waves by the man who represents the father in authority if not in fact, is here in changed form. Nostromo escapes the cruel relative at fourteen, flees across the traditional body of water to a strange land, Sulaco, where he simply "came ashore one evening," and then finds the equivalents of both the kind stepparents *and* strange adventures. Old Giorgio, the Genoese Garibaldino, compares Nostromo's age to that of his dead son. Doña Teresa, Giorgio's wife, constantly claims the prerogatives of a mother. "He was escaping from her, she feared . . . she railed at his poverty, his exploits, his adventures, his loves and his reputation; but in her heart she had never given him up, as though indeed, he had been her son."[46] When he relates his great mission to her as she is dying and receives only her indignation, he himself admits her claims: " 'What angry nonsense are you talking, mother?' " His final refusal to fetch a priest for her weighs heavily upon him, for he "had been orphaned so young that he could remember no other woman whom he called mother."[47] Dr. Monygham pronounces a judgment which reflects the classic Oedipal situ-

---

[44] *Ibid.*, p. 571 (511).

[45] *Ibid.*, p. 466 (416).

[46] *Ibid.*, pp. 281–82 (254).

[47] *Ibid.*, p. 526 (469–70).

ation: " 'Women are so very unaccountable, in every position and at all times of life, that I thought sometimes she was, in a way, don't you see? in love with him—the Capataz.' "[48]

Again and again there is evidence that a reputation for supernatural exploits has gathered around the name of this Italian sailor, just as popular report endowed the heroes of every age with miraculous deeds. He has a special talent for appearing "whenever there is something picturesque to be done." At the moment of gravest danger he saves President Ribiera from the mob; he appears at the inn of old Viola as the enraged populace turn their guns upon it; his mere presence is enough to quell the people. He alone is cited for the task of removing the silver; Captain Mitchell mourns his supposed death because only he is capable of achieving the desperate ride to Cayta. And his vanity thrives on the adulation of both aristocrat and democrat. He is not only Nostromo, the "boatswain," he is Nostro uomo, "our man," which abbreviated in Italian becomes Nostr'uomo.

Though he presents a physical appearance above the ordinary and though his actions reveal heroic potentiality, Nostromo still does not possess the stature of a hero. For all his extraordinary ability he is only a man of the people, a captain of the cargadores. The cargadores themselves are an "outcast lot of very mixed blood, mainly negroes, everlastingly at feud with the other customers of low grogshops in the town."[49] And Nostromo serves as their aloof and condescending taskmaster, supe..ior to them in ability and vanity but not in origin.

The deficiencies which are present in the Capataz are corrected in the person of Martin Decoud, the Journalist of Sulaco. This young man, born in Costaguana of a family later settled in Paris, is an aristocrat, a dilettante, and, like Gould, a self-deceptive idealist. He luxuriates in his position as spectator, in his indifference, his lack of faith, his skepticism. But he deceives himself because he is neither indifferent nor uncommitted. Conrad often uses the word "imagined" when speaking of Decoud's lack of self-knowledge. "Martin Decoud . . . imagined himself to derive an artistic pleasure

---

[48] *Ibid.*, p. 354 (319).   [49] *Ibid.*, p. 15 (14).

from watching the picturesque extreme of wrong-headedness into which an honest, almost sacred conviction may drive a man."[50] "He imagined himself Parisian to the tips of his fingers." That he believes he is a man without faith and principles is apparent from his letter to his sister; that he is capable of intense passions is also apparent from his earnestness in carrying out his initial mission to Sulaco, from his deep love for Antonia Avellanos, from his editorials in *Porvenir* (for which he is marked for execution when the Monterist faction takes Sulaco), from his mission to accomplish Separation, and from his final suicide.[51] Conrad always treats Decoud's pose of "idle cumberer of the earth" with irony. But in Decoud's passionate moments—in his isolation and uncertainty—we can see many of the author's major concerns. Nostromo is the romantic hero, the simple, naïve man who sees events in terms of good and evil, the hero by temperament. Decoud, on the other hand, is capable of the tragic vision, the awareness of ambiguity and irony in life. He alone possesses the exquisite sensibility which realizes that he is part of an immense indifference of things. He is the hero by birth, Aristotle's "type ennobled," the man who can fall from a superior height because the superior height is his rightful social position.

Moreover, the hero is traditionally and historically a national figure, who is willing to subordinate his individual concerns for the larger good of the community. At the outset he is a free agent, who either by choice or special election, is gradually caught up in a chain of causality. He must assume the burden of the quest through which he meets and conquers the dragon that oppresses and blights the land. The regeneration of civilization may be the result of his success.

Sulaco approximates the fallen world of myth; its symbolic curse is expressed in the image of the burden from which no man is exempt. The landscape is often described as being under the weight of clouds or of shadows. The "burdened Indians," the people "all under burdens," accept their lot with patience and silence; their actual loads are representative of the weight of the past which is

---

[50] *Ibid.*, p. 221 (200).

[51] For a discussion of Decoud's two "potential" selves see Albert Guerard, "Nostromo," *Conrad the Novelist* (Cambridge, Mass., 1958), pp. 201–2.

intangible. By Separation, Decoud expects to free the land so that the rest of Costaguana cannot hang "like a millstone round our necks," so that Sulaco may be freed from the stupidity of the past. Nor does Decoud's expectation of Antonia's love negate the selflessness of his actions. We can see in her presence the guiding feminine symbol by means of which Decoud must overcome his own physical limitations. She is the virgin princess of myth and fairy tale whose hand is the final reward for all successful action in the social sphere.

Nostromo, too, regards his quest—the removal of the silver—as an attempt to promote the common good. In accepting the quest, he realizes that he is accepting a curse. And the rewards are in reality insignificant—an incorruptible reputation—compared with the danger involved. Dr. Monygham pricks his vanity by saying that " 'for taking the *curse of death* [emphasis added] upon my back, as you call it, nothing else but the whole treasure would do.' "[52] Moreover, the curse of the silver does involve a symbolic death and recalls the curse of Doña Teresa's "lost soul."

Neither Decoud nor Nostromo—the first accepting the call to adventure of the historical narrative; the other, the call of the traditional story—has yet confronted the possibilities of his own nature. Neither man has been sufficiently alone to look inward in order to make the discoveries which will enable him to understand himself and, perhaps through understanding his own identity, to aid his fellow men. The moment these two set themselves adrift in the lighter with its cargo of silver, they are more alone than either has ever previously been. Their withdrawal from human society is the first step in the complete cycle of the hero's adventure into the unknown. Moreover, the journey by sea in a lighter suggests the hero's journey into the interior regions of the mind. What we have in the novel are external referents which are symbolic translations of internal events. As Joseph Campbell tells us, "The first step, detachment or withdrawal, consists in a radical transfer of emphasis from the external to the internal world, macro- to microcosm, a retreat from the desperations of the waste land to the peace of the everlasting realm that is within."[53]

---

[52] *Ibid.*, p. 288 (259).

[53] Joseph Campbell, *The Hero with a Thousand Faces* (New York, 1956), p. 17.

That Conrad has unconsciously blurred the boundary between the real voyage and the interior journey of the psyche becomes apparent as soon as the two men leave the shore. The standards of the visible world lose their meanings as soon as the night-sea is encountered. "The effect was that of being launched into space." In the last 11 pages of chapter 7, images and metaphors suggesting sleep, dream, and unreality increase in number. To Decoud the stillness affects his senses "like a powerful drug"; he begins to lose his belief in his own individuality and at times doesn't know "whether he were asleep or awake." The past, as well as the present, seems betrayed by the indifference of the dream. "All his active sensations and feelings, from as far back as he could remember, seemed to him the maddest of dreams. Even his passionate devotion to Antonia into which he had worked himself up out of the depths of his scepticism, had lost all appearance of reality."[54] Such intense silence approximates death. "In this foretaste of eternal peace they floated vivid and light, like unearthly clear dreams of earthly things that may haunt the souls freed by death from the misty atmosphere of regrets and hopes."[55]

Nostromo, hearing Hirsch weeping, believes that he is dreaming. Even the gulf on which they float becomes personified—as inanimate objects or intangibles do in dreams or fairy tales: ". . . the gulf under its poncho of clouds remained breathless, as if dead rather than asleep";[56] ". . . the great waters spread out strangely smooth, as if their restlessness had been crushed by the weight of that dense night."[57] Note that these images also reveal a burdened cosmos.

The only sensations which affect these two men are intangibles. "Solitude could almost be felt." Not only does everything appear dreamlike and unreal, not only does the subject-object relationship between man and nature seem obliterated by the oppression of the blackness upon their senses, but also Nostromo and Decoud begin to be identified with the superstitions of the area. The story of the legendary gringos, whose bodies, "spectral and alive," haunt the desolate Azuera, is recalled at that moment by Nostromo. Their task

---

[54] Conrad, *Nostromo*, p. 290 (267).   [56] *Ibid.*, p. 294 (265).

[55] *Ibid.*, p. 210 (262).   [57] *Ibid.*, p. 290 (261).

is more dangerous than "sending a man to get the treasure that people said was guarded by devils and ghosts in the deep ravines of Azuera."[58] Not only the dreams that manifest an individual's own unconscious, but also the popular lore which persists in the local culture is here significant. They have left the workaday world where communication between individuals and knowledge of physical constants are based upon evidence furnished by the senses. The night-sea journey demands a method of understanding beyond that employed by the timed world.

The irrationality of the whole situation provides a superb example of man's fate in an irrational world. They find both sense experience and intellect useless in floating in impenetrable darkness. Unable to determine whether or not they are moving, they yet cannot control their direction. Symbolizing the wider theme of the *bateau ivre*, the rudderless (literally, "drunken") boat, their actions externalize in fictional form the experience of all mankind in an indifferent nature. " 'This is a blind game with death,' " says Nostromo—but so, too, is life. When Hirsch, the hide merchant, is discovered hidden upon the lighter, his fate also remains "suspended in the darkness of the gulf, at the mercy of events which could not be foreseen."[59]

That darkness and shadow suggest the unconscious, the buried life, is made very explicit. At the moment Nostromo snuffs the candle, Decoud realizes the uniqueness of his position. "Intellectually self-confident, he suffered from being deprived of the only weapon he could use with effect. No intelligence could penetrate the darkness of the Placid Gulf."[60] He has begun to confront the interior world of his existence in this dreamlike setting. And so jealous is the Capataz of his reputation that Nostromo resents a situation in which courage is not good enough. " 'I have a good eye and a steady hand; no man can say he ever saw me tired or uncertain what to do; but, *por Dios*, Don Martin, I have been sent out into this black calm on a business where neither a good eye, nor a steady hand, nor judgment are any use.' "[61]

Each man begins to see that the other's presence does and will

---

[58] *Ibid.*, p. 292 (263–64).

[59] *Ibid.*, p. 305 (275).

[60] *Ibid.*

[61] *Ibid.*, p. 306 (275–76).

affect the completion of his own task. Nostromo, whose main concern is the silver, feels that his honor demands that he save the treasure or sink with it. Decoud's task is to reach General Barrios at Cayta. Politics and historical events have complicated Nostromo's singleness of purpose just as the silver may require that Decoud drown to satisfy Nostromo's vanity.

In myth, as I have noted, the hero must undertake a night-sea journey into an ambiguous region either in the dark interior of the earth or below the waters of the sea. This is a symbolic death that occurs so that he may encounter the forces of evil, the monsters that blight the world of natural cycle; he descends, so to speak, into the belly of the whale or into the mouth of the dragon. In overcoming the monster which is death, he experiences the peace of paradise and a knowledge of the unity of existence. But he must be reborn in order to bring his special truth back to a fallen world, in order to redeem mankind. On a personal level, the ritual quest symbolizes the journey into the self, into the dark interior landscape of the dream which approximates the still waters of the womb. After conquering the dragon that is the Ego, the individual is reborn better able to endure the continual flux of life because he has gained a new knowledge of the self, a new sense of identity.[62]

The collision with the troop ship, the burial of the treasure, and Nostromo's final swim back to the mainland—all these can be equated with the mythic journey into the underworld, the death and rebirth of the Capataz. As a result of the report forced from the frightened Hirsch, who is miraculously saved, Nostromo and Decoud are considered dead. The man whose reputation depends upon saving the silver has purportedly "saved" it at the cost of his own life. Yet the truth is that the freighted boat does not sink, but is with difficulty conveyed to the small island. Nostromo, after burying the silver and leaving Decoud, himself sinks the lighter, destroys all evidence of his own survival, and swims to the shore in order to return to Sulaco.

His emergence from the dark sea where the lighter is "hardly distinguishable from the black water upon which she floated," reveals

---

62 Campbell, *The Hero with a Thousand Faces.*

the figure of a man who has passed through several worlds. First of all, he reaches land before dawn and sleeps the entire day until after sunset. Sleeping for 14 hours, he loses his sense of the linear passage of time in the historical world. The site he chooses reflects the corruption caused by death; it is the quadrangle of an old fort among "ruined bits of walls and rotting remnants of roofs and sheds."[63] As he sleeps, the entire area possesses the ambiguity present between the spiritual or internal world of the dark gulf, the world revealed in sleep or death, and the real world where man is required to act. He lay "as if dead," "as still as a corpse." A rey-zamuro watches his body "from a hillock of rubbish" for "signs of death and corruption." The Capataz sleeps through the "white blaze of noon" and only wakes after darkness has again descended. He is thrust back into the world in which ambiguity and irrationality must be confronted by the knowledge gained from an irrational and ambiguous experience. Only after Nostromo awakes does the bird fly away— and then reluctantly, as if aware of the invisible corruption within or aware that this man has just been reborn from the peace of a symbolic death. And because this man has been "reborn," because he is now without those externalities necessary to his sense of personal identity, he is not fully equipped to handle the exigencies of his situation. Rather, Conrad uses the images of the child just born or of an animal, a regression to the primitive in the individual life or to the prehuman state. He awakes "with the lost air of a man just born into the world."[64] With a "growling yawn" he appears "as natural and free from evil in the moment of waking as a magnificent and unconscious wild beast."[65] Moreover, the strangeness he feels concerning this new order of events shows how complete his rupture from the previous adventure has been. He is "some time in regaining his hold on the world. It had slipped from him completely in the deep slumber of more than twelve hours. It had been like a break in continuity in the chain of experience; he had to find himself in *time and space* [emphasis added], to think of the hour and the place of his return."[66]

---

[63] Conrad, *Nostromo*, p. 459 (413).   [65] *Ibid.*, p. 458 (412).

[64] *Ibid.*, p. 458 (411).   [66] *Ibid.*, p. 460.

But the world into which Nostromo is reborn is a world which believes that he is dead. So this man, whose faithfulness and worth are based upon an exaggerated concern for public reputation, finds his new life dreamlike. As he enters Sulaco, the town seems unreal. "The thought that it was no longer open to him to ride through the street, recognized by every one, great and little, as he used to do every evening on his way to play *monte* in the posada of the Mexican Domingo; or to sit in the place of honor, listening to songs and looking at dances, made it appear to him as a town that had no existence."[67] Obsessed by a feeling of betrayal, he rushes to the custom-house "like a pursued shadow" to be greeted by another unreality—the shadow of Hirsch's hanging dead body. When Dr. Monygham relates recent events, Nostromo listens "as if in a dream," feeling "himself of as little account as the man." Even the ride to Cayta must be undertaken without the support of an admiring audience. It is the achievement of a ghost, or of a man unable to meet the world he once knew on his own terms.

Nostromo as hero, then, has undergone many aspects of the ritual adventure. He has withdrawn temporarily from mankind in order to fulfill the requirements of his task. His withdrawal into the unknown takes the form of the journey by night-sea, a region where the unconscious may project its fantasies without the hindrance of time and space.[68] The darkness of the gulf represents that world beyond the boundaries which sense imposes. His entire adventure upon the gulf is his descent into the belly of the whale, into the peace of death. Although little more than 24 hours have elapsed, Conrad has artistically created the illusion of time held in suspension. His images suggest an immutable world. Nostromo is reborn, supposedly able to redeem the fallen world with his new presence.

But, as we have been told, the mythic journey is within; the gulf is the "realm we enter in sleep. We carry it within ourselves forever."[69] What has been demanded of Nostromo is that he annihilate

---

[67] *Ibid.*, p. 463 (414–15).

[68] Campbell, *The Hero with a Thousand Faces*, p. 79.

[69] *Ibid.*

his ego in order to save Sulaco. When he enters the peace of the gulf, he for the first time faces the possibility of his own failure. Though Decoud is his companion in the adventure, he is at last entirely, profoundly, isolated. The perfect logic of his very simple character breaks down in a situation which cannot be controlled by "a good eye nor steady hand nor judgment." Like the revolutionary Colonel Sotillo he has never realized "the limitations put upon human faculties by the darkness of night,"[70] by the repressed within one's own nature. And he resents having to face the threat of corruption over all humanity in the Conradian scheme of things and over all flesh in the fallen world of myth. He thinks he has been betrayed by the Blancos, the aristocrats who use him, although his own ego destroys him. He resents, finally, any human truth which denies the reality of his past actions. The awareness of failure and the inevitability of death, the "intimate impressions of universal dissolution," cause the collapse of his vanity.

What Nostromo cannot do when he returns is "survive the impact of the world,"[71] as the successful hero should. He cannot readjust himself to the society whose admiration he requires. After his symbolic rebirth, he cannot bridge the gap between the two worlds— the logical simple world he has created for himself and the dark world of the unknown. His new life begins the moment he awakens on the mainland, for he must live both concealed himself and concealing the hiding place of the silver. Decoud's death merely intensifies his own secret life. The disappearance of both the ingots and Decoud causes an "irrational apprehension." Decoud's leaving the spade near the treasure, an act which reveals the hiding space, connotes "utter carelessness or sudden panic," conduct which confounds Nostromo's consistent nature. His simplicity does not embrace a knowledge of the irrational.

Changes take place in him over the years. His public life as Nostromo has ceased, existing only in the memory of those who participated in the fight for Separation. (Several of these men, however, are dead.) He has made another public existence for himself as

---

[70] Conrad, *Nostromo*, p. 322 (290).

[71] Campbell, *The Hero with a Thousand Faces*, p. 226.

Gian' Battista Fidanza: his real name is first used, ironically enough, when he discovers that Decoud is dead and the four ingots of silver are gone. Now he is "unpicturesque, but always a little mysterious." The name which meant "boatswain" or "our man" is replaced by a surname which denotes reliability. But his new public life is only appearance; the real life is hidden. The confidence he inspired can exist only in memory or as a lie. His position as *Capataz de Carga-dores* is assumed by Ramirez, a starving waif grown to manhood and a suitor of Giselle Viola. By stealing the silver, Nostromo grows rich slowly. The world believes Captain Fidanza has a profitable business. He becomes betrothed ostensibly to Linda Viola, but secretly courts Giselle, who he feels will accept his crime. When he is shot, he lies to Giselle about the motive of his return to the Great Isabel. " 'It seemed as though I could not live through the night without seeing thee once more—my star, my little flower.' "[72]

As Nostromo's secrets grow, so his isolation from the community grows. The town for which he undertook the quest is forgotten. In his own eyes, however, he is still Nostromo, still "Incorruptible." He refuses to admit the "soft spot, the place of decay"[73] within, denies the evil in himself and so symbolically denies it in all mankind. And in denying his personal evil, he proves that he cannot transcend the limits of his own ego. At last he dies, admitting the truth only once to Emilia Gould. To himself and the world he has denied, he has "lived his own life on the assumption of unbroken fidelity, rectitude, and courage!"[74]

But the successful hero is the whole man, a creature who realizes that both guilt and innocence, corruption and purity, are mixed inevitably in the human sphere. Nostromo's fault is that he is a man "who, satisfied with his own appearance, presumes to consider himself right and whole, a hero, a king in the seat of judgment."[75] The silver, once given him as an actual task and a symbol of his hero's

---

[72] Conrad, *Nostromo*, p. 618 (554).

[73] Conrad, *Lord Jim*, p. 13.

[74] Conrad, *Nostromo*, p. 625 (561).

[75] Heinrich Zimmer, "The King and the Corpse," *The King and the Corpse: Tales of the Soul's Conquest of Evil*, trans. and ed. Joseph Campbell, Bollingen XI (New York, 1956), 224.

quest, now becomes the measure of his guilt. Like the king of the folk tale who must bear on his back the gruesome corpse of an unknown criminal—a corpse whose ghostly voice propounds riddles for the king to answer—Nostromo must bear the symbolic weight of the treasure. In the tale the decaying corpse represents the dead body of the past, "another one of our egos";[76] the ghostly voice within it which prods the king is:

> . . . still another, the strangest ego of all. It dwells behind, beyond, within the kingly 'I' that we consciously consider ourselves to be, and, making its voice echo from the dead forms around, threatens sudden death to us should we refuse to obey its whims. It sets us tasks and pricks us to and fro, involving us in the hideous game of life and death.[77]

The king, after his strange initiation, becomes aware of his complicity in mankind's guilt as well as in mankind's innocence, and so completes his task. After Nostromo is "reborn" and returns unknown to Sulaco, "deprived of certain simple realities, such as the admiration of women, the adulation of men, the admired publicity of his life, [he] was ready to feel the burden of sacrilegious guilt descend upon his shoulders."[78]

The symbolic weight of the buried silver makes him feel enslaved. The references to weight become gradually combined with images of a man in fetters. At all times he is "as if he had been chained to the treasure." To Nostromo these unreal chains have an almost visible and audible force. It angers him because Giselle cannot hear "the clanking of his fetters—his silver fetters—from afar." But Giselle's love for Nostromo does not bind her as Linda's does; for the latter wants to share her lover's guilt and carries her love "like an increasing load of shameful fetters." Symbolically burdened by the treasure, Nostromo dies actually bearing it. When he is shot by a senile Viola, he is creeping out of the foliage "loaded with silver." Even as he is dying, however, he has but one moment of personal doubt. True to his vision of himself, he dies proclaiming that he has been betrayed.

---

[76] *Ibid.*, p. 223.   [77] *Ibid.*   [78] Conrad, *Nostromo*, p. 470 (420).

Again, the knowledge that the whole man combines reason and lack of it, guilt and innocence, binds the archetypal hero more closely to the community which he has saved. His vision of the eternal has confirmed him in his communal role. In this novel, Nostromo's denial of the irrational world and his conscious refusal to accept his guilt (although he unconsciously bears it) isolate him. The silver destroys any meaningful personal relationships which he might establish. Dying, Doña Teresa, the symbolic mother, the nourishing, all-protecting feminine presence in the universe,[79] predicts his failure. " 'Your folly shall betray you into poverty, misery, starvation.' " This is the curse upon his whole venture. After he has grown rich on the treasure, he transfers his affections from the dark Linda, who was to have been his wife, to the blond Giselle. "Linda, with her mother's voice, had taken more her mother's place."[80] To old Viola she is "like a daughter and wife in one." Linda is rejected by Nostromo because he realizes she would not condone his actions. In the mythical counterpart of this fictional episode, the reward for the hero's victory is the beautiful woman at once mother, virgin, sister. Linda, as adopted sister of Nostromo's second family, as symbolic replacement for Doña Teresa—wife to old Viola and mother to Giselle for whom she feels "maternal tenderness"—and as betrothed for Nostromo, fulfills many of the requirements of this role.

But this role is traditionally filled by the blond woman, the innocent, the representative of the world of reason. According to Mario Praz, the dark woman is usually the temptress, the vampire, the creature who, whether through her own volition or because of something beyond her control, has a pact with the devil for the destruction of the hero.[81] And Linda does partake of this irrationality. She is passionate rather than submissive. When she suspects Giselle's duplicity, she behaves like a vampire; she flings "herself upon the chair in which her indolent sister was lying and impressed the mark of her teeth at the base of the whitest neck in Sulaco."[82] Yet with

---

[79] Campbell, *The Hero with a Thousand Faces*, p. 113.

[80] Conrad, *Nostromo*, p. 591 (529).

[81] Mario Praz, *The Romantic Agony*, trans. Angus Davidson (New York, 1954).

[82] Conrad, *Nostromo*, p. 613 (549).

typical Conradian irony the pattern is again reversed. Linda reveals a depth of emotion consistent with her characterization as the daughter of the woman who was herself a little in love with Nostromo, yet who placed a curse upon his actions. But she is also the lighthouse keeper. She watches the light, which stands on the Great Isabel and shines over the treasure, the dark spot in Nostromo's life. The light, like the candle lit in the gulf, seems to represent reason; it appears as a symbol of communication. It has an important function in guiding the members of the community back to shore. But ironically, although with poetic justice it beams over the silver, it cannot penetrate or reveal the burial place of the treasure. As a force of isolation, the silver remains stronger than the light of communication.

Giselle, on the other hand, appears innocent. In truth, her very submissiveness, her indolence, is "seductive." She attracts Nostromo not only because of her difference from Linda, but because her hair is "like gold" and because her voice, unlike Linda's, reminds him of the "tinkling of a silver bell." Admittedly his love-making is embarrassing to the reader. But it is embarrassing not only because Conrad found the subject matter uncongenial, but also because Giselle never becomes a real woman. She is always a symbol of a traditional but dehumanizing force.

Like Charles Gould, whose mine becomes the substitute for a woman, Nostromo's final isolation is from his hero's reward, from the woman he loves. Gradually the inanimate silver is what he yearns "to clasp, embrace, absorb, subjugate in unquestioned possession." He cannot tell Giselle where the treasure is buried because the "spectre of the unlawful treasure arose, standing by her side like a figure of silver, pitiless and secret with a finger upon its pale lips."[83] Finally, this figure of silver, not the human Giselle, draws him back to the island to meet his death.

Nostromo achieves a dubious type of immortality in the end. Refusing to get a priest for the dying Teresa Viola, and thus denying her her hope of salvation, he speaks of his own dangerous mission. Should he die, he bequeaths his silver buttons to one of his pretty

---

[83] *Ibid.*, p. 605 (542).

Morenita girl friends for her next lover. Then, with a phrase which fulfills its early promise as ironic foreshadowing, he says, " '. . . the man need not be afraid I shall linger on earth after I am dead, like those Gringos that haunt the Azuera.' "[84] While floating upon the gulf, Nostromo juxtaposes the dangers of the adventure and a possible search for the legendary "devils and ghosts" of the other treasure. A slave of the buried silver while he lives, he becomes when he is dead its perpetual guardian: ". . . the genius of the magnificent Capataz de Cargadores dominated the dark gulf containing his conquests of treasure and love."[85] Meaning at once "an extraordinary power" and "a spirit presiding over a person or place," the word "genius" describes the immortality of Nostromo; he is a memory which depends upon Linda's love and the lives of those involved in the historical events of Sulaco, and a spirit of sinister unrest which in popular lore hovers over forbidden treasure. Ironically, he had shunned the love of Linda when he was alive, and no one knows of that unrest when he is dead.

Ultimately our lack of identification with Nostromo affects our conception of him as an ideal hero. That his very human self-deception does not enlist our sympathy can, I think, be attributed to the detachment with which Conrad himself seems to view him. Too simple in intellect and too consistent in behavior, his characterization does not reveal any tension between the active world and the inner, personal one. When he begins to question himself, he manages to shift the burden of his self-doubt onto another. "The silences of his personal despair"[86] do not exist. Before the incident on the lighter, we have only isolated glimpses of a man who, purportedly magnificent in appearance, uncomplex by nature, enormous in vanity, arrives at the right place at the right time. These superficial moments in no ways prepare us for a man who is capable of any depth of emotion or suffering. His persistent posing in public —especially the rather absurd incident with the Morenita—tends to

---

[84] *Ibid.*, p. 286 (258).

[85] *Ibid.*, p. 631 (566).

[86] Campbell, *The Hero with a Thousand Faces*, p. 391.

be ludicrous and immature,[87] a characteristic of the egocentric folk hero rather than the universalized and communal tragic hero. Once the hero of popular report and illiterate societies evolves into a literary character, whether in drama or in a novel, he demands a complexity which Nostromo reveals only in isolated moments. Nor does Conrad's failure to make Nostromo's courtship of Giselle believable help us to appreciate this man of the people. This courtship—although couched in clichés consistent with this sailor's lack of education—is, indeed, a perfect example of the author's inability to cope with a love relationship. Conrad did not use those clichés because he felt they were in character; rather, he used them because he could not handle this type of scene artistically.

Nostromo's greatest advocate in the fictional world of Sulaco further alienates the reader; for this advocate is a fool. Pompous, unimaginative, talkative—all these words describe Captain Mitchell of the O.S.N. And through Captain Mitchell's point of view and in his tedious prose we first hear of Nostromo. Thereafter, the admirable captain's opinion (no less dull for being admirable) pursues the Capataz. He suggests his boatswain for every unusual venture; when another character—Decoud or Mrs. Gould—wishes to praise the Genoese, they do so on Captain Mitchell's recommendation. The reader, then, is unfavorably influenced by a character whose greatest admirer is essentially comic. Certainly Captain Mitchell's standing up to Sotillo is courageous; but somehow the manner in which it is done is primarily humorous. Nor does the gold chronometer which the Captain almost dies for—inscribed though it may be—seem a worthy object for an obsession. Or perhaps this obsession merely reveals how much Captain Mitchell is part of the timed universe of historical events.

Yet the final reason for Nostromo's failure as a hero is that he simply lacks status; unlike Legett, or Marlow, he is not a "Conway boy." He is only a sailor and the men he dominates are mainly Negroes. Because they are traditionally symbols of the unknown—and by extension, evil—in Western culture, the dark races or the darker members of the white race reflect the irrational areas within

---

[87] See Susanne K. Langer, "Life-Symbols: The Roots of Myth," *Philosophy in a New Key* (Cambridge, Mass., 1942), pp. 171–203.

ourselves which have been repressed by civilization. Conrad's own attitude toward the revolutionaries can be seen by the fact that many of the populace possess Negroid characteristics: Pedro Montero and his brother, the General, "were very much alike in appearance, both bald, with bunches of crisp hair above their ears, arguing the presence of some negro blood."[88] The *Negro Liberalism* of the Monterist press frightens Señor Avellanos. Both Decoud and Hirsch regard the insurgents as "negro Liberals," a term manifesting Conrad's own conservative bias. In a sense, Nostromo repudiates the revolutionaries by acting for the aristocratic Blancos, the whites, the reasonable men who are living in "indolence" rather than in "mental darkness" like the lower classes. But he eventually feels that the Blancos have betrayed him, a "man of the people."

In our childhood fantasies and in our dreams we become princes and princesses. If we deign to consider ourselves boatswains, we always manage to elevate ourselves in the end to a royal or divine stature. This never happens to Nostromo, who moves from Capataz to Captain, but never to a position high enough for Blancos' respect.

Perhaps Nostromo would engage our sympathies if Decoud were not compared with him. Whereas we watch Nostromo too often through the eyes of Captain Mitchell, we see Decoud chiefly through two points of view—his own and the author's. As Albert Guerard points out,[89] on the one hand we have the man who denies his own commitment, proclaims his indifference; on the other, the man of action who, while protesting his innocence, does act. He realizes his responsibility and so involves himself. The man who claims to regard himself with ironic detachment receives Conrad's sympathy. The author may judge his pose adversely, but never denies him sympathy. Moreover, Decoud's "love affair" with Antonia, because it is expressed in heroic actions rather than the words of romance, does succeed. That he assigns his motives to his love for her does not diminish either these motives or his love. Rather, it proves the extent of his commitment.

Precisely because Decoud is more actor than spectator his final

---

88 Conrad, *Nostromo*, p. 430 (386).

89 Guerard, *Conrad the Novelist*, pp. 201–2.

suicide is convincing. Once adrift on the gulf with Nostromo, he is affected by the belief that this silent darkness is a "foretaste of eternal peace" and that he is freed by "death from the misty atmosphere of regrets and hopes." The complete loss of all sense of reality makes him "the prey of an extremely languid but not unpleasant indifference." How much greater is the peace of the Great Isabel after Nostromo leaves, where no birds visit and where silence becomes "like a tense, thin cord to which he hung suspended by both hands."[90] A reasonable and intelligent man who had before understood the motives of other men, he beholds "the universe as a succession of incomprehensible images." Everything —including his own individuality—merges into the mindless natural world. Nor is he now supported by that activity in which "we find the sustaining illusion of an independent existence as against the whole scheme of things of which we form a helpless part."[91] One acts on behalf of other men because one anticipates a future good based on human rationality. But the total silence challenges Decoud with a vision of complete irrationality and brute nature. Solitude dispels man's "sustaining illusion." The symbolic language of the mountains changes. When he wished to push his political schemes, they cried to him, "Separate." Now Higuerota hovers above, an image of a silent cosmos indifferently viewing man's puny, corrupt struggles.

Decoud decides to kill himself because his vision of total evil has become overwhelming. This acute recognition of irrationality takes the classic form of the hero's refusal to return to the troubled life he has left. His suicide, then, is not an admission that something has value but rather a denial of responsibility because of the belief in all-pervasive evil. Conrad, while he agrees with the vision, does emphasize man's duty toward his fellows. So Decoud's denial is understandable but inexcusable. It is the crime which is the breach of faith with all humanity; it is Lord Jim's jump from the Patna; it is the individual isolation of each member of the Narcissus as a result of misdirected pity for the evil Negro James Wait. Yet somehow the very intensity of Decoud's despair, the anguish which

---

90 Conrad, Nostromo, p. 557 (498).   91 Ibid., p. 556 (497).

his inward voyage reveals, evokes our sympathy—and if we are to judge from the excellence of the prose rhythms and language, the author's as well. Of such anguish new myths are made.

In this refusal to return to the life of action can be seen many figurations of myths and dreams. Decoud is left temporarily upon a small island in a gulf which seems to deny the visible world; and "numerous indeed are the heroes fabled to have taken up residence forever in the blessed isle of the unaging Goddess of Immortal Being."[92] Ironically, his isle is hardly blessed and is soon to be haunted by Nostromo. Decoud moves from a symbolic to an actual death. "He pulled straight towards the setting sun." Myth usually assigns the unknown, the land of death, to the west; for the limitations of our senses make such spatial imprecision necessary. We must relate what we cannot see or know to an area which we cannot reach, yet which our perceptions can encompass. Finally, piling significant image upon significant image, Conrad has the Journalist of Sulaco shoot himself. He falls back into the sea, which itself is the nothingness of death or the body of water which separates the dead from the living. He has weighted his body with four bars of the San Tomé mine; he carries his burden of inherited guilt with him into the world of silence and death.

Decoud, as complex hero, has based his life upon a belief in his own rationality. Nostromo, as simple hero, has also lived his 24 years upon a consistent pattern which, given his premises of existence, is no less rational. The apparently timeless world presents Decoud with a completely irrational universe, in which his pose of skepticism ceases to be a pose and the actions of a reasonable man are revealed for what they are—useless. Nostromo, too, fails because he refuses to admit that he can behave irrationally. Neither emerges from the quest a whole man aware both of the good and evil, reason and lack of it—the one because his vision overwhelms mere rationality; the other because he refuses to admit personal evil, refuses to annihilate his own ego for the community. Each undergoes rites of initiation designed to create the true hero, the self-effacing man whose deeds are a constant reminder of the timeless beyond the

---

[92] Campbell, *The Hero with a Thousand Faces*, p. 193.

world of forms, of the oneness between the individual and the society of which he is only a part. But the obsessive sense of isolation and fragmentation of each reveals that the tragedy of the composite hero of Nostromo is a tragedy of modern man's loss of identity. Nostromo's two names and the ambiguity of his nickname reveal this same lack of unity. Perhaps the fact that there are two heroes— or, finally, four—shows the extent of modern man's dismemberment of personality.

What Joseph Campbell calls the "mythologically instructed community"—that community which "translates the individual's life-crises and life-deeds into classic, impersonal forms"[93]—does not exist in Sulaco—nor, indeed, in modern society. Instead, Conrad has used images of a world in which myth possessed a vital force, but has skillfully applied these images to the Gould Concession, the world of "material interests" that dehumanizes and is demonic in order to make an ironic statement upon the failure of his own society. The myths which Jerome Bruner calls the "treasure of an instructed community"[94] are replaced by the treasure which forms a new myth of a capitalist society. Nor does this treasure, given a validity by universal patterns, help to form the cohesive society which was the usual result of the hero's quest and the ritual acts of initiation. Rather, it simply supports the decay already apparent in the timed world of historical events. The cycle of political acts is contaminated by the evil inherent in the myth created around the silver in particular, and money or material interests in general. Unlike the magic sword wielded by the successful hero, it is a "weapon of wealth, double-edged with the cupidity and misery of mankind, steeped in all the vices of self-indulgence as in a concoction of poisonous roots, tainting the very cause for which it is drawn."[95]

---

[93] Ibid., p. 383.

[94] Jerome S. Bruner, "Myth and Identity," Daedalus (Spring, 1959), p. 357.

[95] Conrad, Nostromo, p. 406 (365).

The Secret Agent
Cosmic Chaos

In writing *The Secret Agent*, only the single and simple historical fact that there was an attempt to blow up the Greenwich Observatory concerned Conrad. He made no pretense of providing a faithful and inclusive picture of events for his "Simple Tale." That the attempt was made by one Martial Bourdin, that the date was February 15, 1894, are relevant to local history but not to the creative impulse of the novelist. The physical appearance of the fictional Stevie parallels that of his real-world counterpart Bourdin, but it is *why* Conrad's tenacious intelligence seized these descriptive details from historical time in order to transfer them to the objective time of his work that is interesting—not the fact that he did so.

As a dissident and dissonant Pole, and as the son of a Polish nationalist who, with wife and son, was exiled for his part in the rebellion of 1863, Conrad possessed a historical and political consciousness, and he had brooded and meditated upon the meaning of events, upon his own biases, and upon his father's role of "patriot." Michaelis may have some superficial resemblance to Mikhail Bakunin; Vladimir, to General Seliwertsow; or the Assistant Commissioner, to Robert Anderson. But in the alchemical process of transmuting objective data into an imaginative construct, of turning history and political theory into story, the creative consciousness so charged both particular fact and ideological abstraction with multiplicity, with energy, and with new drama that they have become true statements of a man's internal awareness of his historical moment. With a vitality of its own, Conrad's novel gives eternal verity to past, present, and future.

From his contemplation of historical events, Conrad detected an essential similarity between extremes of political behavior, which he then dramatized in his novel. The political conservative and the political reformer, the aristocrat and the anarchist, have ostensibly two distinct ways of looking at the timed world in which history is made. The former looks backward to a golden age, and so history becomes inevitable decline; the latter anticipates a good society in the future, a utopia in which all the evils of the past will be annihilated. Yet both, contemplating the linear movement of history, live in a world of process where the primary movement is a cyclical one. The pattern of birth, maturity, decline, and death in the animal world, the similar rhythm in the plant world, the movement of the solar system—indeed, all the cyclical processes of nature— provide analogies whereby man can find some corresponding continuity within his society and within the self. For a cyclical theory of the world of experience promises some sort of renewal or rebirth. Within primitive or civilized religions, natural cycles have often been associated with the birth, death, and resurrection of a god or gods. If everything is "eternal return," then the two political world views, conservative and reformer, are in reality very similar. The utopia of the reformer is simply the golden age restored by the hero-god, the world redeemed by a mass Messiah in which the conditions of Eden will return and time will become timelessness. In an analogy to ritual—which myth implies sometimes—both conservative and reformer undertake a quest to restore the wasteland of modern society to fertility, to significant belief; in an analogy to dream each state is an attempt to descend into the timeless unconscious in order to achieve some personal identity.

That Conrad meant the reader to make an equation between the reformer and the protector of the established order in The Secret Agent is apparent. Mr. Verloc, the "secret agent" par excellence, makes no distinction between "anarchists or diplomats"; his relationship both with the Embassy and with Chief Inspector Heat consists "in betraying the secret and unlawful proceedings of his fellow-men." Nor is the Professor, whose indignation demands the destruction of the weak, different from Sir Ethelred, whose aristocratic sympathy demands the protection of the weak. Each has the moments of mistrust which come "to all men whose ambition aims at a direct grasp upon humanity—to artists, politicians, thinkers, reformers, or saints."[1] The vanity which explains the behavior of social rebels is "the mother of all noble and vile illusions, the companion of poets, reformers, charlatans, prophets, and incendiaries."[2]

Not only are there similarities in the motives and ideologies of the men whom Conrad presents as the inhabitants of this historical world, but also they betray a likeness in physical deformity. All are, as Albert Guerard points out,[3] unnaturally fat. Or else they possess some feature which contradicts the rest of the body. Vladimir, the First Secretary of the Embassy belonging to the foreign power for which Verloc works, objects to both the secret agent's corpulence and domesticity, but has himself "the air of a preternaturally thriving baby." Michaelis, the anarchist turned idealist, whose "pale cheeks hung like filled pouches," has been fattened in prison to capitalist proportions. He is so inundated by flesh that his elbow gives "no appearance of a joint." Even the moribund sensualist Karl Yundt possesses an almost spectral frame with a "skinny groping hand deformed by gouty swellings." The undersized Professor, as a sign of his enormous intellect—or his enormous vanity—has correspondingly enormous, paper-thin ears. Himself slender, Chief Inspector Heat has a face "marred by too much flesh." And Sir Ethelred, the unexpendable parliamentarian, carries a bulk which is appropriate to so important a personage; his "long white face . . . broadened at the base by a big double chin."[4]

But the imprisonment of each man within the confines of flesh, or within his own body, corresponds to each's imprisonment with-

---

[1] Joseph Conrad, *The Secret Agent: A Simple Tale* (Garden City, N.Y., 1926), p. 82. This is Volume XIII of the Kent Edition of Conrad's collected works.

[2] *Ibid.*, p. 53.

[3] *Conrad the Novelist*, p. 225.   [4] Conrad, *The Secret Agent*, p. 136.

in time. While cherishing some view of the timeless, each manifests either through his indolence or his obsessive concern with the motions of the clock a slavery to this historical world. For the attempted crime against the Greenwich Observatory—an actual event translated by Conrad into the history of his fictional world—is, as Robert Stallman has so aptly stated,[5] a crime against time; it is symbolically an attempt to achieve timelessness.

At the moment when he is viewing the torn remains of the victim—and the supposed perpetrator—of the explosion on the Observatory grounds, Chief Inspector Heat, the defender of the established order, believes that he is "above the vulgar conception of time." The "vulgar conception of time" seems to relate to historical time, "sidereal time."[6] Hans Meyerhoff defines this as our most uniform standard of measurement, thought to be "completely objective in the sense of referring to motions the uniformity of which is independent of human experience."[7] This is time not as the individual experiences it, but as clocks and calendars record it. So Heat doubts that such complete physical disintegration as the victim manifests could be achieved without "inconceivable agony." Is such a death instantaneous?

> He remembered all he had ever read in popular publications of long and terrifying dreams dreamed in the instant of waking; of the whole past life lived with frightful intensity by a drowning man as his doomed head bobs up, streaming, for the last time. The inexplicable mysteries of conscious existence beset Chief Inspector Heat till he evolved a horrible notion that ages of atrocious pain and mental torture could be contained between two successive winks of an eye.[8]

Yet Heat in reality cannot confront the irrationality which the subjective awareness of time implies. He is a man for whom the "absurdity of things" in "concrete instances becomes exasperating beyond endurance." His experience of time must coincide with the measured units in physical nature. The sight of the Professor, an

---

5 "Conrad Criticism Today," *Sewanee Review*, LXVII (Winter, 1959), 144.

6 Hans Meyerhoff, *Time in Literature* (Berkeley & Los Angeles, 1955), p. 12.

7 *Ibid.*

8 Conrad, *The Secret Agent*, p. 88.

anarchist who carries enough explosive to send himself and twenty others into eternity, annoys him because he cannot understand the person obsessed by hate and despair, the man who does not proceed by orderly rational rules of conduct, the man who anticipates a world for which the senses are inadequate. Any moment in which he or members of his department lose sight of a reformer seems a break in continuity, "sudden holes in space and time." He is so much a slave to the "vulgar conception of time," time measured by the clock, that he had previously assured his superior that his men can lay their hands upon any anarchist at any "time of day or night." Indeed, once the crime is committed, he is forced to proceed to a satisfactory solution as quickly as possible. Shortly before eleven in the morning the first telegram from Greenwich reports the crime; by ten-thirty in the evening the case is officially closed when the Assistant Commissioner reports to Sir Ethelred, his superior.

The Professor, on the other hand, is apparently above the "vulgar conception of time." He carries an explosive attached to a detonator so that he may be both completely destructive and completely free. "With a swift, disclosing gesture he gave Ossipon a glimpse of an india-rubber tube, resembling a slender brown worm, issuing from the armhole of his waistcoat and plunging into the inner breast pocket of his jacket."[9] He depends not upon life, "a historical fact surrounded by all sorts of restraints," but upon death, where time as it is measured in nature does not exist. Yet even he is subject to the tyranny of time. First of all, he can never destroy the social order completely, never achieve a "clean sweep," but only carry with him into eternity a few men from the mass of mankind. Nor does the detonator attached to the explosive work instantaneously. Rather, twenty seconds elapse between the moment the ball is pressed and the resulting explosion. The passion of the Professor's life rests in creating a "perfect detonator." Ironically, the india-rubber tube is described metaphorically as a "slender brown worm," recalling to the reader the creature which in Western religious tradition is responsible for mankind's loss of a timeless and incorrupt-

---

[9] *Ibid.*, p. 66.

ible world.[10] Although convinced that he is a force for death, the moral agent for destruction—called "incorruptible"—cries out in despair that he requires " 'The time! Give me time!' " As a creature who exists in the historical, objective world, he is, as Ossipon indignantly reminds him, a " 'scurvy, shabby, mangy little bit of time.' "

> "You profess yourself to be one of the strong—because you carry in your pocket enough stuff to send yourself and, say, twenty other people into eternity. But eternity is a damned hole. It's time that you need. You—if you met a man who could give you for certain ten years of time, you would call him your master."[11]

Ultimately what the Professor wishes is to achieve some status, some sense of identity in a timed world, some "power and personal prestige" by means of his control of time. He demands recognition for his slightest merits, for his poverty, for his exalted conception of his own genius. If the world chained to time and convention cannot reward him, then he must change those conventions and manipulate time by means of destruction. And what finally obsesses him is that the multitude cannot be destroyed, that they " 'have everything on their side,' " even death, his weapon. For death, which promises a timeless state for which we have no evidence in nature—and death resulting from madness and despair—is the Perfect Anarchist's lever for the "regeneration of the world."

Ossipon's conception of the better world is of an eternity which is characterized not by timelessness but by unlimited time. Being a former medical student, he still submits to the conventions of science if not of society. Science, by whose fixed laws man has measured time in nature, may be able to extend man's personal experience of time. And the timeless verities by which men live, those truths once revealed by religion, are now provided by science, for which Ossipon has an austere respect. Paradoxically, the "sacrosanct fetish" of the bourgeois British public which Vladimir—albeit

---

10 According to the Christian Fathers, time began at the creation of the world and Adam and Eve did experience diurnal change. But the negative aspect of change, the change for death, physical decay, was foreign to the home of our first parents. Within the frame of reference of this analysis, the experience in Eden belongs not to history, as it does in *The City of God*, but to myth.

11 Conrad, *The Secret Agent*, pp. 305–6.

insincerely—wishes to attack is science, which he equates with the symbol of time, the Greenwich Observatory. But Ossipon, too, is a " 'scurvy, shabby, mangy little bit of time.' " His encounter with Winnie Verloc—after the latter has killed her husband—his subsequent deceit, and his theft of her money do affect his inner experience of time. He no longer is able to establish a sense of continuity between the world of time as he personally knows it and objective time as it is measured by the scientific laws to which he subscribes. After discovering the dead body of Verloc, he and Winnie are forced to hide while a constable flashes his light at the window of Verloc's shop. "While the footsteps approached, they breathed quickly, breast to breast, with hard, laboured breaths, as if theirs had been the attitude of a deadly struggle, while, in fact, it was the attitude of deadly fear. And the time was long."[12] Only twenty minutes have passed from his meeting Winnie to his discovery of the body and his ascertaining Winnie's guilt; yet Ossipon is "terrified at the rapidity with which he had been involved in such danger—decoyed into it."[13] Since such personal reflections can be subject to no uniform tests of measurement, this qualitative aspect of time, which depends on one's consciousness of it, is called "subjective relativity" by Professor Meyerhoff.[14]

Ossipon, however, does map out a plan to get rid of Winnie and does so with apparent equanimity. By means of a cruel deception he abandons her on the ten-thirty train, a process which involves his dependence upon an objective schedule. He must keep his eye on the clock in order to pursue the plan with accuracy. But he cannot, during this interval, ignore his own irrational fears. Everything about this woman reminds him of time. He anticipates her fits of weeping and watches "the symptoms with a sort of medical air, as if counting seconds."[15] He imagines her at one point "turned round him like a snake, not to be shaken off. . . . She was death itself—the companion of life."[16] Not only does she represent the creature who tempted Eve, and hence caused man's imprisonment

---

12 *Ibid.*, p. 286.   13 *Ibid.*, p. 289.

14 Hans Meyerhoff, *Time in Literature*, p. 22.

15 Conrad, *The Secret Agent*, p. 299.   16 *Ibid.*, p. 291.

in a past-present-future world, but she also represents the world beyond life where train schedules cannot exist.

His subsequent acts do manifest the symptoms of incipient madness. Time, which in its subjective aspect of continuous flow is described as a stream, begins to be totally meaningless to him. He walks back from the station, begins to cross a bridge, and stops "for a long time" to contemplate the river, "a sinister marvel of still shadows and flowing gleams mingling below in a black silence."[17] Only once more is he made actively aware of objective time. At half-past twelve the clock tower booms. "He looked at the dial." After this, he walks aimlessly all night throughout the city. Finally, his particular actions reverse the normal bodily functions with which we greet the natural order of the day and night. He sleeps "in the sunlight." After Winnie's death, he is found carrying a paper eight days old. His last lecture to the Professor on the scientific possibilities of extending time is followed by another aimless walk in which he disregards everything. "Scientifically afraid of insanity"—a state where no time can be measured—because of the pressure of events, this conqueror of women begins to neglect his various conquests. And yet he must continue to inhabit a world subject to the "tyranny of time."

Of all the anarchists, Michaelis, the humanitarian sentimentalist, most ignores time. This man, who believes that all "idealization makes life poorer," dreams of a "world like a beautiful and cheery hospital." While anticipating a utopia for the weak, he is able to ignore clocks and chronometers because of an old and aristocratic patroness, herself defying "time with scornful disregard, as if it were a rather vulgar convention submitted to by the mass of inferior mankind."[18] Although engaged only in forcing a lock to release some prisoners, Michaelis was jailed for life in the burst of popular sentiment following the death of a constable possessing a family. For fifteen years he experienced the close confinement of a prison cell. The cell in which he is fattened to monstrous proportions from too much food combined with lack of proper exercise approximates a world exempt from the demands of normal life. Because it is

---

[17] *Ibid.*, p. 300.   [18] *Ibid.*, p. 104.

described as "hygienic," it may be compared to his ideal future "hospital." Because it is confined and "damp and lightless," it has analogies to the grave, which in terms of the individual unconscious suggests a return to the womb.

> He talked to himself, indifferent to the sympathy or hostility of his hearers, indifferent indeed to their presence, from the habit he had acquired of thinking aloud hopefully in the solitude of the four whitewashed walls of his cell, in the sepulchral silence of the great blind pile of bricks near a river, sinister and ugly like a colossal mortuary for the socially drowned.[19]

In the collective experience of various societies, the worlds of the living and the dead are separated by black waters which become the equally dark waters of the womb in the dream experience of a single life. But Michaelis, growing like an unnatural fetus, is not allowed a satisfactory rebirth into the scientific world of measured time. When his lady patroness sends him for a cure to Marienbad, he is forbidden "access to the healing waters." Rather, he retires to a small house in the country where the four walls again recall his womb/tomb–like cell. He spends most of his waking hours "Fitted with painful tightness into an old wooden armchair, before a worm-eaten oak table in an upstairs room of a four-roomed cottage with a roof of moss-grown tiles."[20] Regardless of time, regardless of the changes from night to day, he works upon his "Autobiography of a Prisoner," a "book of Revelation in the history of mankind." "He could not tell whether the sun still shone on earth or not."[21] Ignoring time, he writes for society and men in time, for the world of historical events, in order to achieve a timeless future. But these anarchists are, indeed, idle and indolent creatures, incapable of significant collective or individual action. Michaelis attempts to live his timeless future in a timed present; he has escaped into the eternity of his own disintegrating personality, of his own idealizations, and of his dreams of the future which now completely dominate his will.

The Assistant Commissioner, who is "not easily accessible to illusions," is paradoxically compared to the classic example of the

---

[19] *Ibid.*, p. 44.   [20] *Ibid.*, p. 120.   [21] *Ibid.*

idealist; he is described as an "energetic Don Quixote"—whom W. H. Auden has called the "dedicated man, the Knight of Faith who would restore the Age of Gold."[22] The nearest that he has ever come to the past golden age in this world, however, has been in a tropical colony of the Empire. Here he was engaged in bringing the "order and legality" of a white society to a primitive dark-skinned colony. Such a preliterate society is not subject to the clocks of modern civilization. Marriage chains him not only to a woman, but to a desk and to time as well. He must return to England. Only between five and seven each day in a whist game can he forget the demands of his role. He is not only dependent upon subordinates like Chief Inspector Heat, who is subject to the "vulgar conception of time," but he is also dependent upon "too many masters," among them Sir Ethelred, that Presence who is himself mastered by clocks and calendars.

Sir Ethelred's aristocratic lineage is not measured by historical considerations but rather by natural forces; ". . . the unbroken record of that man's descent surpassed in the number of centuries the age of the oldest oak in the country."[23] He is compared to a figure from his own romantic and feudal past. "The Great Personage might have been the statue of one of his own princely ancestors stripped of a crusader's war harness, and put into an ill-fitting frock coat."[24] But the demands of modern civilization force him to measure every moment. Details which consume time must be ignored: only events which have a bearing upon history are worthy of his consideration. The Assistant Commissioner is limited to seven minutes in giving the salient facts of the Greenwich affair. The entire interview is twenty-five minutes. Conrad conscientiously frames the Great Personage with his "pale circumference of a face" against a clock, which is personified. "The gilt hands had taken the opportunity to steal through no less than five and twenty minutes behind his back."[25] Words used to describe the timepiece—"sly, feeble tick," "steal," "behind his back"—imply deceit; yet the clock moves

---

22 W. H. Auden, "The Sea and the Desert," *The Enchaféd Flood* or *The Romantic Iconography of the Sea* (London, 1951), p. 18.

23 Conrad, *The Secret Agent*, p. 136.

24 *Ibid.*, pp. 137–38.   25 *Ibid.*, p. 144.

by a standard which is uniform, which has been measured. What is not subject to any scientific measurement is Sir Ethelred's reactions to experience, experience in which he "has no time."

Only one character is apparently free of time. And that is Stevie, the brother of Winnie, an idiot who is dominated by the irrational, by the unconscious in which, according to Jung, spatial and temporal relationships are uncertain.[26] Ironically, Stevie is entrusted with the device which is to destroy the Greenwich Observatory "from which geographers and navigators of nearly all nations count their longitude."[27] But Stevie succeeds only in blowing himself up. He defies even the twenty-minute limit set upon the bomb by falling, thus causing an immediate explosion.

When alive, Stevie had spent most of his time "seated very good and quiet at a deal table, drawing circles, circles, circles; innumerable circles, concentric, eccentric; a coruscating whirl of circles that by their tangled multitude of repeated curves, uniformity of form, and confusion of intersecting lines suggested a rendering of cosmic chaos, the symbolism of a mad art attempting the inconceivable."[28] His art not only manifests the almost universal symbol of eternity, but also reveals the symbol for the cyclical theory of time in which every state will repeat itself. Life is followed by death which itself is but a prelude to some rebirth. Experience is ordered by the concept of the "eternal return." In the cyclical theory of time, the constant threat of death is alleviated by the promise of rebirth whether individual or generic; the circle is the symbol of continuity and identity within the individual personality. An essential irony of the book is that the symbol of eternity, of life-death-rebirth, of unity of personality is associated with the idiot. His art is a "mad art." The catherine wheels which Stevie, in a fit of vicious sympathy, sets off on the stairs of a milk firm, have a cluster of associations. They are, indeed, wheels. But they recall the martyrdom of St.

26 C. G. Jung, "The Phenomenology of the Spirit in Fairytales," *The Archetypes and the Collective Unconscious*, trans. R. F. C. Hull, Bollingen XX (New York, 1959), 224. (Vol. IX, 1, of *The Collected Works of C. G. Jung*.)

27 *Webster's New International Dictionary of the English Language*, ed. William Allan Neilson (Springfield, 1955), s. v. "Greenwich."

28 Conrad, *The Secret Agent*, p. 45.

Catherine and that wheel from whose circumference spikes project. They suggest that the circles of modern society are wheels of torture.

The primary symbol of an impotent and indolent mankind caught within time is the city of London. Brooding over the entire novel is this monstrous presence of stone and brick and darkness which recalls the equally vivid evocation of Dickens' *Bleak House*. The structure of imagery used by each author in his narrative suggests a world devoid of meaning, a world which has parallels in the existential hell of various religions. According to Northrop Frye, the city which myth reveals as desirable to our mortal eyes—in Christian myth, the heavenly Jerusalem—is apocalyptic.[29] Inhabited by gods, it is a "world of total metaphor, in which everything is potentially identical with everything else, as though it were all inside a single infinite body."[30] Its opposite, inhabited by demons, is the world which "desire totally rejects."[31] But the apocalyptic and demonic worlds of "undisplaced myth"[32] are both static worlds in which time does not exist. The novel, on the other hand, presents us with a world close to our own human experience; here myth becomes adapted to our common experience. It is a world of continuous process, a world within the cycle of time, in which the clusters of imagery are unidealized[33]—indeed, are essentially nightmarish. And the city of Conrad's flabby, deformed, emotionally stunted humanity contains mythic patterns which are more reminiscent of hell than of heaven. Analogies to ritual and dream are present, but ritual which leads to no significant rebirth, dream which asserts neither individual identity nor continuity of personality nor wholeness of conscious and unconscious being. It is a world totally devoid of meaning where parody and irony distort man's image, and only misery and bondage are certain.

To deny that this city is, first of all, a particular vision of urban reality, a forceful and detailed description of the author's "solitary and nocturnal walks all over London,"[34] is to ignore one of the levels of the novel's appeal. I do not mean to suggest within the

---

[29] Frye, "Archetypal Criticism: Theory of Myths," *Anatomy of Criticism*, p. 144.

[30] *Ibid.*, p. 136.   [31] *Ibid.*, p. 147.   [32] *Ibid.*, p. 140.   [33] *Ibid.*, p. 223.

[34] Joseph Conrad, "Author's Note," *The Secret Agent* (Garden City, N.Y., 1926), p. xiii.

context of my analysis that descriptive and narrative value is the least important or least satisfying from the reader's perspective. Nor is the word "level" used here with any connotations of hierarchy. The symbolic and archetypal becomes meaningless if we ignore the literal description of the city, its objective reality within the fact of the novel; Conrad himself would have been the first to question any critical statement which categorically asserted that he was consciously employing archetypal patterns. Like "Realism, Romanticism, Naturalism" he would consider these patterns "one of the temporary formulas of his [the artist's] craft."[35] To him the author's task is "to make you hear, to make you feel—it is, before all, to make you see."[36] And *seeing* not only involves the vibration, color, and form of outer reality, but also through "its life's movement, its form, and its colour, reveal[s] the substance of its truth."[37] Conrad would, indeed, be one of the first to sympathize with the critic's attempts to prove that motifs exist, that urban reality can be a springboard for archetypal symbols, that, finally, the unconscious is as "true" as the conscious. Ultimately he would admit, like Mann after him, that conscious intention is but a part of creation:

> . . . Realism, Romanticism, Naturalism, even the unofficial sentimentalism (which like the poor, is exceedingly difficult to get rid of,) all these gods must, after a short period of fellowship, abandon him—even on the very threshold of the temple—to the stammerings of his conscience and to the outspoken consciousness of the difficulties of his work. In that uneasy solitude the supreme cry of Art for Art itself, loses the exciting ring of its apparent immorality. *It sounds far off.* It has ceased to be a cry, and is heard only as a *whisper*, often *incomprehensible*, but at times and faintly encouraging.[38]

In its topography London possesses similarities to the confusions of classical labyrinths, an irrational world defying straightness.

> With a turn to the left Mr. Verloc pursued his way along a narrow street by the side of a yellow wall which, for some inscrutable reason, had No. 1 Chesham Square written on it in black letters. Chesham

---

[35] Joseph Conrad, "Preface," *The Nigger of the "Narcissus": A Tale of the Forecastle* (Garden City, N.Y., 1926), p. xiv.

[36] *Ibid.*   [37] *Ibid.*   [38] *Ibid.*, p. xv. Emphasis added.

Square was at least sixty yards away, and Mr. Verloc, cosmopolitan enough not to be deceived by London's topographical mysteries, held on steadily, without a sign of surprise or indignation. At last, with business-like persistency, he reached the Square, and made diagonally for the number 10. This belonged to an imposing carriage gate in a high, clean wall between two houses, of which one rationally enough bore the number 9 and the other was numbered 37; but the fact that this last belonged to Porthill Street, a street well known in the neighbourhood, was proclaimed by an inscription placed above the ground-floor windows by whatever highly efficient authority is charged with the duty of keeping track of London's strayed houses.[39]

Not without importance is the name of the subway station where Mr. Verloc and Stevie emerge to go to the Greenwich Observatory —Maze Hill. Even the glory that was Greece appears with much diminished luster in the modern metropolis where "a butcher boy, driving with the noble recklessness of a charioteer at Olympic Games, dashed round the corner sitting high above a pair of red wheels."[40] The stock metaphor derived from a heroic age gives irony to the particular vision of urban reality which Conrad creates. The Professor's home is "lost in a wilderness of poor houses." Described as an "enormity of cold, black, wet, muddy, inhospitable accumu-lation of bricks, slates, and stones, things in themselves unlovely and unfriendly to man,"[41] its formlessness and its ugliness and its darkness recall the nightmare. As a world of mere objects, it is un-related to the human beings who live within it. Or its decay and confusions have denied humanity. "On one side, the low brick houses had in their dusty windows the sightless, moribund look of incurable decay—empty shells awaiting demolition."[42] Brett Street, where Verloc keeps his shop of shady wares, is part of the maze, out of the way of ordinary life. So Winnie does not hear of the explosion at the Observatory because the echo of the newsboys' cries "drifting along the populous thoroughfares, expired between the dirty brick walls without reaching the threshold of the shops."[43] After Winnie kills her husband, she feels completely isolated in the city street. "She was alone in London: and the whole town of marvels and

---

[39] Conrad, *The Secret Agent*, pp. 14–15.

[40] *Ibid.*, p. 14.   [42] *Ibid.*, p. 82.

[41] *Ibid.*, p. 56.   [43] *Ibid.*, p. 204.

mud, with its maze of streets and its mass of lights, were sunk in a hopeless night, rested at the bottom of a black abyss from which no unaided woman could hope to scramble out."[44] Even the sun over London—the center of that Empire "on which the sun never sets"—looks "bloodshot." It is a "rusty London sunshine" shedding "lukewarm brightness." In its "diffused light" neither "wall, nor tree, nor beast, nor man casts a shadow."

The primary characteristics of this city are, then, its confusion and its irrationality, the darkness which signifies the unconscious life. Light—which, Jung tells us,[45] is the triumph of consciousness—rarely visits this area. The daylight appears tainted by fog; the sun, "bloodshot." The buildings of this city—particularly the shop of shady wares—seem "to devour the sheen of light." Night itself, when it comes, gives this city the aspect of that ultimate irrationality and darkness beyond life.

> Down below in the quiet, narrow street measured footsteps approached the house, then died away, unhurried and firm, as if the passer-by had started to pace out all eternity, from gas-lamp to gas-lamp in a night without end; and the drowsy ticking of the old clock on the landing became distinctly audible in the bedroom.[46]

Note that the passage juxtaposes eternity, which is timeless, and the world of objective time, represented by the clock. The night of the natural order, however, becomes "night without end" in the realm beyond that order. Moreover, measured by human feet, eternity here is simply another London of crooked ways and gas-lamps. Again, the image of the gas-lamp dominates the story, presenting us with an atmosphere in which much of the light is derived from an artificial source. Nor can this man-made light dispel the sense of formlessness or lost direction when "the town's colossal forms" seem "half lost in night." Ultimately, the London of the novel is a metropolis of "diffused light" or of the "blurred flames of gas-

---

[44] *Ibid.*, p. 270.

[45] C. G. Jung, "The Dual Mother," *Symbols of Transformation*, trans. R. F. C. Hull, Bollingen XX (New York, 1956), p. 348. (Vol. V of *The Collected Works of C. G. Jung.*)

[46] Conrad, *The Secret Agent*, p. 57.

lamps" or of darkness "as vast as a sea." "Without shadows," it is, indeed, soulless.

The preceding simile adds another dimension to the cluster of images which surround London. This demonic city is both formless and dark, resembling at once death and the irrationality of the unconscious life. In its ritual analogies, archetypal criticism employs water as the significant symbol of rebirth. Rain, in its associations with nature's renewal in spring, appears in this novel as fog and mist, both of which help block out the energy-giving rays of the sun. Indeed, Verloc anticipates the spring through the "faint buzzing of a fly—his first fly of the year—heralding better than any number of swallows the approach of spring."[47] Nor does the city present the customary greenness of the season: "It was a raw, gloomy day of the early spring; and the grimy sky, the mud of the streets, the rags of the dirty men harmonized excellently with the eruption of the damp, rubbishy sheets of paper soiled with printers' ink. The posters, maculated with filth, garnished like tapestry the sweep of the curbstone."[48] While the air is permeated by fog and mist, the waters which cover the ground make the street "like a wet, muddy ditch." The Assistant Commissioner, looking into the street, sees it lie "wet and empty, as if swept clear suddenly by a great flood. It was a very trying day, choked in raw fog to begin with, and now drowned in cold rain. The flickering, blurred flames of gas-lamps seemed to be dissolving in a watery atmosphere. And the lofty pretensions of a mankind oppressed by the miserable indignities of the weather appeared as a colossal and hopeless vanity deserving of scorn, wonder, and compassion."[49] When he descends into the city, it seems an "immensity of greasy slime and damp plaster interspersed with lamps, and enveloped, oppressed, penetrated, choked, and suffocated by the blackness of a wet London night, which is composed of soot and drops of water."[50] Verb forms like "drowned," "choked," "dissolving," "enveloped," "oppressed," "suffocated" suggest death. Used together with words denoting darkness, and nouns and adjectives by which clear water becomes adulterated—"raw fog," "greasy slime," "soot and drops of water"—

---

[47] *Ibid.*, p. 27.   [49] *Ibid.*, p. 100.
[48] *Ibid.*, p. 79.   [50] *Ibid.*, p. 150.

all these combine to reveal a society in which stagnation and darkness and impotence destroy any possibility of either physical or spiritual rebirth.

Another fluid, the water of life, is circulating blood. In the demonic world the image of spilled blood becomes a manifestation of the water of death.[51] In *The Secret Agent* there is, first of all, the most obvious variation of spilled blood—the completely mutilated corpse of Stevie, whose remains are gathered into a waterproof sheet. Metaphorically, with macabre humor, the fog and Stevie's body are equated. Chief Inspector Heat loses his appetite because "he had swallowed a good deal of raw, unwholesome fog in the park."[52] Then he beholds this "raw material for a cannibal feast." Both fog and corpse are the unhealthy nourishment provided by a nightmare world.

But the spilled blood of the first victim merely anticipates that of the second. The minute following the murder of Verloc seems to be one of complete silence until Winnie, who "cared nothing for time," suddenly becomes conscious of a ticking sound. Drops of blood fall "on the floor-cloth one after another, with a sound of ticking growing fast and furious like the pulse of an insane clock."[53] The falling blood possesses no objective or measured beat. Nor does it possess the regularity of circulating blood. Rather, it signifies a state achieved beyond time, a death which is both insane and final. The blood from the wound becomes equated with the destructive quality of water. Afterwards, Winnie rushes into the street "as if the trickle had been the first sign of a destroying flood."[54]

Although Conrad did not select London as the scene of his novel so that the archetypal critic might have empirical data to support critical arguments, the insular nature of Britain does accidentally contribute to the mythic structure of imagery. With his careful selection of the scene the author unconsciously furthered the reader's very conscious interpretation. Bodies of water usually separate two states of existence. The infant hero of the exposure myth—

[51] Frye, "Archetypal Criticism: Theory of Myths," *Anatomy of Criticism*, p. 150.
[52] Conrad, *The Secret Agent*, p. 86.
[53] *Ibid.*, p. 265.   [54] *Ibid.*

Sargon, Moses, Karma, Perseus—is set adrift in a basket or cask by a hostile grandfather or parent.[55] The adult hero about to complete his quest crosses a river, or a body of water, which separates life and death. When he has achieved his task, he may return from the underworld. If we assume the narrative myth to be the outward projection of inward events—figures of speech which represent the unconscious of the race—then the cask and water of the exposure myth become the womb and the amniotic fluid in which the fetus grows to birth. Death becomes a return to that state, with the coffin now representing the womb. Mr. Verloc, of unknown origins, comes "like an influenza" to London, the nightmare city of darkness and mist. And this city becomes metaphorically both death and sinister, stagnant water. After Mr. Verloc's murder Winnie forms the resolution to drown herself.

> The street frightened her, since it led either to the gallows or to the river. She floundered over the doorstep head forward, arms thrown out, like a person falling over the parapet of a bridge. This entrance into the open air had a foretaste of drowning; a slimy dampness enveloped her, entered her nostrils, clung to her hair. It was not actually raining, but each gas-lamp had a rusty little halo of mist. The van and horses were gone, and in the black street the curtained window of the carters' eating-house made a square patch of soiled blood-red light glowing faintly very near the level of the pavement.[56]

First of all, Winnie acts like a drowning woman. Then, all the images describing water are demonic, or distortions of conventional motifs: "slimy dampness," "rusty little halo of mist." Even light is "soiled blood-red" as opposed to the bright light of reason or the purifying light of purgation. After meeting Ossipon, Winnie believes she can escape death; she can flee across the Channel to the continent; she can leave the city of darkness and mud. Soon deserted by him, she does take the steamer to France at midnight. Here a realistic detail—the ship's timetable—assumes a symbolic burden. Ultimately Winnie's love of life is overwhelmed by despair, and she actually drowns herself in the sea.

---

[55] Rank, *The Myth of the Birth of the Hero.*

[56] Conrad, *The Secret Agent*, p. 269.

In his "Author's Note," written twelve years after the initial publication of the book, Conrad discusses the way the details of the plot emerged in his mind. Here he reconstructs the imaginative effects of the image of the city upon the creative temperament.

> Then the vision of an enormous town presented itself, of a monstrous town more populous than some continents and its man-made might as if indifferent to heaven's frowns and smiles, a cruel devourer of the world's light. There was room enough there to place any story, depth enough there for any passion, variety enough there for any setting, darkness enough to bury five millions of lives.[57]

The main figure of speech—that of a monstrous presence—recalls images which had already become part of *The Secret Agent*. Shops are "lapped up" for the night. The enormous town is described as "slumbering monstrously on a carpet of mud under a veil of raw mist."[58]

In biblical myth, Satan, the serpent, identified as the "leviathan of this world," is the monster responsible for man's fall, his subsequent imprisonment within time, his subjugation to death. As Northrop Frye points out, "if the leviathan is the whole fallen world of sin and death and tyranny into which Adam fell, it follows that Adam's children are born, live, and die inside his belly."[59] Urns found in ancient Greece and Crete, medieval folk art reveal repeated examples of spent heroes emerging from the mouths of dragons or serpents. In iconography and in Miracle plays, the mouth of Hell into which Christ, as hero, descends is represented by the open mouth of a hideous monster. Again, Northrop Frye indicates that the "image of the dark winding labyrinth for the monster's belly is a natural one,"[60] an assertion which the myths of the Minotaur and Jonah support. The sterile wasteland, the intricate jungle, the formless or labyrinthine city—all may become part of the extended metaphor for this world which is the world of death, the black world that mythic narrative often assigns to the innards of some monster, be it serpent or dragon or leviathan.

---

57 Conrad, "Author's Note," *The Secret Agent*, p. xii.

58 Conrad, *The Secret Agent*, p. 300.

59 Frye, "Archetypal Criticism: Theory of Myths," *Anatomy of Criticism*, p. 190.

60 *Ibid.*

Moreover, the leviathan of the Bible is "a sea-monster, which means metaphorically that he is the sea. . . . As denizens of his belly, therefore, we are also metaphorically under water."[61] Mr. Frye then illustrates the connection between the Gospel's emphasis on the redemptive importance of fishing, Christ's miracles in calming the sea, and the apostles' symbolic roles as "fishers of men." Nor are Beowulf and Fergus the only folk heroes who perform their deeds under water. According to some versions of Irish folk and fairy tales, Cuchulain is finally killed in a battle against the waves of the sea. "As the leviathan, in his aspect as the fallen world, contains all forms of life imprisoned within himself, so as the sea he contains the imprisoned life-giving rain waters whose coming marks the spring."[62]

London, the city of night, the monstrous being through which men wander aimlessly like Ossipon or with destructive purpose like the Professor or in search of freedom like the Assistant Commissioner, does hold within itself the fogs and mists which are simply the waters of death. It envelops everything in its universal dampness. The river which flows through it is not the fresh water representing the stream of life but a "sinister marvel of still shadows and flowing gleams mingling . . . in a black silence."[63] Furthermore, a parody of the fishing motif of biblical literature and pagan folk tales is also present. At one point the street is equated with a "slimy aquarium" and the Assistant Commissioner and the people, "queer foreign fish." Sir Ethelred, that "great and expanded Personage" who must seriously limit his discussion of the explosion at Greenwich because he has no time, spends most of his waking moments on a bill for the Nationalization of Fisheries. At one point his secretary Toodles tells the Assistant Commissioner that " 'He's sitting alone in his room thinking of all the fishes of the sea.' "[64] He is a mock Fisher King whose own deformity contributes to the blight upon his city. He does not have time to "set . . . [his] lands in order." The only mention of the color of spring and fertility and the dream world, green, has no connection with the natural scene of this novel.

---

[61] Ibid., p. 191.

[62] Ibid., pp. 191–92.

[63] Conrad, The Secret Agent, p. 300.

[64] Ibid., p. 215.

Rather, it describes the closed study of this "big and rustic Presence." "Shades of green silk fitted low over all the lights imparted to the room something of a forest's deep gloom."[65] And the Assistant Commissioner proceeds to refer to Verloc as the "sprat" which will catch the "whale" or "the dog-fish" or "the witty fish" which is Vladimir. The larger fish may be caught, but the sprat is swallowed or, as Toodles' limited knowledge so graphically reveals, ends within the restricted confines of a sardine can.

That the city of London—with its irrationality, its darkness, its persistent dampness, its monstrous presence—symbolizes a kind of modern underworld becomes all too apparent whenever we trace the progress of the man who, more than any other character, resembles the traditional quest hero. The Assistant Commissioner, a "cool, reflective Don Quixote," attempts to find the truth in spite of the private knowledge and machinations of Chief Inspector Heat. But the former's motives are not entirely selfless. In England he is oppressed by the details and desk work of his position. One of the solaces of his existence—his access to the house of the elderly patroness of Michaelis—will be lost if the latter is imprisoned again by Heat.

When he leaves Sir Ethelred, his progress is described as a "descent into the street . . . like a descent into a slimy aquarium." Everything assumes the ambiguity and formlessness which ritual assigns to the underworld and dream to the unconscious. He moves "like an unobtrusive shadow." "He might have been but one more of the queer foreign fish that can be seen of an evening about there flitting round the dark corners."[66] The proverbial ferryman—in the form of a hansom—appears to carry him across the threshold of one world into another. The irony of the whole situation is increased by the revelation of the author's conscious awareness of some of the folk motifs which he is using. When the Assistant Commissioner tenders his coin to the driver, Conrad writes of the driver's response, "But the size of the coin was satisfactory to his touch, and his education not being literary, he remained untroubled by the fear of finding it presently turned to a dead leaf in his pocket. Raised above the world of fares by the nature of his calling, he contemplated their

---

[65] *Ibid.*, p. 217.   [66] *Ibid.*, p. 147.

action with a limited interest. The sharp pulling of his horse right round expressed his philosophy."⁶⁷ The conscious irony, the double meaning of phrases like "Raised above the world of fares," the ambiguity—all these do not diminish the effect that the driver's actions possess in the entire mythic structure.

A sense of annihilation of self is the psychological effect of the journey into the underworld, the inward meaning of ritual events. The Assistant Commissioner, on his selfish quest, experiences some of this dreamlike annihilation as he enters the Italian restaurant, a particular corner of the hell that is London. First, he assumes a kind of disguise which consists in raising the collar of his jacket, and he undergoes a baptism by ditch waters: " 'I'll get a little wet, a little splashed.' " He seems to "lose some more of his identity. He had a sense of loneliness, of evil freedom."⁶⁸ The people who inhabit this "immoral atmosphere" possess no real individuality. They have lost "all their national and private characteristics." As "it was impossible to form a precise idea what occupations they followed by day and where they went to bed at night,"⁶⁹ so in their company "he himself had become unplaced." And this sense of spatial and temporal freedom is "pleasurable." He compares this experience to that of being "ambushed all alone in a jungle"—another unknown area upon which the unconscious life projects its fantasies. But the annihilation of self, this conquest of ego which is momentarily pleasurable, leads nowhere. It merely confirms the Assistant Commissioner's isolation and enhances his egoism. Ultimately he must return to a job he despises and subject himself to the tyranny of public opinion. Heroism among pencils and pens becomes meaningless. Society cannot provide personal satisfaction. Nor can individual fulfillment in this demonic world have any relationship to society. The Assistant Commissioner never redeems his world because he never escapes its bondage himself. The bricks of the city are as immovable as the Fates of Greek tragedy and as impersonal—and much dirtier.

Where human life is subject to imprisonment in an evil city and where madness and despair replace the heroic postures of a tragic tradition, even an idiot may be a hero. In chapter 8—structurally

⁶⁷ *Ibid.*, p. 148.   ⁶⁸ *Ibid.*   ⁶⁹ *Ibid.*, p. 149.

unique because it involves the chronological dislocation of a flash-back—Conrad has created a self-contained parody of the typical quest romance. The classic quest of the self-forgetful hero who assumes a task imposed by the community he is to redeem is paral-leled by the cab journey of a self-sacrificing old lady to an almshouse. And the irony is intensified because of the author's emphasis upon heroic action in this modern night-sea journey of the idiot Stevie, his sister Winnie, and their aged mother. In nine separate instances Conrad refers to the heroism of this old woman whose physical characteristics are hardly reminiscent of the great mother principle. At most, there is a "venerable placidity conferred upon her outward person by her triple chin, the floating ampleness of her ancient form, and the impotent condition of her legs."[70]

That the cab ride is a symbolic descent into the underworld be-comes apparent because of the accumulation of images relating to myth. Even the stereotyped figure of death appears in the form of a large brewer, a Baronet and M.P. This representative of the social order to whom Winnie's mother applies for entrance into the home for brewers' widows is dressed all in black; his voice is "sad"; he is "very, very thin and quiet . . . like a shadow." Once admitted to the charity home, she takes the cab ride which is the journey of the soul across the river separating the living from the dead.

No figure of myth or nightmare can be more sinister than the creature who takes the mother on her "last cab ride." The driver is "maimed," possessing a "hooked iron" instead of a left hand. He does not speak out loud, but whispers with a voice which "seemed to be squeezed out of a blacked throat." His "stern whisper . . . is strained almost to extinction." He, moreover, has the unthinking habit of repeating in his ghostly whisper parts of phrases which have been addressed to him. His countenance, "bloated and sodden" from drink, takes on all the deformity which is the property of the demonic in the collective or personal experience. His payment is "pieces of silver" which "symbolize the insignificant result which reward the ambitious courage and toil of mankind whose day is short on this earth of evil"[71]—Conrad's ironic comment upon the

---

[70] *Ibid.*, p. 153.   [71] *Ibid.*, p. 165.

driver's own unheroic and inglorious labor. Symbolically, it refers, particularly, to Winnie's mother and, generically, to all who must journey to death. These few coins finally find their way into "the depths of *decayed* clothing [emphasis added]." He is truly, as he is quick to inform Stevie, a "night cabby."

The similarities between the infirm horse of chapter 8 and the horse of Raskolnikov's nightmare in Dostoevsky's *Crime and Punishment* have been pointed out.[72] Not a Pegasus but, rather, a steed of "apocalyptic misery"; ". . . the infirm horse, with the harness hung over his sharp backbone flapping very loose about his thighs, appeared to be dancing mincingly on his toes with infinite patience."[73] According to Heinrich Zimmer,[74] the image of horse and man in traditional literature is a common one, reflecting the twofold nature of man, half animal, half god. The gods in their chariots, the knight on his charger—these are but variations of that motif which postulates the essential unity of life. Whether consciously or unconsciously, Conrad has provided us with a parody of the heroic motif of "the feat of strength," when the cab driver lifts the "enormous bony head" of his animal for Stevie's inspection. "He approached instead the motionless partner of his labours, and stooping to seize the bridle, lifted up the big, weary head to the height of his shoulder with one effort of his right arm, like a feat of strength."[75]

Nor is there lack of evidence for Conrad's intention in his less than subtle control of the reader's response to this cab. This is the old lady's "last cab drive." Its destination is a "charity cottage (one of a row) which by the exiguity of its dimensions and the simplicity of its accommodation, might well have been devised in kindness as a place of training for the still more straitened circumstances of the grave. . . ."[76] Retreating from the "charity gateway," the cab is described as a "dark low box on wheels." Before the lighted pub, the vehicle and horse possess "such a perfection of grotesque misery and weirdness of macabre detail, as if it were the Cab of Death itself."[77] Its whole aspect exudes "irremediable decay."

---

[72] Guerard, *Conrad the Novelist*, p. 225.

[73] Conrad, *The Secret Agent*, p. 156.

[74] Zimmer, "A Pagan Hero and a Christian Saint," *The King and the Corpse*, p. 33.

[75] Conrad, *The Secret Agent*, p. 168.

[76] *Ibid.*, p. 160.   [77] *Ibid.*, p. 170.

But equally significant is the author's attempt to manipulate spatial and temporal images to convey a world unlike our own. Although conscious artistry is involved here, Conrad was probably not entirely aware of the cluster's impact. What is important is that the images—whether by intention or by accident—work upon the fringes of our consciousness to convey the atmosphere of another world, a world of misery, darkness, death, infernal—or nightmarish—inhabitants. So shaky is the cab in which the group is riding, so narrow the streets, that to those within "all visual evidences of motion became imperceptible." The cab "rattled, jingled, jolted; in fact, the last was quite extraordinary. By its disproportionate violence and magnitude it obliterated every sensation of onward movement; and the effect was of being shaken in a stationary apparatus like a mediaeval device for the punishment of crime. . . ."[78] In such a conveyance, "time itself seemed to stand still." But time does move. The journey, begun during the light of day, extends into the evening. Symbolically, the old lady has moved into the world of death. "Night, the early dirty night, the sinister, noisy, hopeless, and rowdy night of South London, had overtaken her on her last cab drive."[79] Finally, we are told that "Mrs. Verloc's mother having parted for good from her children had also departed this life."[80] Brother and sister make the journey back together; but the way back leads merely to the same kind of demonic world, one where the only peace comes from illusion or idealization.

In this society in which darkness and irrationality dominate, the idiot Stevie is the hero. But he is also society's victim, sacrificed in order to provide a means of escape for Verloc. The death of Stevie results from a life based upon ritualized patterns of behavior, the assurance that certain acts will recur with idiotic rather than symbolic regularity. Once trained to act in a particular way, Stevie cannot readily absorb the implications or significance of new situations. Mrs. Verloc inspects her brother's face and hands before meals because in former years the ferocious "anger of the father was the supremely effective sanction of these rites."[81] Stevie's usefulness to Verloc is based upon the careful insistence of the sister and

---

[78] *Ibid.*, p. 163.
[79] *Ibid.*, p. 159.

[80] *Ibid.*, p. 169.
[81] *Ibid.*, p. 38.

mother that Mr. Verloc's displeasure should not be aroused nor his patience tried. When the trusted secret agent of the Baron Stott-Wartenheim decides to use his brother-in-law's blind devotion to accomplish the destruction of a "fetish of science," he devotes several days to providing examples for Stevie's emulation. Both retrace the proper route with infinite care. That Verloc fails and Stevie dies indicates the nature of the city where frustration and failure represent the norm.

The imagistic justification for regarding Stevie as both hero and scapegoat in this sinister atmosphere, although not readily apparent, is nonetheless there. In a city without gods—where only the gas-lamps possess dull halos of mist—Stevie's appearance suggests a perversion of divinity consistent with the tone of the entire novel. His chin is blurred by "thin fluffy hair" "like a golden mist." Stevie's actions, though ritualized, do manifest irrationality; yet the irrationality has a logic of its own. His morbid fear of pain and torture begins in sympathy and "immoderate compassion" and finally turns into futile viciousness. The talk of impotent revolutionaries and drunken cabmen alike move him to "pitiless rage." He spends his leisure time—and he, indeed, has all the time in the world—drawing circles which represent "cosmic chaos," timeless eternity, unity of existence which cannot be achieved in this fragmented world or can only be achieved by the self-forgetful hero. Although he does represent "dumb, gullible, sentimental humanity,"[82] in Albert Guerard's words, he is the only character who strongly reacts to the horror of life. " 'Poor brute, poor—people' " represents an intuitive perception into the evil of the demonic world in which he finds himself. He resents its diabolic and cannibalistic nature which has "one sort of wretchedness having to feed upon the anguish of the other—at the poor cabman beating the poor horse in the name, as it were, of his poor kids at home."[83] In a world drowned in darkness, Stevie alone is frank and "as open as day." Even Winnie, even his mother, do not seek "fundamental information." But while Stevie knows truth, he lacks the ability to carry his "universal charity" into any valid action. For his panacea to mankind's ills is always the same.

---

[82] Guerard, *Conrad the Novelist*, p. 229.
[83] Conrad, *The Secret Agent*, p. 171.

He could say nothing; for the tenderness to all pain and all misery, the desire to make the horse happy and the cabman happy, had reached the point of a bizarre longing to take them to bed with him. And that, he knew, was impossible. For Stevie was not mad. It was, as it were, a symbolic longing; and at the same time it was very distinct, because springing from experience, the mother of wisdom. Thus when as a child he cowered in a dark corner scared, wretched, sore, and miserable with the black, black misery of the soul, his sister Winnie used to come along, and carry him off to bed with her, as into a heaven of consoling peace. Stevie, though apt to forget mere facts, such as his name and address for instance, had a faithful memory of sensations. To be taken into a bed of compassion was the supreme remedy, with the only one disadvantage of being difficult of application on a large scale. And looking at the cabman, Stevie perceived this clearly, because he was reasonable.[84]

The revolutionaries and the police are victims of their own idealizations, although apparently rational. Unlike them, Stevie, although outwardly confused, although "apt to forget mere facts," realizes his impotence. Ironically, Conrad tells us that he is "reasonable."

Stevie represents a hero of modern society—not only caught within an order of nature more dead than alive but unable to act with the hero's traditional hubris because of personal limitations. His family ties are equally a perversion of the pattern which is part of the composite myth of the hero as described by Otto Rank, Jung, or Joseph Campbell. The hostile parent who, because of a prophetic threat to his power, sets the elected hero adrift in a basket or cask becomes in this novel an irascible brewer with a tendency to rage, assail closed doors, and fling objects. Their home is a " 'business house,' dark under the roof and scintillating exceedingly with lights and cut glass at the level of the street like a fairy palace."[85] In this family the mother relinquishes some of her nourishing and protecting qualities to the small daughter, who, in turn, becomes herself the equivalent of the stepmother of the exposure myth. Even as a child Winnie had put Stevie to bed, brushed his hair, intercepted the paternal blows "often with her own head." Indeed, she had married Verloc to provide a home for that brother-become-son. The double image

---

[84] *Ibid.*, pp. 167–68.   [85] *Ibid.*, p. 242.

of the flowing river—the first fresh, the second almost stagnant —adequately describes Winnie's earlier love affair and her final marriage to Verloc, an act which transfers her into the mother.

> Affectionate and jolly, he was a fascinating companion for a voyage down the sparkling stream of life; only his boat was very small. There was room in it for a girl-partner at the oar, but no accommodation for passengers. He was allowed to drift away from the threshold of the Belgravian mansion while Winnie averted her tearful eyes. He was not a lodger. The lodger was Mr. Verloc, indolent and keeping late hours, sleepily jocular of a morning from under his bed-clothes, but with gleams of infatuation in his heavy-lidded eyes, and always with some money in his pockets. There was no sparkle of any kind on the lazy stream of his life. It flowed through secret places. But his barque seemed a roomy craft, and his taciturn magnanimity accepted as a matter of course the presence of passengers.[86]

As a wife, she rejoices in her childlessness, her maternal passions (too destructive to be termed "love") dominated by the child "only a little peculiar." In her final self-deception, she projects the role of the stepfather upon Verloc, a role which the latter assumes only financially. As the husband and brother leave the shop—ostensibly to walk, in reality to rehearse the plan for destroying the Greenwich Observatory—Winnie thinks, " 'Might be father and son.' "

Stevie not only possesses the double set of parents of the composite hero story in much perverted form, but also becomes the scapegoat or *pharmakos* of the society, an arbitrary victim of the wasteland that is modern London. Traditionally, the death of the hero, preliminary to his bodily or spiritual rebirth and the regeneration of the community, may take the form of tearing to pieces. The fertility rites of vegetation myths provide ample evidence for this motif. Dionysus, Osiris, Orpheus, Attis—all are listed by Sir James Frazer in his discussions of primitive rites involving mutilation or disintegration.[87] Christ''s crucifixion is the Christian equivalent to the ritual suffering of the individual god-hero, which anticipates the redemption of the race. But Stevie's death—his *sparagmos*—is totally

---

[86] *Ibid.*, p. 243.

[87] Sir James Frazer, *The Golden Bough: A Study in Magic and Religion*, 1 Vol., abridged ed. (New York, 1948).

devoid of any heroism. It does not involve any conscious action or almost superhuman endeavor. Nor is any rebirth—either individual or generic—promised for this city lost in night. Finally, Winnie's macabre vision of the explosion reveals the ultimate distortion both of the image of fructifying rains which herald spring and the rebirth celebrated in fertility rites and of the image of light, symbol of reason, of consciousness, of the sun deity. "Mrs. Verloc closed her eyes desperately, throwing upon that vision the night of her eyelids, where after a rainlike fall of mangled limbs the decapitated head of Stevie lingered suspended alone, and fading out slowly like the last star of a pyrotechnic display."[88] Here light is merely a "pyrotechnic display," a display foreshadowed by the earlier setting off of fireworks and catherine wheels on the staircase of a milk firm. And both displays, in the absurdity of the situation, manifest a humor which results from excessive pain. To make these images tolerable, the author must make the reader laugh.

To emphasize the image of cannibalism in *The Secret Agent* is to see a demonic parody of the sacramental feast in which the hero's body is eaten by his followers in order to revitalize the community. The symbolic Christian phase of this rite, the Eucharist, becomes a mockery here. Stevie's body is the "accumulation of raw material for a cannibal feast." Chief Inspector Heat's breakfast is "a good deal of raw, unwholesome fog." The later reference to the "cold beef," the "funereal baked meats for Stevie's obsequies," which Verloc devours hungrily, reminds the reader of the earlier cannibal feast—and probably was so intended by as careful a craftsman as Conrad. The interpretation which points out the references to ritual enriches the reader's appreciation but was probably not apparent to Conrad. That such motifs were part of the author's literary experience cannot, however, be doubted. Certainly Gustav Morf reveals that Conrad had an intimate knowledge of fables, the Bible, and Grimm's fairy tales, where certain structural patterns are similar to those of myth.[89] And we know his reading experience was immense.

Winnie herself functions not only as a kind of stepmother of the

---

[88] Conrad, *The Secret Agent*, p. 260.

[89] Gustav Morf, *The Polish Heritage of Joseph Conrad* (London, n.d.), pp. 45–78.

exposure myth, the nourishing female and helpful sister, but is also the wife of Mr. Verloc. After all, from a more obvious but no less important perspective, this novel is a domestic drama, a story of personal relationships and lack of communication. As wife, she reveals resemblances to the terrible female, the woman who can never be possessed. Conrad's own inability to make love scenes convincing, his own embarrassment before actual dramatizations of passion, again enhance his characterization of the destructive nature of the relationship between man and woman in a society where common values no longer exist. Characteristics reminiscent of the siren and *femme fatale* are more startling than those recalling the faithful wife. Winnie's apparent loyalty to Verloc is once, and only once, compared to that of the most faithful wife of Greek epic. When the secret agent returns from his final trip to the continent (after his interview with Vladimir), Mrs. Verloc dutifully serves him. "And across the length of table covered with brown oilcloth Winnie, his wife, talked evenly at him the wifely talk, as artfully adapted, no doubt, to the circumstances of this return as the talk of Penelope to the return of the wandering Odysseus. Mrs. Verloc, however, had done no weaving during her husband's absence."[90]

The author's early descriptions of her reveal an attractive, very feminine young woman whose mother boasts of French descent. Traces of this origin "were apparent in Winnie, too. They were apparent in the extremely neat and artistic arrangement of her glossy dark hair."[91] Her enormous external calm, however, is her outstanding characteristic. Yet more often this "unfathomable reserve" gives an air of mystery which Conrad attributes to a person "systematically incurious." In her relationship with her husband, she is "mysterious, with the mysteriousness of living things." The endings of chapters 3 and 8 dramatize their complete estrangement. First, he cannot tell her of the absurd demands of Vladimir; the second scene precedes his final trip to the continent. Again, he cannot unburden himself to her. He is "not a man to break into such mysteries. He was easily intimidated. And he was also indolent, with the indolence which is so often the secret of good nature. He forebore touching

---

[90] Conrad, *The Secret Agent*, p. 183.   [91] *Ibid.*, p. 6.

that mystery out of love, timidity, and indolence. There would be always time enough."[92] Each scene concludes with Mrs. Verloc's inquiring whether or not to put out the light and with Verloc's answer, " 'Put it out.' " Each scene states or implies a fear of darkness, of night, of loss of the brightness which is the primary image of consciousness and reason. And it is this woman who instinctively believes that "things don't bear looking into very much" who in each case actually—and later symbolically—extinguishes the light. Again, her final crime is discovered after she sends Ossipon back into the shop to turn off the lights.

Nor can the reader doubt that Verloc loves her "as a wife should be loved—that is, maritally, with the regard one has for one's chief possession."[93] Loved like a possession, she is, unfortunately, never really possessed. Verloc's outstanding self-deception is that he is loved for himself alone. And it is this belief which finally kills him. For Winnie's reserve merely veils her extraordinary maternal love of Stevie. In a world where the brother plays the son and complete isolation substitutes for sexual fulfillment between husband and wife, love itself is demonic and destructive.

Myth, as a structure of imagery used in narrative, has analogies to dream as well as to ritual. Indeed, according to Northrop Frye, the analogies to dream in ironic literature—that is, fiction—are more prevalent than those to ritual.[94] References are made to the facial similarities of Winnie and Stevie. At the moment preceding Verloc's death, Winnie's face assumes an expression paralleling that of her dead brother: "As if the homeless soul of Stevie had flown for shelter straight to the breast of his sister, guardian, and protector, the resemblance of her face with that of her brother grew at every step, even to the droop of the lower lip, even to the slight divergence of the eyes."[95] Ossipon, at last detecting the truth about the death of the brother and the subsequent murder of the husband, envisages Mrs. Verloc as "the sister of a degenerate, a degenerate herself—of a

---

92 *Ibid.*, p. 180.

93 *Ibid.*, p. 179.

94 Frye, "Archetypal Criticism: Theory of Myths," *Anatomy of Criticism*, p. 214.

95 Conrad, *The Secret Agent*, p. 262.

murdering type."[96] Both end "by turning vicious"—Stevie when his universal charity is confronted by the " 'Bad world for poor people,' " Winnie when deprived of the one genuine passion of her dull life.

But more important are the real differences existing between brother and sister. These differences do, indeed, complement each other to form a whole, but it is a deficient whole. Together the pair might be said to reveal the two sides of the modern personality. I have already suggested that Stevie's actions possess an apparent madness but are fundamentally logical if viewed in the context of an absurd and fallen universe. The profusion of circles which he draws, suggesting "a rendering of cosmic chaos, the symbolism of a mad art attempting the inconceivable," have the merit of reflecting the universal need for eternity on a collective level, or the integration of the personality on an individual level. Though "his thoughts lacked clearness and precision," "he felt with greater completeness and some profundity." And the rational quality attributed to feelings makes him want "to go to the bottom of" matters like that involving the cabman's poverty and paternity and the horse's grotesque, desiccated frame. Winnie, conversely, possesses all the outward manifestations of rationality—order, calm, reserve. Yet her external calm simply reflects an unfathomable mystery, irrational passions which she covers by her "trust in face values," by her belief that "things did not stand being looked into."

Stevie is slight and blond; with his "golden mist" of a beard, almost a child. Both the halo-effect of the new growth of beard and the fact that he is, mentally at least, still a child recall the motif of the child-god who, in his associations with the sun, is an "enlarger of consciousness," a "bringer of light."[97] The Christian adaptation of this pattern can be seen in the Christ child, the halos present in iconography, the constant play upon the two words, "sun," and "son." These children—often culture heroes—reveal, as Stevie does, a knowledge beyond "our present-day consciousness."[98] Stevie's one

---

[96] Ibid., p. 290.

[97] Jung, "The Psychology of the Child Archetype," The Archetypes and the Collective Unconscious, p. 169.

[98] Ibid.

attempt to contribute to his own support is terminated when he is found, on a foggy day, letting "fireworks off on the staircase," fireworks including catherine wheels. Although this sinister circle recalls the martyrdom of a Christian saint, it has, in its desirable associations, a form which is symbolic of totality of experience. Again, Stevie is "as open as day." While Stevie is blond, Winnie is dark. It is she who, in the two instances already cited, turns out the light. It is she who in Jungian terms represents the feminine, the repressed and undifferentiated component of the male personality.

Winnie's role as a nourishing, but ultimately destructive, mother has already been noted. But her role as terrible mother can never be separated wholly from her role as seductress. Indeed, if we allow ourselves to use the Jungian term, which must be inferred from the above discussion of the brother-sister pair, she represents a type of anima projection, unconscious femininity.[99] Stevie's death makes Winnie a free woman, relieves her of her protecting maternal role. "At that precise moment Mrs. Verloc began to look upon herself as released from all earthly ties. She had her freedom."[100] Verloc's death releases her completely from the role of wife. What she desires most of all now is life; what she fears most is death which she, paradoxically, both seeks and represents.

In rushing to the river to kill herself, she confronts Ossipon, the pseudo-scientist, the advocate of the world of facts and empirical data, whose god is Lombroso. But it is Ossipon who is drawn into the whirlpool, who is first seduced. "He was terrified at this savage woman who had brought him in there, and would probably saddle him with complicity, at least if he were not careful. He was terrified

---

[99] The "mother archetype" and the "anima archetype"—spontaneous components of the "collective unconscious"—are not synonymous in Jung's theory, although in the individual experience the projection of the anima is first met in the mother. "The first bearer of the soul-image is always the mother; later it is borne by those women who arouse the man's feelings." (C. G. Jung, "The Relations between the Ego and the Unconscious," *Two Essays on Analytical Psychology*, trans. R. F. C. Hull [New York, 1956], p. 206.) Indeed, Jung points out in *The Archetypes and the Collective Unconscious* (p. 94) that the "mother-complex is never 'pure,' it is always mixed with the anima archetype." Each archetype has both a positive and a negative aspect. The negative aspect, which prevails in the demonic world of *The Secret Agent*, leads to death or to madness.

[100] Conrad, *The Secret Agent*, p. 251.

at the rapidity with which he had been involved in such danger—decoyed into it."[101] He begins to see her not as the self-contained, desirable-because-mysterious wife of Mr. Verloc but as a dark presence. "Near him, her black form merged in the night, like a figure half chiselled out of a block of black stone."[102] Her dark veil covers her face so that only her "big eyes gleamed lustrously, like the eyes of a masked woman."[103] She is "all black—black as commonplace death itself." And in a moment of excitement, as she clings to his legs, "his terror reached its culminating point, became a sort of intoxication, entertained delusions, acquired the characteristics of delirium tremens. He positively saw snakes now. He saw the woman twined round him like a snake, not to be shaken off. She was not deadly. She was death itself—the companion of life."[104] Now he regrets that he has interfered with a force that, according to Jung, "had better been left unconscious."[105] Winnie, indeed, in her irrationality does conform to a type of anima projection. "Everything the anima touches becomes numinous—unconditional, dangerous, taboo, magical. She is the serpent in the paradise of the harmless man with good resolutions and still better intentions. She affords the most convincing reasons for not prying into the unconscious."[106] Although Ossipon is not a "harmless man with good resolutions and still better intentions," he does feel "himself losing his footing in the depths of this tenebrous affair."[107] And his fate is that of the man possessed by the components of the negative anima—madness.

Winnie's freedom is first limited by her maternal love for Stevie, who is described in terms which recall the sun-god, the bringer of light. When she resigns herself to Ossipon and seeks his protection, Conrad notes that she is no longer free. Moreover, Ossipon, too, is described in terms of a perverse sun-god or God the son. He has an "Apollo-like ambrosial head." To Winnie he comes "like a radiant messenger of life;" he is her "saviour." During his ordeal with the panic-stricken woman, he possesses the "face of a man who had

---

101 *Ibid.,* p. 289.   103 *Ibid.,* p. 294.

102 *Ibid.,* p. 280.   104 *Ibid.,* p. 291.

105 Jung, "Archetypes and the Collective Unconscious," *The Archetypes and the Collective Unconscious,* p. 28.

106 *Ibid.*   107 Conrad, *The Secret Agent,* p. 279.

drunk at the very fountain of Sorrow,"[108] an image recalling the description of Christ as "Man of Sorrows." In spite of associations linking him to Christ and Apollo, his appearance is tainted by suggestions of darkness: he has a "flattened nose and prominent mouth cast in the rough mould of the negro type."[109] And his blond hair is a "bush of crinkly yellow." Although Winnie has been freed from the maternal role, she becomes enslaved again, this time assuming an inferior and dependent position—at once seductress and daughter.

Enough has been said of the characteristics of the demonic city, the presence of which hovers over the entire novel. Irrationality and the unconscious, darkness, death as imaged by pools, stagnant water or dark rain or blood or damp mist or simply a devouring, drowning sea—all these describe the modern world of London. But all these describe Winnie Verloc as well, Winnie as mother and femme fatale, Winnie as the negative aspect of the shadowy feminine principle, Winnie who in terror mumbles vaguely " 'Blood and dirt. Blood and dirt.' " London, the devouring monster, which is the jaws of death, is equally the destructive feminine principle. Ossipon sees this same principle in the dark and faceless woman or in her coiling figure. According to Jung, the Old Testament treats cities "as if they were women."[110] The city of desire in Western thought is the heavenly Jerusalem; the city to be shunned, Babylon or Tyre. "Strong, unconquered cities are virgins. . . . Cities are also harlots."[111] Moreover, "The city is a maternal symbol, a woman who harbours the inhabitants in herself like children. It is therefore understandable that the three mother-goddesses, Rhea, Cybele, and Diane, all wear the mural crown."[112] Whether the maternal symbol be apocalyptic—desirable—or demonic—undesirable—depends upon the context.

Earlier I noted the equation between the city and the monster, the city with its labyrinthine streets and the monster, Death, whose innards are described as a dark maze where ambiguity and irrational-

---

[108] Ibid., p. 295.   [109] Ibid., p. 44.

[110] Jung, "Symbols of the Mother and of Rebirth," Symbols of Transformation, p. 208.

[111] Ibid.   [112] Ibid.

ity confront the descending soul. Joseph Campbell, in *The Masks of God: Primitive Mythology*, quotes several authorities cited in an article by W. F. Jackson Knight on "Maze Symbolism and The Trojan Game." One archaeologist reveals that the ancient cities of both England and Crete associated the labyrinth and maze with "the internal organs of the human anatomy as well as with the underworld, the one being the microcosm of the other.[113] 'The object of the tomb-builder would have been to make the tomb as much like the body of the mother as he was able,' he writes, 'since to enter the next world' . . . 'the spirit would have to be re-born.' "[114]

The Secret Agent, then, is a complex of metaphors which link the city and the woman, darkness, and death. It presents a "world of total metaphor," for in the static hell which Conrad creates "everything is potentially identifiable with everything else."[115] Winnie, whose brother is a son, destroys both son and husband because of her illusions; her death by drowning is the final act of destruction, an act which denies rebirth. London, which contains its inhabitants within it, refuses the sun. Even the life-giving spring rains manifest themselves as fog or black puddles. The entire effect is enveloping and permanent darkness.

Analogies to ritual and dream—to myth—in the modern novel might show that personal despair and individual commitment have some significance, that even tragedy is beneficial in human experience. The eternal verities are still, perhaps, eternal verities. But in *The Secret Agent*, life, commitment, and despair lead nowhere except to the death-in-life of London or to actual death. The perversion of religion and society and heroic action manifests itself on every page. The ancient bond between myth and religion cannot exist in a community that has lost all contact with traditional methods of worship. Vladimir does recognize a significant fact of his age when he absurdly goads Mr. Verloc into frenzied action. An attempt to destroy a church will not inflame modern passions; for man's "fetish" is no longer religion but science. Only an act against a

---

[113] Campbell, *The Masks of God: Primitive Mythology*, p. 69.

[114] W. F. Jackson Knight, "Maze Symbolism and the Trojan Game," as quoted by Joseph Campbell, *The Masks of God: Primitive Mythology* (New York, 1959), p. 69.

[115] Frye, "Archetypal Criticism: Theory of Myths," *Anatomy of Criticism*, p. 136.

scientific structure will possess the "character of a religious manifestation." It will arouse the tyrant that is public opinion and result in repressive legislation in a country which has an absurd and "sentimental regard for individual liberty." Ossipon, who invokes "Lombroso, as an Italian peasant recommends himself to his favorite saint,"[116] is the "scientist," but the scientist who is morally corrupt, mentally weak, socially impotent, and scientifically false. How little intellectual support the world of science gives its chief advocate is seen when he cannot cope with the fear which Winnie's acts rouse.

> If Comrade Ossipon did not recommend his terrified soul to Lombroso, it was only because on scientific grounds he could not believe that he carried about him such a thing as a soul. But he had in him the scientific spirit, which moved him to testify on the platform of a railway station in nervous, jerky phrases.
> "He was an extraordinary lad, that brother of yours. Most interesting to study. A perfect type in a way. Perfect!" . . . He spoke scientifically in his secret fear.[117]

Society, however, still requires the sacrifice of those who adhere to the new religion, whether it be science or politics. So this distorted world also has its secular martyr such as the innocuous and grotesquely fat Michaelis whose martyrdom is thrust upon him by the force of public opinion. Sentimental humanitarian, believer in "cold reason," optimist, idealist, and impotent revolutionary—all these describe the man who, physically, is the direct antithesis of the gaunt martyr of medieval art. Yet isolated he is, if not in the African deserts, at least in the society which both punishes and canonizes him. Acclimated to a cell-like, hygienic prison, he is no longer able to accept the intrusion of another voice or argue logically about any problem.

> He was no good in discussion, not because any amount of argument could shake his faith, but because the mere fact of hearing another voice disconcerted him painfully, confusing his thoughts at once— these thoughts that for so many years, in a mental solitude more barren than a waterless desert no living voice had ever combatted, commented, or approved.[118]

---

116 Conrad, *The Secret Agent*, p. 297.

117 *Ibid.*, p. 297.   118 *Ibid.*, p. 45.

Image after image increases the cluster of associations. He is, first of all, a "ticket-of leave apostle" or "like those saintly men whose personality is lost in the contemplation of their faith."[119] Though his physique is less than cherubic, he is "angelic," possessing the "temperament of a saint." His rather confused convictions had appeared to him in prison "like a faith revealed in visions" and now master him "like an act of grace." With "mildly exalted eyes" he talks to himself even among the wealthy. Again, the chief labor of his life, pursued with "delightful enthusiasm," is his autobiography, the " 'Autobiography of a Prisoner' which was to be like a book of Revelation in the history of mankind."[120] Made almost stationary by flesh, confused in thinking, he represents no threat to a city imprisoned within its own darkness. Nor is he a rallying point to other exponents of his static faith. Martyrdom, self-sacrifice to strengthen a cause for which one believes, becomes simply the ordinary state of the fractured personality.

What characterizes Michaelis also characterizes the other individuals who inhabit the society which has martyred him—all are partial men without identity or status. Although the novel itself is an eloquent example of communication, the creatures within it have lost the sense of personal or communal unity. There is isolation on every level—among colleagues, among friends, among families, even between husband and wife. Verloc cannot make Vladimir see the fine distinction between an " 'agent provocateur' " and a bomb-throwing anarchist; Ossipon and the Professor are only brothers over the skin; Chief Inspector Heat has his private information; the Assistant Commissioner also acts officially in an unorthodox—though efficient—way. Winnie's mother cannot explain her motives to her daughter, who herself does not explain to her husband that he is not loved for himself alone. Winnie and Verloc—she believing that "things did not stand looking into," he that "there would be always time enough" to fathom the mystery of his wife—actively avoid trying to understand each other. The image of darkness is the most prevalent manifestation of this isolation in personal relationships.

---

[119] *Ibid.*, p. 107.   [120] *Ibid.*, p. 120.

Perhaps affecting the same pattern of associations is the image of the shadow, the dreamer in a waking world. That the waking world happens to be a night and nightmare world does not lessen the significance of the image. Even so large a presence as that of Sir Ethelred is described as "shadowy." Leaving the Great Personage, the Assistant Commissioner proceeds "with the air of a thoughtful somnambulist." Verloc, feeling his stable position menaced in the extreme, loses further contact with reality. More and more he gazes at his wife with "a somnambulistic expressionless gaze" or "as though she had been a phantom." He acts "like a man in a nightmare." Ossipon regards his vague commitment to Winnie as "madness, a nightmare." And she responds "dreamily." Or else she becomes frantic "as if started suddenly out of a dream of safety." After her death, however, Ossipon's new involvement in time and life ends in madness. The mere mention of a newspaper now causes him to start "like a scared somnambulist."

Linked to the group of words suggesting unreality and illusion are all those relating to masks. Mist and fog mask the sun; darkness veils day. The necessity for action causes Mr. Verloc to regard Stevie "with morose thoughtfulness that lately had fallen like a veil between Mr. Verloc and the appearances of the world of senses."[121] Most conspicuously, it is Winnie whose own calm has meant to conceal her irrational passions. When she believes herself freed by Stevie's death, she veils her face "like a masked and mysterious visitor of impenetrable intentions." Her husband removes the veil, "unmasking a still unreadable face, against which his nervous exasperation was shattered like a glass bubble flung against a rock."[122] After his death, her face and form take on symbolic proportions in her encounter with the pseudo-scientist. Her underlying passions rise to the surface, but her face is masked—at once suggesting the mystery of the unconscious and her essential isolation. ". . . Mrs. Verloc, veiled, had no face, almost no discernible form." One of the most ironic sections of the novel deals with Winnie's final confrontation of Ossipon, whom she meets as she is rushing to kill herself. He still believes that Verloc has perished in the Greenwich ex-

---

[121] *Ibid.*, p. 174.   [122] *Ibid.*, p. 256.

plosion. Their verbal exchange suggests the complete inability of each to comprehend another human being; each, like Michaelis, is talking to himself although each believes he has established a line of understanding. When Ossipon eventually does find Verloc's body, he sees Winnie not as a suffering fellow creature, but as a specimen from a textbook by Lombroso. "Through her black veil her big eyes gleamed lustrously like the eyes of a masked woman."[123] He comprehends emotionally only the blackness and cannot read the eyes, themselves glowing "lustrously."

The mask with which Winnie seems to confront the others may also be the symbol of her own self-estrangement. Once free, she cannot grasp the independence which life implies. Faced with her inner nature apart from any husband or brother, she cannot admit her own sexuality, love of life, instincts. What she cannot meet—and conquer—is the monster within herself. And the mask which she assumes to the world becomes the real woman without her realizing it.

The mask image and the image of stone merge in the figure of a terrified Ossipon, who, concealing his fear, presents a face "like a fresh plaster cast of himself after a wasting illness."[124] As the mask conceals, so the stone, with its connotations of hardness and rigidity, becomes the perfect metaphor for the individual who does not wish to reveal himself as a flesh and blood being in this inhuman landscape. Emotions become atrophied and ossified because of lack of use, indolence, and inability to communicate. Yeats's words may well apply here: "Too long a sacrifice / Can make a stone of the heart." Earlier Verloc, lying in bed beside his wife, reads her reserve, her mystery as if she were "a recumbent statue in the rough." Through indolence, he becomes unwilling to penetrate the surface; through self-deceit she becomes unwilling to reveal the truth about her love for Stevie, her inability to love her husband. Eventually Winnie's incoherence reminds Ossipon of "a figure half chiselled out of a block of black stone."[125] This simile admirably reveals her fragmentation as a result of her bridled emotions. When she finally unmasks herself, her face is "like adamantine," made stern by fear.

---

[123] Ibid., p. 294.   [124] Ibid., p. 293.   [125] Ibid., p. 280.

And, again, Ossipon cannot read the rigidity of terror. Terrified in return, he further isolates her as a case study in degeneracy created by his own estranging fear and selfishness. He perceives her piecemeal.

> He gazed scientifically. He gazed at her cheeks, at her nose, at her eyes, at her ears. . . . Bad! . . . Fatal! Mrs. Verloc's pale lips parting, slightly relaxed under his passionately attentive gaze, he gazed also at her teeth. . . . Not a doubt remained . . . a murdering type.[126]

Static, isolated, divided, impotent, none of these people possess the superior force and gigantic will which we associate with the heroic. But if they are not heroic, neither are they simply entertaining creations. The chief accusation against an archetypal study of *The Secret Agent* may be that I have taken the work too seriously—a charge Conrad's own words seem to corroborate. To assuage the misgivings of John Galsworthy, whose own prose style may be most kindly described as "conventional," Conrad wrote,

> After all, you must not take it too seriously. The whole thing is superficial and it is but a tale. I had no idea to consider Anarchism politically, or to treat it seriously in its philosophical aspect; as a manifestation of human nature in its discontent and imbecility. The general reflections whether right or wrong are not meant as bolts. . . . They are, if anything, mere digs at the people in the tale. As to attaching Anarchism as a form of humanitarian enthusiasm or intellectual despair or social atheism, that—if it were worth doing—would be the work for a more vigorous hand and for a mind more robust, and perhaps more honest than mine.[127]

To R. B. Cunninghame Graham he called his revolutionaries "shams."[128] We may readily accept his statement to Sir Alexander Methuen that he was writing "*purely a work of imagination*" which "has no social or philosophical intention."[129] We must accept with equal praise or blame his statement in the same letter that his work

---

[126] *Ibid.*, p. 297.

[127] Letter to John Galsworthy, September 12, 1906, as printed in G. Jean-Aubry, *Joseph Conrad: Life and Letters*, 2 Vols. (New York, 1927), 11, 37–38.

[128] Letter to Cunninghame Graham, October 7, 1907, *ibid.*, 11, 60.

[129] Letter to (Sir) Alexander Methuen, November 7, 1906, *ibid.*, 11, 38.

"may even have some moral significance"—a truly Conradian irony.
The detachment, the enormous sense of control, the apparent lack
of authorial compassion, the verbal games and epithets noted by
Albert Guerard,[130] all tend to support the judgment that Conrad
was not emotionally involved in this artistic creation. But the very
necessity for the control apparent in every line implies a deep sense
of commitment and involvement. Where no danger lurks for the
author, no verbal guard is necessary. In "An Epistle to a Lady,"
Swift admirably summed up the real tensions between authorial
distance and authorial identification, between what seems and what
is:

> Like the ever-laughing Sage,
> In a Jest I spend my Rage:
> (Tho' it must be understood,
> I would hang them if I cou'd:)

In his "Author's Note"—prefaced to the novel long after initial
intention was adulterated by the actual work, but certainly as valid
as the consoling letter to Galsworthy—Conrad wrote,

> For the surrounding hints were not lacking. I had to fight hard to
> keep at arm's length the memories of my solitary and nocturnal
> walks all over London in my early days, lest they should rush in
> and overwhelm each page of the story as these emerged one after
> another from a mood as serious in feeling and thought as any in
> which I ever wrote a line. In that respect I really think that "The
> Secret Agent" is a perfectly genuine piece of work. Even the
> purely artistic purpose, that of applying an ironic method to a subject
> of that kind, was formulated with deliberation and is the earnest
> belief that ironic treatment alone would enable me to say all I felt
> I would have to say in scorn as well as in pity.[131]

From this quotation two important points need to be noted. His
insistence, first of all, is upon the "ironic treatment," not upon the
"satiric treatment." In satire the author's position is always clear: he
wishes to correct by making either ludicrous or loathsome. Irony, on
the other hand, manifests an ambiguity of attitude; neither author
nor audience is unequivocal in his response. Grotesqueness cannot

---

130 Guerard, Conrad the Novelist, pp. 227–28.

131 Conrad, "Author's Note," The Secret Agent, p. xiii.

be unrelieved; men cannot become monsters. The distance between an author and each character is a constantly shifting one—on the one hand, apparently antipathetic; on the other, sympathetic. Conrad himself realized the necessity for ambiguity, for he felt that what he had to say must be said "in scorn as well as in pity." Nor is the boundary between scorn and pity always clearly defined.

Second, there are few characters so base or so comic that the reader does not detect some compassion, some awareness of pity and understanding. Winnie's reserve, phrases in apposition like "the widow of Mr. Verloc, the sister of the late faithful Stevie (blown to fragments in a state of innocence and in the conviction of being engaged in a humanitarian enterprise),"[132] and the Dickensian tag line, "things don't bear looking into very much"—these may provide the artistic calculation necessary for utter detachment. And were these devices dominant, Winnie would indeed be a flat character in a satiric novel. But Conrad does admit the claims and fascinations of Winnie's humanity in his "Author's Note." Within the text itself, Winnie's life manifests a single-minded, unquestioning, almost heroic loyalty to her duty. Though her energy is fixed upon the needs of an idiot, her devotion does withstand all the pressures of her existence, an "existence foreign to all grace and charm, without beauty and almost without decency, but admirable in the continuity of feeling and tenacity of purpose."[133] No matter how comic the final meeting with Ossipon may appear, their complete inability to comprehend each other turns what might be sheer farce into a grotesque vision of truth. When a human life awaits the end of a sentence, our emotions can never admit that they are simply being manipulated for entertainment. Winnie's struggle for life does, ultimately, involve the reader. That she should wish to save such a life is perhaps the greatest horror—or the greatest comedy.

Nor can the novel communicate its nightmare to us unless we regard the author's position as an ironic one. Such macabre comedy approximates *Galgenhumor*, gallows humor, humor in the midst of horror, the point at which despair becomes humorous. It is this genuine despair which finally redeems the distorted physical beings

---

[132] *Ibid.*, p. 266.   [133] *Ibid.*, p. 244.

whom Conrad called "shams." Shams they may be as revolutionaries, but as human beings they are all capable of an awareness of their own isolation, the lostness which a dead world imposes upon the living. Only on the surface—no matter how broad the surface—are they comic. Though Mr. Verloc's anxieties exist several levels below the flesh, they are a very real threat to his indolence, his comic appearance, and his "fat-pig style." His own illusions about his marriage or his value as a secret agent cannot sustain him. In his fear of the darkness, his real concern for his menaced security, his genuine inability to touch his wife's emotions, he reflects some of the malaise symptomatic of the modern disintegrating personality. His fatness is confined to his "mortal envelope," or is a symbol of his sick society. Even Ossipon, at once the most despicable and most physically attractive character, is finally redeemed from mere satire by the fact that his own actions drive him insane. Nor can Mrs. Verloc's mother's sacrifice be ignored because the old woman herself possesses triple chins, an ample, ancient form, and swollen, useless legs.

These are people imprisoned in the time that is modern society, a London which is more dead than alive. Having fallen from the ideal of heroic action in a golden age, they still cannot act in order to rise to a utopia. Physical grotesqueness is the mask for their one-sided, fractured, estranged selves. Or it is the symbol of the absurd world of darkness and madness in which they are caught. In such a society, the idiot becomes both hero and scapegoat; a perverse god, he promises no individual renewal or rebirth. Religion becomes the worship of power or science. Nor does the parody of the night voyage, the journey into the interior regions, reveal a meaningful struggle with personal despair. Rather, the perversion of ritual with dream patterns here increases the irony, raises that despair to the point where it must be made humorous in order for the reader to bear it. Amusement must severely dilute sympathy which is, after all, "a form of fear."

CHAPTER FOUR

Under Western Eyes
Mirror of a Double Quest

The autocratic Russia that Joseph Conrad hated as a Pole, and that his imaginative creation Razumov served, existed within historical memory. A Russian named V. K. de Plehve, an infamous director of the state police and Minister of Interior in 1902, was actually murdered by one Sasonov in 1904. Nor are most students of Conrad unaware that this world of revolutionaries and despots also produced a double agent named Azeff, whose activities on behalf of conspirator and police alike might well have served Conrad as a model for Razumov. In pursuing the "very soul of things Russian,—*Cosas de Russia*,"[1] Conrad was dealing with a world physically and emotionally nearer the very soul of things Conradian than the world of Sulaco and *Cosas de Costaguana*. Embittered by Poland's historical submission to the czars, Conrad had himself written an equivalent of his imagined source for *Nostromo*; both "The Crime of Partition" and "Autocracy and War"[2] were, indeed, his "Fifty Years of Misrule."

In a well-documented and well-argued study of Conrad's political novels, Eloise Knapp Hay is most distressed to find "hints and

---

[1] Joseph Conrad to John Galsworthy, January 6, 1908, *Joseph Conrad: Life and Letters*, ed. G. Jean-Aubry (New York, 1927), II, 64–65.

[2] Joseph Conrad, *Notes on Life and Letters* (Garden City, 1925), pp. 83–133.

sources for Conrad's characters and allusions almost everywhere [newspaper articles, novels, histories, memoirs] I looked."[3] The fantastic chapters by Herzen or the biographies of men like Bakunin offer a plethora of Conradian characters. But "hints and sources" are finally irrelevant. This is to say that perhaps what Conrad detected in *Cosas de Russia* was simply its humanity: Russia and Geneva are spatial entities that reflect interior events—two parts of the nature of man.

My purposeful mingling of life and art reflects what seems to me to be Conrad's intention. The narrator of *Under Western Eyes* presents himself as a rather dull and pedantic English teacher of languages who more often than not must energize for us episodes and confrontations that he knows only at second hand. What he does insist upon is the historical validity of his narrative, that "to invent the mere bald facts of . . . [Razumov's] life would have been utterly beyond my power."[4]

> But I think without this declaration the readers of these pages will be able to detect in the story the marks of documentary evidence. And that is perfectly correct. It is based on a document; all I have brought to it is my knowledge of the Russian language, which is sufficient for what is attempted here. The document, of course, is something in the nature of a journal, a diary, yet not exactly that in its actual form. . . . Some of the entries cover months of time and extend over dozens of pages. All the earlier part is a retrospect, in a narrative form, relating to an event which took place about a year before.[5]

And this record "is connected with an event characteristic of modern Russia in the actual fact."[6]

However, as Albert Guerard points out,[7] the man who self-consciously disclaims his aesthetic gifts then proceeds to narrate the story for us with skill, creating more than adequate transitions, effacing himself when necessary, immersing us in the drama or pushing us away to make us observers as detached as himself. Words, which

---

[3] *The Political Novels of Joseph Conrad* (Chicago and London, 1963), p. 279.

[4] Joseph Conrad, *Under Western Eyes* (Garden City, N.Y., 1926), p. 3.

[5] *Ibid.*, pp. 3–4.   [6] *Ibid.*, p. 7.

[7] Guerard, "Two Versions of Anarchy," *Conrad The Novelist*, p. 250.

he protests "are the great foes of reality," are so structured by him that Razumov's story, his self-communion, moves from personal history to universal myth. And Conrad's own situation is analogous to that of his narrator, his English teacher of languages. His imaginative and sympathetic presence has so pervaded the pages that what is important are not the real events occurring in a world of action that may or may not have anticipated the novel, but the construct of words by which history may be transformed into art. If "words are the great foes of reality," it is because they here belong to the artist's world more than to the actor's.

When we move from actual history into the fictional history of *Under Western Eyes*, two spatial dimensions emerge by which some of the meaning of the novel is to be conveyed. On the one hand, there is the West, a vague geographical entity which may simply mean Geneva or may mean the world west of Russia.[8] Though at times the narrative makes us assume that we are directly within the mind of the Russian Razumov, we are always under Western eyes, having our experience filtered for us by the old Englishman who steadfastly maintains both his inability to understand and his inability to communicate to his readers. He obtusely counterpoints the "simple" Russian experience with the "complex" Western one. "Difference of nationality is a terrible obstacle for our complex western natures,"[9] he protests. Or when he finds no real sympathy for Madame de S—— permeating his narrative, he stops his emotional diatribe to justify his method.

> The object of my digression from the straight course of Miss Haldin's relation (in my own words) of her visit to the Château Borel, was to bring forward that statement of my friend, the professor's wife. I wanted to bring it forward simply to make what I have to say presently of Mr. Razumov's presence in Geneva, a little more credible—for this is a Russian story for Western ears, which, as I have observed already, are not attuned to certain tones of cynicism and cruelty, of moral negation, and even of moral distress already silenced at our end of Europe.[10]

---

[8] *Ibid.*, p. 244.

[9] Conrad, *Under Western Eyes*, p. 116.

[10] *Ibid.*, pp. 163–64.

When the city Geneva itself charges our image of the West with its own peculiar atmosphere, the image is equally derogatory. What in the individual character is unreliable, pompous, and dull, becomes in society complacent, orderly, and mediocre. The "respectable and passionless abode of democratic liberty" is without feeling, without character, without inspiration. It is "the very perfection of mediocrity attained at last after centuries of toil and culture."[11] As Guerard reminds us, the counterpoint of Swiss and Russian would seem to be ". . . not merely one of the secure and the suffering, but also of the respectable and the anarchic, the decent and the messy, the complacent and the compassionate, the mercenary and the mystical, the 'saved' and the tragic, the abstract and the human."[12]

When we translate the spatial relationships into temporal ones, the two worlds face history so that they are again back to back. Geneva has attained its "prosaic virtue" "after centuries of toil"; her orderly landscape is studded with statues and names of the great of the past—the *philosophes*, Rousseau. When the old teacher tries ineptly to assuage Mrs. Haldin's grief by moving from her personal tragedy—the death of her son—to historical events, he claims:

"We too have had tragic times in our history."
"A long time ago. A very long time ago."
"Yes."
"There are nations that have made their bargain with fate," said Miss Haldin, who had approached us. "We need not envy them."[13]

But later, when the narrator wishes to protect Natalia against the ineffectual machinations of Peter Ivanovitch, she again emphasizes the fact that for the West history has already been written; lives in England and Geneva are part of a causal chain whose first link was forged long ago.

". . . You belong to a people which has made a bargain with fate and wouldn't like to be rude to it. But we have made no bargain. It was never offered to us—so much liberty for so much hard cash. . . ."[14]

---

[11] *Ibid.*, p. 203.

[12] Guerard, "Two Versions of Anarchy," *Conrad the Novelist*, p. 245.

[13] Conrad, *Under Western Eyes*, p. 114.   [14] *Ibid.*, p. 134.

Unlike the Englishman, the Russian is born to an inheritance to be gained in the future. The land itself anticipates what Razumov envisions. "Under the sumptuous immensity of the sky, the snow covered the endless forests, the frozen rivers, the plains of an immense country, obliterating the landmarks, the accidents of the ground, levelling everything under its uniform whiteness, like a monstrous blank page awaiting the record of an inconceivable history."[15] Such immensity is a promise of timelessness, either through a suspension of historical processes on earth by which all men will achieve in a utopian future what Western religion had earlier promised in a heavenly eternity or through death where the traditionally sanctioned celestial city of God obliterates time-consciousness.

In this novel, too, Conrad juxtaposes the autocrat, supporting the established order, and the revolutionary. When Razumov, in a moment of agitation, is embraced by his father, he is overwhelmed by "contemptuous tenderness." "This simple-minded, worldly ex-Guardsman and senator whose soft grey official whiskers had brushed against his cheek, his aristocratic and convinced father, was he a whit less estimable or more absurd than that famine-stricken, fanatical revolutionist, the red-nosed student?"[16] Razumov considers both anarchic: both the "lawlessness of autocracy" and the "lawlessness of revolution" menace Razumov's "being in the willed, in the determined future." Both possess qualities of the numinous, the mysterious, the irrational; what Conrad at several points calls "mystic." The narrator attributes the same qualities to those forces which alternately threaten to engulf Natalia Haldin when he uses the metaphor "the shadow of autocracy" and "the shadow of revolution." And "cynicism" we are told is both a "mark of Russian autocracy and of Russian revolt."

Where the autocrat and the revolutionary diverge is in their separate emphasis upon what the historical fact of the land promises for the future. For the autocrat, the peace of eternity is a reward to be gained in heaven above; but a strong ruler, they argue, can bring a measure of peace. For that reason, some turned "to autocracy for the peace of their patriotic conscience as a weary unbeliever,

---

[15] *Ibid.*, p. 33.   [16] *Ibid.*, p. 308.

touched by grace, turns to the faith of his fathers for the blessing of spiritual rest."[17] So the autocrat looks to the traditional religion with its rewards and punishments to support his lawlessness on earth; and humble men, like Sophia Antonovna's father, attribute acts of appalling virulence to "the hand of God." General T——, the man to whom Razumov gives Haldin up, cannot maintain his wonted reserve when he reiterates his hatred of rebels, " 'People that deny God himself—perfect unbelievers.' " The General's own home reminds Razumov of that timeless realm to which the government will soon dispatch Haldin: it possesses a "grave-like silence"; the clock itself is "mute."

The revolutionary, however, hopes for a heaven on earth where all men will share in the joys of existence, a "new future" brought about by the "sacred will of the people." Haldin kills so that a " 'new revelation shall come out of Russia. . . . The Russian soul that lives in all of us. It has a future. It has a mission. . . .' "[18] Haldin does not conceive of the soul in the theological sense—as that immaterial essence that animates life and survives the death of the body. Rather, he uses the religious word to designate the infusing spirit of rebellion, the idea "which never dies." The God in which Haldin believes is not the transcendent Providence of General T—— or Prince K——, but "what's divine in the Russian soul." For his mother and sister he is the "hope of the future," but of a utopian future very much in this world.

That this vision of an auspicious future becomes permeated with a cluster of religious imagery seems but one of the ways Conrad both ironically allows the deluded revolutionaries to sanction their activity and parodies the situation in which a nightmarish world must borrow from traditional structures to enhance values that are no longer operative.[19] In this world of utopian revolutionaries, Haldin is a "saviour"; his initial contact with the driver Ziemianitch issues

---

17 *Ibid.,* p. 34.   18 *Ibid.,* p. 22.

19 Eloise Knapp Hay states that the Russian Messianic myth underlies the nationalism of both autocrat and revolutionary, "Russia's sacred mission among the nations of the world" (*The Political Novels of Joseph Conrad* [Chicago & London, 1963], p. 284). In the autocrats of the novel, I detect the most traditional belief in God—as much English as Russian. The revolutionaries, on the other hand, provide a sanction or rationalization for their actions by transferring to these events the symbolism of

from his "teaching." "The spirit of the heroic Haldin had passed through these dens of black wretchedness with a promise of universal redemption from all the miseries that oppress mankind."[20] Social revolution rather than purgatorial penance will provide the "purifying flame" through which slum-dwellers will be saved. When the self-deluded revolutionaries shift Haldin's mantle, his "poisoned robe," to Razumov, the latter is actually called "saviour" by the student madcap Kostia. If Haldin is the "saviour" and sacrificial victim, that other "heroic fugitive," Peter Ivanovitch, himself plays many roles in which he dramatizes his religious function. Not only is he the "apostle of feminism," but he is also constantly referred to as "inspired"—that is, breathed upon by deity. With apostolic zeal he attempts to instil Natalia Haldin with the new religion consonant with "the high conception of our future."

> "Nowadays the devil is not combated by prayers and fasting. And what is fasting after all but starvation? You must not starve yourself, Natalia Victorovna. . . . Sin is different in our day, and the way of salvation for pure souls is different too. It is no longer to be found in monasteries but in the world, in the. . . ."[21]

Even the narrator comments upon his "austere decency—something recalling a missionary." Variously, he is the "noble arch-priest of Revolution"; he suggests "a monk or a prophet"; he "preached generally the cult of the woman."

But if the revolutionaries mouth or inspire the imagery of godhead, Razumov sees them equally as fallen angels. Sophia Antenovna appears to him as the "true spirit of destructive revolution," his "personal adversary." (Ironically, Satan, meaning "adversary," should have God or Christ to oppose him.) She possesses the anarchic passion that he has not yet admitted exists. She espouses the activist philosophy carried into effect by Haldin. " 'Life, Razumov, not to be vile must be revolt.' " In her "unappeasable passion" she reminds Razumov of Mephistopheles, who himself chose to

---

Christianity. This, however, is characteristic of all Western utopian movements and revolutions, whether in Russia, Mexico, or Christianized Africa. For a study of the way political movements use the imagery and content of Christianity, see Norman Cohn, *The Pursuit of the Millennium* (New York, 1961).

[20] *Ibid.*, p. 279.   [21] *Ibid.*, pp. 127–28.

" 'burn rather than rot.' " The slant of her "Mephistophelian eyebrows," her crimson blouse, her pose of eternal restlessness—these
suggest the demonic. Yet in the civilized world, we are reminded by
the narrator, the

> Evil One, with his single passion of satanic pride for the only mo-
> tive, is yet, on a larger, modern view, allowed to be not quite so
> black as he used to be painted. With what greater latitude, then,
> should we appraise the exact shade of mere mortal man, with his
> many passions and his miserable ingenuity in error, always dazzled
> by the base glitter of mixed motives, everlastingly betrayed by a
> short-sighted wisdom.[22]

All the misdirected energy of the woman, all her nobility of suffering evoke a sympathy that the "morality of the Western reader"
cannot easily grant. Sophia Antonovna at least knows that she is on
the devil's side when autocracy dictates orthodox truth.

That the religious imagery takes the form it does—that of Christianity—simply reveals an environmental bias imposed upon basic
human patterns, a cultural emphasis that is Western in the largest
sense. Conrad may, of course, appeal to images suggesting folk tradition; but these function like the Christian figures of speech to
manipulate our response to a particular person or situation. So often
described as innocent or childish or simple, the Russian soul is subject to fairy-like enchantment. Sophia Antonovna sees the infant of
Mother Russia " 'lapped up in evils, watched over by beings that are
worse than ogres, ghouls, and vampires.' "[23] Revolution is calculated
to free that Russian soul from pagan superstition. Madame de S——,
"a lady of advanced views, no longer very young, once upon a time
the intriguing wife of a now dead and forgotten diplomat,"[24] wishes
to give her pretenses the dignity of history; she imagines herself a
Mme. de Stael ministering to the needs of a Voltaire. Peter Ivanovitch believes that "everyone who approaches her falls under the
spell" of her spirit and charm. But for the narrator and Razumov
who see beyond her "mystic significance," she is a witch. Her relationship to Peter Ivanovitch strikes Razumov as a nauseating per-

---

[22] *Ibid.*, pp. 304–5.

[23] *Ibid.*, p. 254.   [24] *Ibid.*, p. 125.

formance, making a mockery of the supposed audacity of his mission to Geneva.

> What could be the relations of these two people to each other? She like a galvanized corpse out of some Hoffman's Tale—he the preacher of feminist gospel for all the world, and a super-revolutionist besides! This ancient, painted mummy with unfathomable eyes, and this burly, bull-necked, deferential . . . what was it? Witchcraft, fascination. . . . "It's for her money," he thought. "She has millions!"[25]

But if her ineffectuality—and that of the utopians in general—is Conrad's negative comment upon the role of the revolutionaries, the mere fictional existence of the woman increases Razumov's self-flagellation. His practiced deceptions and guilt feelings cannot withstand the suggestions of her physical presence. Her "death-like immobility," the "grinning skull effect" of her painted face, her "death's head smile," remind him again and again of a corpse. And this man, for whom the simple mention of Haldin's name is enough to conjure up a shadow of the haunting presence, is deceived into believing that she, ghoulishly among the living, has some vital connection with the dead. She inadvertently plays upon his anxieties by claiming to "see your very soul." Later he deliberately tortures himself in taunting Sophia Antonovna to have Madame de S—— "conjure" Haldin up for her.

In *Under Western Eyes*, the hero of myth who is the actor and savior in the social sphere finds his romantic parody in the person of Victor Haldin. The application of Christian myth to social revolution does reflect Conrad's ironic comment upon the creatures of his making, who nonetheless live a plausible nightmare in an equally plausible world of misery and alienation, in a world nearer hell than heaven. But Victor Haldin is betrayed very early in the novel, thus transforming both the burden of meaning and the burden of despair to Razumov and thus avoiding the technical problems presented by the composite hero of *Nostromo*, the Nostromo-Decoud of "familiar memory." Razumov at the beginning of the novel belongs neither to the world of the autocrat nor to that of the revolutionary.

---

[25] *Ibid.*, pp. 215–16.

Though the narrator uses Razumov's diary as the "documentary evidence," as the written source for the facts of his narrative, though the presence of this source indicates that the events of the novel are already a part of fictional history, Razumov lives in what might be considered on the subjective level as an eternal present. He possesses no personal past. Indeed, the unknown parentage of Razumov enhances the mythic ironies of his existence. The two sets of parents of the traditional hero both exist in this novel in the rumors that circulate about the student, rather than in fact.

> Mr. Razumov was supposed to be the son of an Archpriest and to be protected by a distinguished nobleman—perhaps of his own distant province. But his outward appearance accorded badly with such humble origin. Such a descent was not credible. It was, indeed, suggested that Mr. Razumov was the son of an Archpriest's pretty daughter—which, of course, would put a different complexion on the matter. This theory also rendered intelligible the protection of the distinguished nobleman.[26]

But if Prince K—— (who, as the events of the novel bear out, is Razumov's bodily father) does not enact the usual hostile parent's role here, it is because he refuses to admit his paternity explicitly. He does not abandon his son to the wilds of the forest or to the deep sea; rather, he simply dismisses him to all of Russia. Certainly Razumov's initial and instinctual appeal to Prince K—— in the former's oppressive desire "to be understood" is sufficient reason to assume that Prince K—— fulfills the role of the only mortal authority figure that Razumov is allowed to recognize.

When Razumov tells Victor Haldin that all his "ties are social," he appeals to the image of his second mother, a symbolic rather than a personal one. "His closest parentage was defined in the statement that he was a Russian."[27] ". . . The hard ground of Russia, inanimate, cold, inert, like a sullen and tragic mother hiding her face under a winding-sheet—his native soil!—his very own—without a fireside, without a heart!"[28] This emotionless entity is the equivalent of the step-mother of the exposure myth of the abandoned hero. In trying to rationalize to Victor Haldin why he is not among the

---

[26] *Ibid.*, p. 6.   [27] *Ibid.*, pp. 10–11.   [28] *Ibid.*, pp. 32–33.

vanguard for revolutionary progress, Razumov speaks of his tradition which is "historical." " 'What have I to look back to but that national past from which you gentlemen want to wrench away your future?' "[29] To a man confronting his own utter loneliness for the first time, the endless space associated with the "historical fact" of the land only enhances moral isolation.

But if Razumov has no unique past, his future is equally barren. With a pitiless logic he wishes simply for "personal prestige," academic distinction that will convert the "label Razumov into an honored name." The symbol of that prestige is the "silver medal" offered as a prize by the Ministry of Education. For such an existence in the future requires no heroic action, no exceptional disruption, only the continuity of a daily regimen, a willed immersion in the "trivialities of daily existence." "The exceptional could not prevail against the material contacts which made one day resemble another. Tomorrow would be like yesterday."[30] His main preoccupation, then, is the present of his academic life.

The man who has no personal past, the man to whom Victor Haldin mistakenly shares the knowledge of his deed is a partial being. The reserve on his face, which Victor reads in his own terms as "strength of character," is merely indifference or lack of commitment. To the Razumov who feels "no bitterness against the nobleman his protector" and who can yet watch the daughters of that nobleman Prince K—— in the fashionable streets without apparently recognizing his repressed emotions, everything can be achieved by the deliberate exercise of one's reason. For him, "Life is a public thing"; there are no secrets (though the circumstances of his own birth are secret) nor hidden corruptions. The advent of Haldin, the presence of that spirit of "unrest" in his dark room, causes him to encounter for the first time the possibility of the irrational, the necessity of absorbing the destructive and unseen within the structure of the every day. Confronted with "an existence which seemed no longer his own," he must ask,

"What is the good of exerting my intelligence, of pursuing the systematic development of my faculties and all my plans of work?"

---

[29] *Ibid.*, p. 61.　　　　　[30] *Ibid.*, p. 54.

. . . "I want to guide my conduct by reasonable convictions, but what security have I against something—some destructive horror—walking in upon me as I sit here? . . ."[31]

His journey within must now be endured with all its consequences.

If the necessity of the novel is to adapt the forms of true myth, the experience of pure revelation, to the demands of the plausible, then Razumov, as hero, might be said to undertake initially two actual quests which eventually metastasize into many others: the first, the minor journey to get Ziemianitch to drive Haldin to safety, an act which prefigures the betrayal; the second, the longer journey to Geneva, which culminates in the mutilation of Razumov by Necator and the consequent accident in the street. But each quest exploits motifs that appear in the larger quest toward self-knowledge. Though formally the trials may seem to belong to separate narrative sequences in each of which Razumov has a different role, symbolically and psychologically each marks a phase of the journey into the unconscious. Here, as in the classic form of the hero myth, "a blunder—apparently the merest chance—reveals an unsuspected world, and the individual is drawn into a relationship with forces that are not rightly understood."[32] Razumov goes for Ziemianitch, at all times inwardly refusing the call to adventure, the potentiality for significant action that Haldin offers. The entire affair is projected against a landscape which, as in a mythopeic society, is "made alive with symbolical suggestion";[33] yet "symbolical suggestion" can only function ironically in a modernity in which the cultural emphasis has shifted from content to structure.

Razumov moves from the darkness of his room into the darkness of night, and everything takes on the distortions of the dream. He is aware that "no rational determinations had any part in his exertions." The "sledges glided phantom-like and jingling through a fluttering whiteness on the black face of night."[34] Even other passers-by seem unreal. "They came upon him suddenly, looming up black in the snow flakes close by, then vanishing all at once—

---

[31] *Ibid.*, p. 78.

[32] Campbell, *The Hero with a Thousand Faces*, p. 51.

[33] *Ibid.*, p. 43.   [34] Conrad, *Under Western Eyes*, p. 26.

without footfalls."[35] Or else human figures assume a sub-human appearance in this world of the lowest dregs, the "night birds of the city." The owner of the den that Ziemianitch frequents is a "horrible, nondescript, shaggy being with a black face like the muzzle of a bear."[36] His descent into Ziemianitch's own "abode"—a "long cavernous place like a neglected subterranean byre"—parodies the night-sea journey into the caverns of the earth. Ziemianitch, the "bright soul" of revolutionary ideology, at once a "purveyor of souls" and a "driver of the devil," partakes of the qualities of the classical Hermes. Like the latter, he is also a "driver of thieves." And the joke that Ziemianitch unwittingly plays upon Razumov is worthy of that trickster god of Greece: he is dead-drunk, a "vile beast," so devoid of reason by virtue of his indulgence that he does not respond to Razumov's beating. In this "cellar-like stable," the abode of shadows, the only knowledge that Razumov achieves is the knowledge that does, perversely, help him preserve his society. He decides to betray Haldin to the police, thus helping to maintain the status quo, thus denying the utopian visions of the revolutionaries, thus refusing to admit that night and the unseen are as much a part of his universe as the rational day-world of his studies. Haldin and his ideas become associated in the image-patterns with darkness, smoke, and the irrational; Razumov's own powers, with clarity and truth. "What are the luridly smoky lucubrations of that fellow to the clear grasp of my intellect."[37] In order to confirm him in what he considers an "act of conscience," he draws near a frivolous crowd in the street that is "well-lighted." General T——'s home restores his confidence: ". . . all the lights . . . [are] turned on"; he need not fear the hallucinations and visions of the darkness here. Moreover, he is supported in his confession by the man he believes to be his father. The physical light of the room ironically does nothing to dispel the secrets of his birth. The sense of moral loneliness that is dispelled is only momentary, only appearance.

Perhaps it is fitting to note that I have equated the decision to betray Haldin as the inflow of special knowledge that the hero achieves as a result of his first encounter with the timeless world of

---

[35] *Ibid.*, p. 26.   [36] *Ibid.*, p. 28.   [37] *Ibid.*, p. 35.

dream and myth. Conventionally the experience in the underworld enables the hero to save the sick or sterile country he has left. The first irony of Razumov's return from the hell of Ziemianitch's cavern is obvious; he decides that "absolute power should be preserved . . . for the great autocrat of the future";[38] in other words, it is Haldin, the revolutionary, not the present system that is the "contagious pestilence," the "withered member" that must be cut off. In making this decision Razumov has, in fact, acted the social role but has neither understood the depth of vision made open to him, nor significantly admitted its dark and invisible side. Unconsciously, he realizes that something has changed; what he cannot yet do is emotionally cope with the consequences of the change.

> ". . . Can you conceive secret places in Eternity? Impossible. Whereas life is full of them. There are secrets of birth, for instance. One carries them on to the grave. . . . And there are secret motives of conduct. A man's most open actions have a secret side to them. That is interesting and so unfathomable! For instance, a man goes out of a room for a walk. Nothing more trivial in appearance. And yet it may be momentous. He comes back—he has seen perhaps a drunken brute, taken particular notice of the snow on the ground—and behold he is no longer the same man. . . ."[39]

Speculating insecurely upon the possibility of "secret places," he is, however, still able to tell Haldin that his "tradition is historical." Having just experienced Ziemianitch and the irrational world of darkness, he still describes himself as "a man with a mind" which for him means a "cool superior reason," "a flow of masterly argument." Razumov, having just consigned Haldin to death, still cannot admit the simultaneous existence of two selves; the tumult of new impressions is too much for his "cool superior reason" to absorb, so he rejects them.

His second trial, his second experience with the timeless realm of his unconscious, occurs immediately after Haldin rushes off to his determined fate. Conrad has described Haldin again and again to indicate to the reader the extent of Razumov's denial of the assassin's existence. As a hallucination lying in the snow, this man has more substance than he has lying on Razumov's bed. Elsewhere

---

[38] *Ibid.*, p. 35.   [39] *Ibid.*, p. 59.

he is simply a "shadow" and Razumov is a "fellow with a phantom." As Haldin hears the distant clock tolling twelve, he disappears from Razumov's sight and hearing "as noiseless as a vision," "a fleeting shadow." It is no mere chance that the moment he leaves, Conrad chooses to have Razumov drop and break his watch, that symbol of objective time which wrongly records three minutes to twelve. Significantly, Razumov—who has built his existence upon a fidelity to order—cannot now trust the observations of the clock; could, indeed, never trust them. For the next twenty-four hours he is completely cut off from the historical world except for the distant tolling of the clock. So immersed is he in the subjective world of his own creation that he apprehends that clock only vaguely.

> Razumov looked wildly about as if for some means of seizing upon time which seemed to have escaped him altogether. He had never, as far as he could remember, heard the striking of that town clock in his rooms before this night. And he was not even sure now whether he had heard it really on this night.[40]

For the minutes between twelve and one—while he is waiting for Haldin to be arrested—he can neither work nor sleep. The ambiguity of the experience of darkness begins to overwhelm his exalted "cool superior reason." His mind "borders on delirium": he has a vision of General T—— lurking in a dark gateway; he hears himself "saying, 'I confess,' as a person might do on the rack."[41] During the next twenty-three hours he acts like a man in a dream; he mechanically composes his testament of faith; he tries to sleep but wakes several times "from a dream of walking through drifts of snow in a Russia where he was as completely alone as any betrayed autocrat could be; . . . But after each shuddering start his heavy eyelids fell over his glazed eyes and he slept again."[42] Daylight does not relieve his sense of "suspended animation." He hears no sound; all his senses remain completely inert "as though life had withdrawn itself from all things and even from his own thoughts."[43] Again, the diurnal movements of the solar system are his only indication that the timelessness within the room is not external reality. "He was mildly surprised to discover himself being overtaken by night. The

---

40 *Ibid.*, p. 65.   41 *Ibid.*   42 *Ibid.*, p. 66.   43 *Ibid.*, p. 68.

room grew dark swiftly though time had seemed to stand still."[44] Only after midnight, twenty-four hours after Haldin's departure, does he consciously throw off his immersion in the interior landscape. His previous life of surface and order reasserts itself in restoring him to a temporal and spatial existence he can understand. ". . . The habit of reflection and that desire of safety, of an ordered life, which was so strong in him came to his assistance as the night wore on."[45] Now, however, though Haldin has ceased to exist in physical immediacy if not in animate life, Razumov will not be allowed to go on living as if the former had never existed.

Folklore and myth mirror in narrative form the trials of the hero who undertakes the quest into the underworld in order to achieve the elixir of life. More often than not, the adventures and the obstacles overcome reflect upon the dubious morality of the adventurer. Trickery is often used to achieve the desired end. But that morality is only dubious to the culture dominated by a Hebraic-Christian past. The hero's route is ambiguous; his means of attainment, sometimes questionable; but his role is always clearly defined. He is a savior who must accept a symbolic or an actual death in order to revivify his stricken society. But, as I have noted, Razumov inhabits a plausible world where no amount of evidence can support the presence of gods and demons: there are only god-like men or demonic ones who serve willy-nilly the shifting demands of the State. In this world, Razumov is forced to assume a double role. He engages upon two nightmarish quests at the same time, each of which negates the other, each of which will help to maintain a world that promises a timeless apocalyptic future (whether in heaven or on earth), but that can provide only demonic unrest, anarchy, revolt. The first quest is thrust upon him because he is the only man Haldin has ever mentioned in his letters to his mother and sister as one of those " 'unstained, lofty, and solitary existences.' " The deluded revolutionaries believe that as Haldin's accomplice in the murder of de P——, he must be in physical danger. He becomes a symbol to them of the dragon-killer, the man of action, the man who will save Russia for its future role as a paradise

[44] *Ibid.*, p. 69.   [45] *Ibid.*, p. 71.

on earth. His reserve deceives the revolutionaries as it had deceived the assassin. Tekla, whose fidelity to revolutionary principles fulfills a personal need to subjugate herself, echoes his heroic function. " 'You are strong. You kill the monsters.' " The obtuse narrator speaks of Natalia's failure to understand her brother's reputed friends: "He had fascinated her by an assumption of mysterious reserve."[46] She herself tells him that " 'It is in you that we can find all that is left of his generous soul.' "[47] Simultaneously, Razumov is the secret agent for the autocrats, having inspired Councillor of State Mikulin with the advantages that can be subtly tapped from the superb loneliness of his position. To save the lawlessness of arbitrary power, the student must gain information concerning the cabals of revolutionaries in the West. He moves to "save" two worlds, neither one of which can provide his solitary existence with the recognition his orderly life requires and both of which destroy his rationalization that "life is a public thing."

Primitive myths and those of civilization abound in figures of more than human prowess whose purpose is to aid the hero on his journey, to provide him with the tools of his successful confrontation with the dragon that is Death. Whether talking animals, winged steeds, hermits, ladies of the lake, or aged crones—all assure the hero that beyond the dangers of the unseen there is a return for the successful man to the secure, ordered, comprehensible world. They represent

> . . . the benign, protecting power of destiny. The fantasy is a reassurance—a promise that the peace of Paradise, which was known first within the mother womb, is not to be lost; that it supports the present and stands in the future as well as the past . . . that though omnipotence may seem endangered by the threshold passages and life awakenings, protective power is always and ever present within the sanctuary of the heart and even imminent within, or just behind, the unfamiliar features of the world.[48]

That the man whom Razumov has betrayed is the figure whom the student's guilt-ridden imagination summons as an eternal comrade,

---

[46] *Ibid.*, p. 202.   [47] *Ibid.*, p. 346.

[48] Campbell, *The Hero with a Thousand Faces*, pp. 71–72.

a constant presence, is obvious. Not reassurance but self-torture is, however, the psychic validity for the dream figure who constantly accompanies him. Razumov's first hallucination of Haldin, "solid, distinct, real," appears immediately before Razumov goes to Prince K——. So struck is the student by the vision of the irrational that he immediately seeks a "well-lighted street." Later he cannot escape the presence: ". . . always Haldin—nothing but Haldin—everywhere Haldin: a moral spectre infinitely more effective than any visible apparition of the dead."[49] But even his delusion that his bedroom is the only area free of the phantom-presence of his victim vanishes when Mikulin enlists his aid. He begins to think of the fact that he "no longer belonged to himself." Then his mind leaps to the possibility of acquiring distinction as a "reforming servant of the greatest of states." But his optimism is short-lived.

> Calm, resolved, steady in his great purpose, he was stretching his hands towards the pen when he happened to glance towards the bed. He rushed at it, enraged, with a mental scream: "It's you, crazy fanatic, who stand in the way!"[50]

The mere mention of Haldin's name disconcerts him. When Madame de S—— claims that she " 'can see your very soul,' " Razumov assumes that she sees the constant specter of Haldin by his side. "Her shiny eyes had a dry, intense stare, which, missing Razumov, gave him an absurd notion that she was looking at something which was visible to her behind him."[51] Without understanding the extent of Razumov's identification with his victim, the narrator, as he sees the student walking, describes his appearance as "extraordinary hallucined, anguished, and absent"; he has the "expression of a somnambulist struggling with the very dream which drives him forth to wander in dangerous places."[52] The narrator does not know that, in truth, Razumov is driven; that his wandering in the dangerous circles of exiles does not stem from a conscious or a waking choice; that his actions have none of the deliberate acceptance of the hero rising generously to meet the challenge.

---

[49] Conrad, *Under Western Eyes*, pp. 299–300.

[50] *Ibid.*, p. 302.   [51] *Ibid.*, p. 224.   [52] *Ibid.*, p. 317.

The incorporeal Haldin who accompanies Razumov is an ironic inversion of the supernatural guide of myth functioning here, of course, on a perverse quest. Where revolutionary politics provides the absolutes once sanctified by a metaphysical system of values, the anarchist becomes the martyred redeemer and may inspire his followers with the divine touch of a prophet. So against his will and reason, the betrayer deserves his ultimate effect upon the utopians because of the latters' mistaken and deluded assumptions. So Haldin has, in fact, bequeathed his soul to Razumov. When, however, Haldin speaks of his soul, he disclaims the non-material and immortal essence having an existence separate from the body that it survives. Consonant with his distortion of Christian theology, his soul is that part of the living man " 'which aspire[s] to perfection of human dignity' " and which seeks its immortality on this earth within the bodies of other men who themselves aspire to a terrestrial Eden. Nor can the death of the individual man destroy it or cause it to endure independently. According to Haldin,

> "Men like me leave no posterity, but their souls are not lost. No man's soul is ever lost. . . . What will become of my soul when I die in the way I must die—soon—very soon perhaps? It shall not perish. . . . My spirit shall go on warring in some Russian body till all falsehood is swept out of the world. The modern civilization is false, but a new revelation shall come out of Russia. . . . The Russian soul that lives in all of us. It has a future. It has a mission. . . ."[53]

Later, when he is nearer to death than he anticipates, he claims that " 'They can kill my body, but they cannot exile my soul from this world.' "[54] Thinking of the popular superstitions connected with the souls of murdered men, Razumov misinterprets his victim's promise to "haunt" the sensible world. But Haldin scornfully turns this aside.

> "Haunt it! Truly, the oppressors of thought which quickens the world, the destroyers of souls which aspire to perfection of human dignity, they shall be haunted. As to the destroyers of my mere body, I have forgiven them beforehand."[55]

---

[53] *Ibid.*, p. 22. [54] *Ibid.*, p. 58. [55] *Ibid.*

Unfortunately, Razumov is both, and, paradoxically, it is this man upon whom Haldin has thrust his mission. Haldin has made Razumov his second self, his promise of immortality.

But if Haldin has externalized his immortal being in Razumov, Razumov has been possessed by his own second self, the phantom of Haldin. It is the tenacity of this possession and Razumov's consequent anxiety that cause the reader to sympathize not with the victim but with the Judas-like betrayer. The latter's first hallucination —during his mission to get Ziemianitch—has been mentioned. When Haldin leaves to keep his unknown assignation with the agents of General T——, Razumov cannot lie upon the vacated bed for almost twenty-four hours. When he finally does, he thinks only, " 'I am lying here like that man.' " After he goes to Geneva, many of his responses to the false assumptions of the others involve his recollections of Haldin's earlier responses. Immediately before Haldin assassinates de P——, he recalls "an almost irresistible longing to lie down on the pavement and sleep."[56] When Razumov later tells Sophia Antonovna of "his" deed, he repeats this same desire. Indeed, his whole narrative is peppered with the tag phrases derived from his initial experience, phrases reiterated "like a man who has been dreaming aloud." Finally, after Razumov composes his long letter to Natalia and before he goes to confess to the gathering of revolutionaries at Laspara's house—his symbolic death—Conrad intentionally has his character behave exactly like Haldin. In the student's re-enactment of the previous episode, he is "the puppet of his past, because at the very stroke of midnight he jumped up and ran swiftly downstairs as if confident that, by the power of destiny, the house door would fly open before the absolute necessity of his errand."[57] He is "saved" by the "betrayed man," redeemed by the victim who had first given him his dangerous mission within this "prison of lies" and, hence, his ironic journey to self-awareness.

If Conrad meant to show by Razumov's almost cyclical assumption of Haldin's responses that Haldin is, in fact, a second self, he also wished to make some dramatic statement concerning the nature of the second self. As I have already mentioned, the appearance of

56 *Ibid.*, p. 17.   57 *Ibid.*, p. 362.

the utopian revolutionary in Razumov's room, "all black against the usual tall stove of white tiles gleaming in the dusk,"[58] inspires for the first time the suggestion that unseen powers pervade the universe, that life cannot be a "public thing." He for whom "present institutions" appear "rational and indestructible" acknowledges the "horrible discord of this man's presence." The assassin's life means "disruption"—not alone in the social sphere but in the personal sphere as well. Razumov's mission to Ziemianitch is undertaken at night. Both the cavernous haunts of the latter's drunkenness and the room in which Haldin confesses to Razumov are described as worlds of shadow. Too often now he feels "a suspicious uneasiness such as we experience when we enter an unlighted strange place— the irrational feeling that something may jump upon us in the dark —the absurd dread of the unseen."[59] Compared with this confusion, the world of Razumov's student labors is one of light but, because of Haldin, of light now "extinguished."

Like the removal of the silver on the dark gulf in *Nostromo*, Haldin's advent starts a sequence of events "which no sagacity can foresee and no courage can break through."[60] The man who has killed for his belief and scattered death "like a butcher" has intruded himself upon Razumov's single, solitary existence, and the interior world can no longer be denied. First comes an unprecedented realization of loneliness. In an uncharacteristic intrusion of his personal voice, Conrad permits himself a comment in the narrator's objective document; it is a statement very like that which oppressed Decoud's last days of awareness.

> Who knows what true loneliness is—not the conventional word, but the naked terror? To the lonely themselves it wears a mask. The most miserable outcast hugs some memory or some illusion. Now and then a fatal conjunction of events may lift the veil for an instant. For an instant only. No human being could bear a steady view of moral solitude without going mad.[61]

But Razumov is not struck like Decoud and Kurtz with the secret horror of new knowledge; rather, he simply cannot as yet absorb the real nature of his internal journey and his search for personal com-

---

58 *Ibid.*, p. 14.   59 *Ibid.*, p. 35.   60 *Ibid.*, p. 83.   61 *Ibid.*, p. 39.

mitment. His long-repressed emotional life has not yet begun to take its vengeance upon him. If at this point he chooses the personal father who must deny him, rather than the social "brother" he shares with all of revolutionary Russia, he does so without speculating upon it, without making deliberate choices, instinctively. Moreover, once the deed of betrayal is past, he deceives himself momentarily into believing that nothing was changed. "After he had gone a little way the familiarity of things got hold of him. Nothing was changed."[62] But Haldin's continued presence in the dark room quickly disabuses Razumov of this belief. For the room itself has taken on the characteristics of the realm of the unconscious: it is without "sound," possesses a "dead stillness." Later, it will distort Razumov's apprehension of objective time. In this room Haldin appears "like a dark and elongated shape—rigid with the immobility of death."[63] From now on, each new day brings Razumov a "strange dread of the unexpected."

Otto Rank, in his writings on the Double,[64] distinguishes between the second self, or Double, that primitive man saw in his reflection or shadow and the Double that appears in the literary externalization of an opposing self. Primitive man saw this self positively as a spiritual being, "an assurance of eternal survival for his self, a promise of immortality."[65] Modern man, who has overdeveloped his rational faculties at the expense of his emotional being, whose conflicts appear in his failure to reconcile thoughts and action, places a negative value upon the opposing self. Too often it reveals the contemporary split personality. Instead of seeing the second self as the immortal survival of the living man, threatened modern man tends to see it as a prediction of mortality. In Haldin's pronouncements we can see a political corruption of the primitive's emphasis upon future personal survival; Haldin's immortality depends upon his "spirit warring in some Russian body" and upon his sister's re-

---

[62] *Ibid.*, p. 53.   [63] *Ibid.*, p. 55.

[64] Otto Rank, *Beyond Psychology* (New York, 1958) and *Psychology and the Soul*, trans. William D. Turner (New York, 1961). See also "Der Doppelganger," *Imago*, III (1914). For another discussion of the relationship of the shadow to the "idea of the soul" see Lucien Lévy-Bruhl, *L'Ame primitive* (Paris, 1927).

[65] Rank, "The Double as Immortal Self," *Beyond Psychology*, p. 64.

maining "faithful to his departed spirit," not upon the continuation of an individual spiritual self.

In Razumov, however, the modern separation of the self, the divided personality, is obvious. The thinker,[66] the reasonable man, does not accept his own emotional being until his intense repression of that life asserts itself in a chain of unexpected events. There are various moments when Razumov's response to what he regards as preposterous circumstances reflects itself in a sense of personal division. The strange drawing room of Madame de S—— inspires such uneasiness. "He felt, bizarre as it may seem, as though another self, an independent sharer of his mind, had been able to view his whole person very distinctly indeed."[67] Self-torment causes him to reveal his guilt to Natalia Haldin at the precise moment that he is safest, but the struggling emotions that nourish his temporary madness are obvious even to the English narrator: "He seemed to me to be watching himself inwardly, as though he were trying to count his own heartbeats, while his eyes never for a moment left the face of the girl."[68]

On the literal or narrative level, the second or opposing self is Haldin, the actor, the revolutionary; on the mythical level, Haldin's shadow seems an ironic inversion of the hero's supernatural helper. But psychologically Haldin, both man and hallucination, is the representative of the man of feeling who is able to weep, unlike his betrayer; he is the repressed part of Razumov's divided personality. It is too easy to assign Razumov's visions to his guilt feelings (although I have and although, of course, they are); they are also the emanations of the buried emotional life.

But when the Christian belief in immortality begins to be juxtaposed to the possibility of natural and supernatural evil, the anarchic self, the spirit of "unrest," is externalized in the form of a Devil in pure myth or of a demonic human being in the forms of literature in which myth must be made to suit the demands of nature.[69] Only

---

[66] Haldin himself notes the division between actor and thinker, but this division obviously does not appear in a single person and does not inspire any dynamic sufferings. We see Haldin too rarely as a fully realized character to detect any split within the self, any tortured self-analysis causing anxiety or concern.

[67] Conrad, *Under Western Eyes*, p. 230.   [68] *Ibid.*, p. 349.

[69] Frye, "Archetypal Criticism: Theory of Myths," *Anatomy of Criticism*, p. 158.

implicitly does Haldin give body to the images of an allegorized morality. When Razumov is confessing to Natalia Haldin, he almost incoherently alludes to the alternative to an active Providence —the "personal Devil of our simple ancestors. But, if so, he has overdone it altogether—the old Father of Lies—our national patron—our domestic god, whom we take with us when we go abroad."[70] Neither Natalia nor the narrator (who thinks him deranged) know that he refers to the bodiless Haldin whom he carries eternally with him. Haldin is, again, a "haunting, falsehood-breeding spectre" because it is the dead man's description of Razumov in a letter to his sister that has completely deluded the other utopians into perpetuating a lie.

It is Razumov, not Haldin, whose person the author has burdened with the largest share of demonic images and motifs. As early in narrative time as his return to his room from General T——'s house, he has a "diabolical impulse to say [to Haldin], 'I have given you up to the police.' "[71] He avoided with difficulty "a burst of Mephistophelian laughter" at the point of hysterically reminding Haldin of life's "secrets and surprises." He teases Peter Ivanovitch "with a satanic enjoyment of the scorn prompting him to play with the greatness of the great man—."[72] He hears from Sophia Antonovna how Ziemianitch, "the driver of thieves and devils" who finally kills himself, has brooded over the beating he has received from Razumov, ultimately believing that it was given by the devil "in person," "a dark young man." (For Sophia Antonovna, herself a restless wanderer from Eden, devils exist on earth to make a hell of it. Indeed, she has a diabolic propensity for guessing the truth without realizing it—that "the devil" is "some police-hound.") In writing that extraordinary letter to the sister of his victim, Razumov speaks both of Victor Haldin's belief in living through his sister, who will someday marry, and of his own irrational desire to steal that sister's soul.

"Victor Haldin had stolen the truth of my life from me, who had nothing else in the world, and he boasted of living on through you

---

[70] Conrad, *Under Western Eyes*, p. 350.

[71] *Ibid.*, p. 55.   [72] *Ibid.*, p. 228.

on this earth where I had no place to lay my head. She will marry some day, he had said—and your eyes were trustful. And do you know what I said to myself? I shall steal his sister's soul from her."[73]

But he discovers that he has ended by loving her; in " 'giving Victor Haldin up, it was myself, after all, whom I have betrayed most basely.' "[74] But " 'he saves me,' he thought suddenly. 'He himself, the betrayed man.' "[75] Victor Haldin is, then, not merely the spirit of "unrest," but the redeemer to the man who has betrayed him; like Razumov himself he is both "a scoundrel and an exceptionally able man."

According to Guerard, Razumov's written confession violates the authenticity of the author's characterization. Here the student "claims to have been a much more cynical person in his relationship with Natalia Haldin, then we have had any reason to suspect!"[76] In the brief meetings with Natalia Haldin, most of them related by the English narrator in whose presence they occur, we do not detect evidence of this diabolism. Moreover, when Tekla warns him against subjecting Natalia to Peter Ivanovitch's influence, Razumov's response is "chill and gloom." Guerard assumes that Razumov's final confession may be a vestigial remain of an earlier plan that Conrad devised and later abandoned: "The temptation to steal the soul may be described as another 'lost subject.' "[77]

An important point in Razumov's statement of demonic intent is that it reflects a continual disparity between the totally rational role that Razumov dramatizes for the world and what in fact he does do or feel. We have seen that Razumov's moments of tensest emotion and greatest suffering are perceived by others as moments of complete equanimity and self-possession. When Haldin foists his crime upon Razumov's isolation, the former detects only " 'frigid English manners,' " but Razumov's journal indicates that he "kept down a cry of dismay." After Razumov's agonized personal confession, the narrator wonders at his "appalling expressionless tranquillity." But the difference between tranquillity and excessive control depends

---

[73] *Ibid.*, p. 359.   [74] *Ibid.*, p. 361.   [75] *Ibid.*, p. 362.
[76] Guerard, "Two Versions of Anarchy," *Conrad the Novelist*, p. 240.
[77] *Ibid.*, p. 242.

very much upon through whose perception the events of the narrative are reported. That he is not tranquil subsequent events and actions prove. Razumov is a man who has practiced repression for so long a time that when feelings do push to the surface, they are expressed in language perhaps hyperbolic. Even the restraint of the epistolary form cannot hide the incoherence of the syntax of the letter. He does not speak of stealing Natalia's soul while in her presence. He cannot face the burden—or the unburden—of complete communication now, any more than he could throw himself before an outstretched Haldin "to pour out a full confession in passionate words that would stir the whole being of that man to its innermost depths; that would end in embraces and tears; in an incredible fellowship of souls—such as the world had never seen."[78] He cannot embrace Natalia and weep with her any more than he could earlier respond to Victor or call him "brother." He can, however, realize the nature of the hidden world and its irrationality as he could not in the past. That he places a negative value upon that irrational—that he, in other words, demonizes it—simply reveals how much he is a recipient of Western culture.

Moreover, as I have suggested, Conrad's metaphorical equation of Razumov's desires to corrupt Natalia with the Devil reflects the influence of Haldin's anarchic presence upon Razumov's too-controlled, too-civilized personality. Each time a demonic image occurs to clarify Razumov's situation, it involves some human response below the level of rationality: Razumov has a "diabolical impulse" that "frightens him"; he avoids "with difficulty a burst of Mephistophelian laughter!" Finally, possessed by Haldin's spirit sufficiently to re-enact the latter's experiences, divided between the orderly and the anarchic, assigned Haldin's "dragon-killing" role by the false assumptions of others, obsessed with his own sense of guilt, his personal "evil"—in a phrase, "stretched on the rack"—it is no wonder that he instinctually assigns to himself a more horrendous intention than he could consciously devise.

Razumov alone asserts his demonism; but at the same time an appropriate image attributes to every character in the text a similar

---

[78] Conrad, *Under Western Eyes*, p. 40.

diabolism. I have already discussed the restlessness and spirit of revolt dominating the presentation of Sophia Antonovna. What would seem contradictory is the application of demonic motifs to the autocratic government against which the revolutionaries strive. The old English teacher of languages, conventionally concerned with the proper complexion of events, insists upon intruding his learned voice into Mikulin's plans for putting Razumov into his service. It is he who alone suggests that the aristocracy is demonic.

> To the morality of a Western reader an account of these meetings would wear perhaps the sinister character of old legendary tales where the Enemy of Mankind is represented holding subtly mendacious dialogues with some tempted soul. It is not my part to protest. Let me but remark that the Evil One, with his single passion of satanic pride for the only motive, is yet, on a larger, modern view, allowed to be not quite so black as he used to be painted. With what greater latitude, then, should we appraise the exact shade of mere mortal man, with his many passions and his miserable ingenuity in error, always dazzled by the base glitter of mixed motives, everlastingly betrayed by short-sighted wisdom.[79]

While the narrator really wishes to excuse Mikulin's actions by this rampant didacticism, he is, in fact, drawing our sympathy to Razumov, who at this point has reached the nadir of his experience by compounding betrayal with counter-betrayal, by becoming a police agent.

Finally, what is important is not that Razumov's behavior is diabolic, or that Sophia Antonovna is Mephistophelian, or even that the autocrats practice a game as evil as the revolutionaries; what is important is that in its spaceless immensity, in its search for some valid timelessness whether within the mind, within history, or within eternity, in its constant "burning," Russia and all Russians reveal characteristics that our Hebraic-Christian heritage assigns to the Devil. In his satanic allusions, Conrad is moralizing anarchy, rebellion, lawlessness, "unthinking forces"—indeed, all that we include in the word "irrational." It is the recognition of the irrational that changes Razumov from an apparently satisfied but obviously partial human being who accepts his "thinking nature" unthinkingly, into

---

[79] *Ibid.*, pp. 304–5.

a divided man seeking unity. Earlier, he proclaims his "superiority" as a "thinking reed":

> "I am reasonable. I am even—permit me to say—a thinker, though to be sure, the name nowadays seems to be the monopoly of hawkers of revolutionary wares, the slaves of some French or German thought—devil knows what foreign notions. But I am not an intellectual mongrel. I think like a Russian. I think faithfully—and I take the liberty to call myself a thinker. It is not a forbidden word, as far as I know."[80]

Ultimately he discovers that "to think like a Russian" is to admit Haldin, Ziemianitch, the drunken driver, Councillor Mikulin and "the lawlessness of autocracy," and the pretty woman in the streets whose nationality and nature is symbolically summed up by her dress; she is "covered in the hairy skins of wild beasts down to her feet, like a frail and beautiful savage. . . ."[81] The irony of his situation is that, externally in the intellectual context of a Christian society but in a world abandoned by God, his suffering takes its meaning from God's Adversary rather than God's Son. Where revolution becomes religion and where man may serve two gods or two devils or a god and a devil whose traditional attributes are reversed, personal suffering becomes socially meaningless.

Apart from any particular function that the demonic imagery sustains for the meaning within the text, it does tell us something about Conrad's creative impulse. Guerard, as I have noted, regards Razumov's stated intention to possess Natalia Haldin's soul as a possible "lost subject" of the novel. The other "lost subject" is revealed in an oft-quoted letter to Galsworthy written during Conrad's initial immersion in that novel in which he was "trying to capture the very soul of things Russian,—*Cosas de Russia*":

> Listen to the theme. The Student Razumov (a natural son of Prince K.) gives up secretly to the police his fellow student, Haldin, who seeks refuge in his rooms after committing a political crime (supposed to be the murder of de Phehve). First movement in St. Petersburg. (Haldin is hanged, of course.)
> 2d in Geneve. The Student Razumov meeting abroad the mother and sister of Haldin falls in love with that last, marries her,

---

[80] *Ibid.*, p. 90.   [81] *Ibid.*, p. 40.

and, after a time, confesses to her the part he played in the arrest of her brother.

The *psychological developments* leading to Razumov's betrayal of Haldin, to the confession of the fact to his wife and to the death of these people (brought about mainly by the resemblance of their child to the late Haldin), form the real subject of the story.[82]

Haldin's narrative vengeance was to have been effected by the "resemblance of Razumov's and Natalia's child to the betrayed man."

As the novel exists, Haldin's vengeance takes the form of his haunting shadow, or phantom, his soul. Razumov's hallucinations result at once from his guilt feelings and from the externalization of the irrational life he has always suppressed; they are his own second self. This opposing self is what modern over-rational man has substituted for the bodily spiritual self that originally was a guarantee of his personal immortality. The new impulses that Haldin's presence inspires within Razumov become demonic in Conrad's abortive attempts to moralize this second self. But, according to Rank, another form of the Double is the child, a promise of survival consequent upon man's substitution of a procreative for a bodily immortality. Just as the Devil infused the primitive idea of immortality with the suggestion of evil and death, so the child became both a promise of some future life and also a recognition that that future life is not to be the survival of a bodily self.[83] So we see that the initial intention that Conrad abandoned, his later emphasis upon Razumov's desire for demonic power over Natalia Haldin, and the continual presentation of Haldin's presence as a "phantom," a "spirit of rebellion," and a "soul" are variations upon the same human situation[84] and the same creative impulse. In effect, not the intention but the content of the intention has changed. Both the earlier intention and the final result are ironic comments upon the possibility of immortality in the modern world. In a parody of the

---

[82] Joseph Conrad to John Galsworthy, January 6, 1908, *Joseph Conrad: Life and Letters*, II, 64–65. Emphasis added.

[83] Rank, *Psychology and the Soul*, pp. 33–69.

[84] One does not have to go very far to discover examples in which novels using the idea of the second self either structurally or thematically employ all these patterns of imagery and contain within the narrative the presence of a child as a manifestation of procreative immortality. Emily Brontë's *Wuthering Heights* and William Faulkner's *Absalom, Absalom!* are two very obvious examples.

metaphysical quest for bodily immortality, Haldin's "soul" achieves an ironic rebirth in Razumov's reluctant presence, makes Razumov an actor in a world in which he has never acted and which he does not yet understand. But psychologically the revenge wreaked by the second self, the repressed within, appears in hallucinations and visions rather than in the bodily presence of an actual fictional child. Since Conrad's letter to Galsworthy indicates that he is concerned with "psychological effects," surely the final form offers every advantage in its dramatization of Razumov's anxiety-ridden, suffering responses—suffering that is not only thematically but artistically necessary as well in order to engage our sympathy for a betrayer and a "double agent."

After Part I, which ends on Councillor Mikulin's question to Razumov, " 'Where to?' " there is a spatial leap from Russia to Geneva, a chronological jump into the historical past of the narrator's meeting with Natalia Haldin (which antedates the narrative past of Razumov's betrayal), and a dramatic change from the Englishman's reliance upon events he has read about in the diary of Razumov to his own vague participation in affairs. When the reader returns directly to Razumov's acceptance of his counter-quest in Part IV and his answer to Mikulin's question, Razumov's meetings with the gamut of "revolutionary tyranny" have already become, for the reader, part of the fictional past. That there is no lessening in the ambiguity that Razumov feels during the long period of trial from Haldin's intrusion to his own "escape" from Russia is apparent from the abundant vocabulary implying unreality. The assumption of another role—that of counter-revolutionary—is no more conducive to a sense of security than that of revolutionary. Razumov's mission to Geneva strikes him as "a game of make-believe." That Kostia believes enough in the make-believe of revolutionary action to steal from an over-indulgent father strikes the compromised student as preposterous. " 'It's a dream,' " he thinks. As if he were completely detached, as if he were, in fact, two Razumovs, he gives

> himself up to watching the development of the dream with extreme attention. It continued on foreseen lines, inexorably logical—the long drive, the wait at the small station sitting by a stove. They did not exchange half a dozen words altogether. Kostia, gloomy

himself, did not care to break the silence. At parting they embraced twice—it had to be done, and then Kostia vanished out of the dream.[85]

His "last waking act" is throwing the money that he gratuitously inspires Kostia to steal upon a landscape completely devoid of "human habitation," a "great white desert of frozen, hard earth."

> . . . and then the dream had him again: Russia, Saxony, Würtemberg, faces, sights, words—all a dream, observed with an angry, compelled attention. Zurich, Geneva—still a dream, minutely followed, wearing one into harsh laughter, to fury, to death—with the fear of awakening at the end. . . .[86]

Actual space has only a dream reality.

Since the narrative sequence involving Razumov's actions up until his final confession and self-sacrifice has already been related in Parts II and III, Conrad can telescope in a few paragraphs and a handful of images the meaning of these events to Razumov. Chronological dislocation in the artistry of a skilled craftsman has also served to enhance the sense of timelessness that is a dominant quality of the dream or of the unreal world. So we as readers are drawn into the interior world of Razumov's emotions at the same time that the narrator's emphasis upon space reminds us that there is an external reality. But we are never allowed to forget the ironic fact that Razumov's dream-like quest (taken to revive a stricken society) is a double one, that he functions as a hero in two social structures each of which demands the destruction of the other, that his actions parody those of the traditional hero of myth because, in each case, they are forced upon him by the false assumptions of others and because the world in which he functions is nightmarish. All of the images of unreality and timelessness symbolically reveal how prolonged his mental suffering is. And it is the extent of that brooding and torture within objective time and space that increase reader and authorial sympathy for him.

Razumov's sense of an "hallucined existence" is not simply operative in Russia. As we have seen, he carries it with him into the

---

85 Conrad, *Under Western Eyes*, p. 315.
86 *Ibid.*, pp. 315–16.

"heart of democracy" where there are "no thieves"—let alone assassins—where the green is "orderly," where "in its unsuggestive finish" Geneva is "the very perfection of mediocrity attained at last after centuries of toil and culture."[87] On the one hand, he is confronted by the Boulevard des Philosophes, symbolizing a dedication to reason as well as "prosaic virtue." On the other hand, he notes that Geneva's "universal hospitality" invites the presence of a Château Borel, a "house of folly, of blindness, of villainy and crime." Here most of Razumov's temptations come, of course, in that temple-like structure, "embowered in the trees and thickets of its neglected ground,"[88] which the revolutionary passions of Madame de S—— have seized for her bizarre councils. Château Borel is the fitting meeting place of fugitive revolutionaries. Its empty immensity mocks the "inheritance of space" from which the visionaries come; its darkness and dirt and chaos suggest the liberated spirit of criminal anarchy, a static hell which makes a suitable place for devils; its presiding feminine genius parodies the helpful crone or fairy godmother of myth and tale. In addition to her witch-like qualities, Madame de S—— is summed up by a profusion of images connoting death: she is like a "galvanized corpse out of some Hoffman's Tale," "ghoulish" and "ghostly," "a wooden figure" rigid with "the rigour of a corpse," with a "death's head smile." Even her energy is of a stagnant kind. That Peter Ivanovitch speaks of her spiritualizing propensities, of her "true light of femininity," only intensifies the irony of Razumov's experience of her darkness.

Here, too, Razumov, accepted by all as the accomplice of Haldin and, hence, as a heroic actor, first encounters the whole spectrum of secret revolutionaries including Tekla, who ascribes to him the most ancient and honored of heroic tasks—that of "killing monsters"—and Sophia Antonovna, whose Mephistophelian eyebrows define her as Razumov's temptress and "personal adversary" and who has an extraordinary instinct for perpetuating falsehood. Here he meets Natalia Haldin, whose soul he wishes to steal but who in reality possesses his as her brother's agent. Each unconsciously acts as a temptress because she accepts the role that he is playing, the role that the

---

[87] *Ibid.*, p. 203.   [88] *Ibid.*, p. 142.

"falsehood-breeding spectre" Haldin and the "Father of Lies" have forced upon him. Because they accept him so readily, he is able to justify the duplicity of his actions by shifting the responsibility for them to Haldin and, thus, avoid the acceptance of his own guilt. Indeed, in absorbing the identity of his new role, in arguing himself into his new belief, he perseveres in the delusion that he can prepare himself for all eventualities. "As long as he managed to preserve a clear mind and to keep down his irritability there was nothing to fear. The only condition of success and safety was indomitable will-power, he reminded himself."[89] But the quality of Sophia Antonovna's information concerning Ziemianitch's beating, remorse, and suicide, together with the half-truths that are concluded from these facts, make Razumov again conscious of the "invincible nature of human error," "as if the devil himself were playing a game with all of them in turn."[90] Within the "shadow" of the Château, his "personal adversary" forces him to relive the unexpected intrusion of Haldin. She sees into the intensity of his suffering—though he manages with difficulty his usual "sinister immobility of feature." While myth assures us that each adventure that the traditional hero meets within the shifting landscape of trials increases his self-awareness, Razumov's encounters temporarily reinforce the depths of his self-deception. As late as this meeting, Razumov can still rationalize that "In this world of men nothing can be changed. . . ."

Yet that moment when Razumov is completely accepted by the revolutionists, the moment he believes that he is safe, is precisely when he makes his confession. For a man who had believed that "life is a public thing," the loss of "frankness of intercourse with his kind"—that is, all Russians—the adoption of a duplicitous life and the need to lie are oppressive. He wishes to be free of the "fumes of falsehood." But the "tainted air" is intimately connected with the specter of Haldin which his guilt feelings project into the omnipresent "shadow" or the "second self" and which accompanies him on his quest for understanding. No wonder, then, that when Madame de S—— claims " 'I can see your very soul,' " he has "an

---

[89] *Ibid.*, p. 248. [90] *Ibid.*, p. 284.

absurd notion that she was looking at something which was visible to her behind him."[91]

Moreover, the mythic progress of the novel is also a progress from physical solitude to moral loneliness; this loneliness enhanced by the revelation that he has no one to whom he can confess. It is that intense solitude and the desire to communicate with another human being that sends him to Prince K——, the father who has denied him. It is that solitude upon which Councillor Mikulin fastens when he determines to use Razumov as a counter spy. "The obscure unrelated young student Razumov, in a moment of great moral loneliness, was allowed to feel that he was an object of interest to a small group of people of high position."[92] It is that solitude that finally drives him to confess to Natalia Haldin: " 'Do you know why I came to you? It is simply because there is no one anywhere in the whole great world I could go to. Do you understand what I say? No one to go to. Do you conceive the desolation of the thought—no one—to—go—to?' "[93]

Razumov's final sufferings have some of the formal trappings of convention. After his confession to Natalia, and before that at Laspara's house, he is drenched by a torrential rain—"washed clean" enveloped by rain as by a "luminous veil in the play of lightning," as by the veil of Natalia Haldin which he has taken with him from her room, baptized into a new life by self-knowledge and by his recognition of love for Natalia. He goes at midnight—the same hour Haldin left his room to meet destruction—climbs two flights of stairs from the lower darkness into the subdued light of the meeting. There, having voluntarily submitted himself to the judgment of the collected utopians, he undergoes a symbolic *sparagmos*. He "expected to be torn to pieces" like the fertility gods of the mystery rites, but he is only made deaf by Necator, the "slayer of gendarmes," whose participation in the dreams of the future masks his psychotic sadism, his own life as a double agent. Like the crucifixion of Christ, this act is accompanied by thunder and lightning. As a result of his injuries, multiplied by his inability to hear a tramcar that runs over him, he becomes totally dependent upon Tekla who

---

[91] *Ibid.*, p. 224.   [92] *Ibid.*, pp. 307–8.   [93] *Ibid.*, pp. 353–54.

is his first, his new-found, and his only "relation." "She sat down calmly, and took his head on her lap; her scared faded eyes avoided looking at his deathlike face."[94] Her maternal pose recalls that of Mrs. Haldin who "seemed to watch a beloved head lying in her lap."[95] Tekla becomes, in effect, Razumov's final mother. She takes him back to that Russia which his early loneliness had caused him to regard as his only parent; there he lives in retirement "in the south," talking to those revolutionaries who because of "forgiveness or compassion," or simply because of guilt feelings, visit him.

That Razumov achieves the illumination that is the culmination of his internal struggle is apparent. He realizes by his behavior that the life of reason is not enough, that there are irrational forces—among them guilt feelings—that projected into the cosmos appear as supernatural ones. " 'In giving Victor Haldin up, it was myself, after all, whom I have betrayed most basely. . . . It is through you that I came to feel this so deeply. After all, it is they and not I who have right on their side!—theirs is the strength of invisible powers.' "[96] And he undergoes the ego-crushing experience of love for another human being which his perpetual reserve will not allow him to articulate. Only in his journal, however, can he address Natalia who has herself become another part of himself because she has become Victor Haldin's "soul." As the narrator phrases it:

> In this queer pedantism of a man who had read, thought, lived, pen in hand, there is the sincerity of the attempt to grapple by the same means with another profounder knowledge. After some passages which have already made use of in the building up of this narrative, or add nothing new to the psychological side of this disclosure (there is even one more allusion to the silver medal in this last entry), comes a page and a half of incoherent writing where his expression is baffled by novelty and the mysteriousness of that side of our emotional life to which his solitary existence had been a stranger. Then only he begins to address directly the reader he had in his mind, trying to express in broken sentences, full of wonder and awe, the sovereign (he uses that very word) power of her person over his imagination, in which lay the dormant seed of her brother's words.[97]

---

[94] *Ibid.*, p. 371.   [95] *Ibid.*, p. 355.   [96] *Ibid.*, p. 361.   [97] *Ibid.*, pp. 357–58.

Love for her saves him, moreover, because it effects his release from the "blindness of anger and hate."

But in his role as world-redeemer, Razumov functions far less successfully. First, no significant sexual union occurs by which the hero unites himself to the promised bride who is one of the rewards for completed action in the social sphere. Indeed, his achievement is the ultimate rejection of the redeemer role Victor Haldin has thrust upon him, a rejection of the world of lies or illusions by which the others live. Not his union with the conspirators, but his essential independence from them is what Razumov asserts. " 'Only don't be deceived, Natalia Victorovna, I am not converted. Have I then the soul of a slave? No! I am independent—and therefore perdition is my lot.' "[98] He now thinks of himself as a rebel, as "independent," and so as lost. His mutilation is a kind of death, from which he is reborn into a world which seems to accept his ideas only because he is physically helpless. Moreover, these ideas are not defined, but rather take their validity from the guilt feelings of the revolutionaries, who ironically still foist roles upon him. He can never be independent again, but returns to the "cradle of Russia" which is "lapped up in evils, watched over by beings that are worse than ogres, ghouls, and vampires."[99] He becomes, as it were, the little child again in charge of that parody of Mrs. Haldin's maternal solicitude, the *dame de compagnie* of Château Borel, Tekla.

Natalia Haldin's failure to accept the personal implications of her brother's political position and, by extension, her own, is another Conradian denunciation of revolutionary mercy. Immediately preceding Razumov's anguished confession she denies the "duty of revenge."

> "I believe that the future will be merciful to us all. Revolutionist and Reactionary, victim and executioner, betrayer and betrayed, they shall all be pitied together when the light breaks on our black sky at last. Pitied and forgotten; for without that there can be no union and no love."[100]

Looking toward the future, she—no more than her mother—is unable to reconcile the truth of the past and present with the visions

---

[98] *Ibid.*, pp. 361–62.   [99] *Ibid.*, p. 254.   [100] *Ibid.*, p. 353.

of politics. She commits herself to the "community of mankind" by returning to Russia as a dedicated revolutionary, but she has forgotten all concrete manifestations of that humanity. She "loves suffering mankind" but not a suffering man. She takes on the heroic role of the brother without having really fathomed the depths of knowledge, without being able to accept the god and devil within a single man. She seeks to perpetuate Victor Haldin's "visionary soul" but cannot detect the partial nature of that soul which needs Razumov's for completion. Her future becomes "historical."

That the hero's tempters themselves experience adventures which prefigure their assumption of revolutionary roles is one of the ironies of the book's structure. Peter Ivanovitch's captivity and escape present in capsule form the motifs of Razumov's larger night-sea journey. They too appear in written form, but as an obvious exemplum of "mystic treatment" riddled with self-analysis for the communal eyes of a sympathetic public rather than as a journal for the inward eye of its author. His years of dissolute existence are shattered by the death of a society girl whom he intended to marry. But the social tyranny of his society makes his world a nightmarish one. After having been imprisoned for his conspiratorial activities, he escapes from a Siberian camp into the "forest." To indicate that this spatial dimension is to be defined as a world beyond the everyday limits of experience, Conrad uses the adjective "endless." It is the path of trials which Peter Ivanovitch must travel to derive his world-redeeming elixir as a savior in the social sphere and his illumination in the personal realm. The romantic equivalent of supernatural aid comes from "a quiet pale-faced girl" whose lover has died in prison; the mythic weapon of supernatural power is not a sword like Arthur's Excalibur, but a file—which suits the modern claustrophobic inferno of the self and soul, and which the "heroic fugitive" proceeds to lose. Indeed, his clanking chains, themselves still half-attached, parody the magic winged shoes or cloak of invisibility by which other heroes have been better able to withstand the terrors of their adventures. Within the strange night-world of the forest which defies the logic of civilization, he is brutalized: he becomes "very fierce"; his clothes "drop off him"; it "seemed as though he had lost the faculty of speech"; he goes eastward "instinctively."

His naked tawny figure glimpsed vaguely through the bushes with a cloud of mosquitoes and flies hovering about the shaggy head, spread tales of terror through whole districts. His temper grew savage as the days went by, and he was glad to discover that there was so much of a brute in him. He had nothing else to put his trust in. For it was as though there had been two human beings indissolubly joined in that enterprise. The civilized man, the enthusiast of advanced humanitarian ideals thirsting for the triumph of spiritual love and political liberty; and the stealthy, primeval savage, pitilessly cunning in the preservation of his freedom from day to day, like a tracked wild beast.[101]

He is himself the monster that as hero he must confront and kill. The flies around his head are both the torments of the devil and his infernal halo. Finally, saved from the beast within by the tears of pity of a liberating female presence, he cannot marry her because she is the "newly-wedded wife of the village blacksmith."

The world-redeeming elixir which he carries back into the real world is nothing more than the "gospel of feminism," the "cult of the woman," the "conviction of woman's spiritual superiority." But Peter Ivanovitch practices it under the "rites of special devotion to the transcendental merits of a certain Madame de S——, a lady of advanced views, no longer young, once upon a time the intriguing wife of a now dead and forgotten diplomat."[102] Because the images Conrad assigns to her make her a static figure of death in a sepulchral landscape, she caricatures the traditional goddess of eternal life from the timeless "once-upon-a-time" world: she is old, not young; widow, not virgin; witch-like, not beautiful. Because she is financially useful to the advocates of social revolution, she might be regarded as the prophetic presence who guards the treasure from which all spiritual and terrestrial power flows. But though "her carmine lips vaticinate[d]," her utterances are abstract and meaningless: one must "spiritualize the discontent." Moreover, the redeeming pity that both she and Peter Ivanovitch celebrate in theory, they cannot extend to so poor a figure as Tekla, the constant victim of their domestic tyranny. Though Peter Ivanovitch advocates salvation through action to Natalia Haldin, the necessity to "descend into the arena," he himself does not act but rather hides behind

<hr>

[101] *Ibid.*, p. 122.　　　　　　　　[102] *Ibid.*, p. 125.

his empty rhetoric as he hides behind the mask of his dark glasses and his formless beard.

Perhaps the greatest hindrance to our sympathetic acceptance of Peter Ivanovitch's role is the way Conrad alternates between the former's stale rhetoric and the narrator's understated comments. First, Peter Ivanovitch himself sees his book as a document designed to elevate humanity. In his conscious public pose he manifests another form of personal egotism devoid of self-knowledge. The narrator describes Peter Ivanovitch by the tag phrase "heroic fugitive"; his book contains "mystic significance." But the narrator cannot remember the "weight and length of the fetters riveted to his limbs."[103] When he describes the moment of his freedom, he imagistically draws a tableau suitably histrionic, which the narrator quotes verbatim: " 'My fetters'—the book says—'were struck off on the banks of the stream, in the starlight of a calm night by an athletic taciturn young man of the people, kneeling at my feet, while the woman like a liberating genius stood by with clasped hands.' "[104] And the narrator's dry addition is "obviously a symbolic couple."

Finally, Peter Ivanovitch, the suffering and tormented man, is never seen. He appears only behind the mask of his dark glasses and is viewed constantly from the perspective of an unsympathetic observer. Though his self-analysis may be as tormented as Razumov's, the English teacher of languages—and Conrad—never allows us a glimpse of the searching self. Perhaps one might say that Peter Ivanovitch's quest is all outward on a narrative and active level only; Razumov's, all inward.

The man whom Conrad devises to tell the story of Razumov is more than a measure for authorial and/or audience evaluation of character and situation. If Razumov's most obvious second self is Haldin, the emotional being whom Razumov must accept within himself to become a complete man, the narrator is also a second self, the man Razumov might have become had not the "restless and unsound" Haldin "startled him one dark night." The narrator proclaims himself, after all, a "mere professor," "a teacher of languages." The Razumov who inspires confidence in others because

---

[103] *Ibid.*, p. 120.   [104] *Ibid.*, p. 124.

of his reserve, the Razumov who has a public life only, the Razumov whose parentage is defined by the label *Russia*, wants to be "a celebrated old professor, decorated, possibly a Privy Councillor, one of the glories of Russia—nothing more!"[105] Razumov's repressed emotional life manifests itself during the early pages of the novel in his extraordinary reserve, that reserve that inspires Haldin's confidence, that causes Razumov, seething within, to listen to Haldin without any external ruffle, that, finally, enables him to ingratiate himself into the revolutionary cabals of Switzerland. Surely the English narrator, to whom Natalia Haldin gives Razumov's journal —the pages of which are the "document" that provide the story of *Under Western Eyes*—surely he is meant to respond to the written passages describing Haldin's apparent respect for Razumov's "peace of bitter calmness." When the latter is confronted by the discord of the assassin's presence, his silent astonishment evokes an admiring retort. " 'To be sure, I cannot expect you with your frigid English manner to embrace me.' "[106] Again, Victor's confidences do not excite this fellow, " 'Collected—cool as a cucumber. A regular Englishman.' " Only the most imperceptive reader, a reader as obtuse as the narrator pretends to be, may not comprehend that the comparison between the editor of the journal and its writer is both valid and desirable.

The narrator himself admits his own reserve. After he tells Natalia of her brother's death, he notes "I was grateful to Miss Haldin for not embarrasing me by an outward display of deep feeling."[107] When tears do begin to flow "unrestrained" and Natalia turns her back to him, he slips "away without attempting even to approach her." He often excuses his reactions and silences to Natalia's words because by his attention she believes that he "understood her much better than . . . [he] was able to do. . . . The attention she could see was quite sincere, so that the silence could not be suspected of coldness. It seemed to satisfy her."[108] But he reveals that, in truth, he does not understand her, a failure resulting from the obvious national differences between the Russian temperament and the English, the emotional and the logical, the "simple" and the "complex." His anxious curiosity about the details of Razumov's first

---

105 *Ibid.*, p. 13.   106 *Ibid.*, p. 16.   107 *Ibid.*, p. 112.   108 *Ibid.*, p. 118.

meeting with Natalia only reveals itself verbally, in his questions. "My physiognomy has never been expressive. . . ." With irony only the reader can detect, the narrator has unqualified admiration for Razumov's coolness when Natalia tells of their first meeting.

> "Mr. Razumov seems to be a man of few words. A reserved man— even when he is strongly moved." . . . I said that I took this for a favourable trait of character. It was associated with sincerity—in my mind.[109]

Finally, the narrator again and again reports his feelings for Natalia, feelings he attributes both to his desire to "save" her from the clutches of the inhabitants of Château Borel (only the later possession of the journal informs him of the necessity of "saving" her from Razumov) and to his pity for her lonely future. He purports to realize that she, who is "very capable of being roused by an idea or simply by a person,"[110] could never find him that "person." While denying his qualifications as a suitor—he is too old, his ideas are not "Russian"—he constantly reiterates his attraction to her. ". . . I became aware, notwithstanding my years, how attractive physically her personality could be to a man capable of appreciating in a woman something else than the mere grace of femininity."[111] Her "masculine handshake" is "seductive to him." "Her voice was deep, almost harsh, and yet caressing in its harshness."[112] Before his final gimpse of Razumov in Natalia's apartment, he rationalizes his attitude toward the girl.

> If anyone wishes to remark that this was a roundabout way of think-ing of Natalia Haldin, I can only retort that she was well worth some concern. She had all her life before her. Let it be admitted, then, that I was thinking of Natalia Haldin's life in terms of her mother's character, a manner of thinking about a girl permissible for an old man, not too old yet to have become a stranger to pity.[113]

The mental habits imposed by his long "bachelor" life as a teacher of languages will not now allow him to explode as Razumov does in his confession and letter. He cannot transcend the restraint of

---

[109] *Ibid.*, p. 173.   [110] *Ibid.*, p. 102.   [111] *Ibid.*

[112] *Ibid.*   [113] *Ibid.*, pp. 318–19.

a lifetime. In the end he is only an observer—he insists upon this role several times—with only one moment of misdirected rage after Razumov's confession to Natalia (Razumov does not even see him at this encounter). The final moment of self-deception comes when he reveals his "success" as observer and passive confidant: Natalia Haldin will return to Russia to perpetuate her brother's revolutionary ideology. Perhaps, however, this is simply ironic self-deprecation.

Like Razumov, the narrator has absolutely no one to whom he can communicate his most intense experiences. His internal life can be inferred from his brief statements about himself and his longer speculations about others. Much of his attraction to Natalia results from his solitary existence. And though the most Conradian statements concerning moral loneliness are given to him in his role of editor, the seductive qualities that the girl exudes are those which can appeal to a man who has retreated from involvement. They all unconsciously relate to her brother. Her main conversational gambit is that brother who is committed to an idea and, as he later discovers, to action. What the narrator stresses in describing her is the masculine, rather than the feminine. It is the Victor Haldin within Natalia that calls forth his greatest enthusiasm and his few groping attempts at personal involvement. The brother's soul living on within the sister serves the same function in attempting to give wholeness to the narrator's life as Haldin's second self does in making Razumov look within. The presentation of the Englishman's attempts at integration is less obvious, but no less real. And his failure is significant because it is a reflection of a self Razumov never becomes, a bodily self from which Razumov is saved by Haldin's intrusion which, paradoxically, also damns him.

That both narrator and protagonist create fictional worlds which are then unified into the author's novel seems obvious. The Englishman not only edits Razumov's journal, given to him by Natalia, but also filters this story of Russians through his Western perspective. Denying that he has "high gifts of imagination and expression" —he is, after all, merely a "teacher of languages"—he yet presents his "documentary evidence" with the skill of a novelist.

> If I have ever had these gifts in any sort of living form they have been smothered out of existence a long time ago under a wilderness of words. Words, as is well known, are the great foes of reality. I have

been for many years a teacher of languages. It is an occupation which at length becomes fatal to whatever share of imagination, observation, and insight an ordinary person may be heir to.[114]

His intellectual obtuseness, however, is always so manipulated by Conrad that the reader can perceive the difference between fictional delusion and reality. While wondering why Razumov has committed his story to paper, he yet succeeds in blundering upon a partial truth. "There must be a wonderful soothing power in mere words since so many men have used them for self-communion. Being myself a quiet individual I take it that what all men are really after is some form or perhaps only some formula of peace."[115] Here are two men for whom the usual social and familial relationships of human groups do not exist. One, forced into guilty action, resorts to the words of a journal as an outlet for his submerged longings for communication; the other, while justifying his lack of involvement upon words, allows his repressions the sublimation of sympathetic identification only. The second "edits" the words written by the first to calm himself, to "reconcile him to his existence" —though, of course, Razumov's early repressions make him aware of the "danger of that strange self-indulgence."

Later, the narrator very reliably gives a second reason for Razumov's indulging in the luxury of a journal.

The very words I use in my narrative are written where their sincerity cannot be suspected. The record, which could not have been meant for anyone's eyes but his own, was not, I think, the outcome of that strange impulse of indiscretion common to men who lead secret lives, and accounting for the invariable existence of "compromising documents" in all the plots and conspiracies of history. Mr. Razumov looked at it, I suppose, as a man looks at himself in a mirror, with wonder, perhaps with anguish, with anger or despair. Yes, as a threatened man may look fearfully at his own face in the glass, formulating to himself reassuring excuses for his appearance marked by the taint of some insidious hereditary disease.[116]

Like the Puritans, for whom no daily activity was too trivial to find utterance in their "spiritual autobiographies,"[117] Razumov's journal

---

[114] *Ibid.*, p. 3. [115] *Ibid.*, p. 5. [116] *Ibid.*, p. 214.

[117] Perry Miller and Thomas H. Johnson, eds., *The Puritans* (New York, 1938), pp. 461–62.

serves to reveal the workings of the self to the participant. But whereas the Puritan sought to detect patterns within daily life that indicated the possibility of his personal salvation, achieved only through the grace of God, Razumov's record mirrors the progress of the self in quest of its own identity and of a soul in quest of completion. And it is the glass within which Razumov may predict his future. The teacher of languages begins by attributing his failure to understand Razumov and the revolutionaries upon his Western complexity, his "European remoteness," but in the end he is able through the anguished journal to make the moral distinction between Razumov's final resurrection through suffering and the self-delusive behavior of the others. Razumov's agonizing "I want to be understood" must finally be comprehended when filtered through the vision of a man the student hardly knew. But the hesitancy of the narrator in defining Razumov's role as a journal-writer, the "I think" and "I suppose" of the quoted paragraph, may indicate that the journal is also the mirror within which the narrator could see, if he wished, his own inadequacy, could predict the despair which threatened himself as well.

Ultimately what seem like lapses in narrative technique are occasions by which Conrad may reaffirm the emotional links between the minds of the two men. Part III, as Guerard points out, begins with an omniscient narrator who limits his knowledge to the consciousness of Razumov, but gradually Razumov walks into the perception of the first-person narrator.[118] It is as if the second self that is the narrator so intimately absorbs Razumov's being that there is for three pages no real distinction between the minds of the two men.

The most persistent and consistent image appears in the title *Under Western Eyes*, perhaps simply a metaphor that the story takes place in a West European country or that it appears through the perspective of a man of the West. "He had lowered at last his fascinated glance; she too was looking down, and standing thus before each other in the glaring light, between the four bare walls, they seemed brought out from the confused immensity of the Eastern borders to be exposed cruelly to the observation of my Western

---

[118] Guerard, "Two Versions of Anarchy," *Conrad the Novelist*, p. 249.

eyes."[119] Such is the emphasis upon that feature of the face that almost every character is described in terms of it. Razumov, when he first encounters Victor Haldin in his room, wishes the assassin would take away himself and his "ugly eyes." And he remembers Haldin lying upon his couch with his arm flung over his eyes—as if preventing the soul from emerging to pursue the man who will betray him. But the shadow that represents the soul has already begun to pursue him. Haldin himself inspires Razumov with the desire to seek Natalia, who will perpetuate his soul and who has "trustful eyes." The narrator rejoices that Natalia's eyes are "frank and open" whereas General T——'s goggle eyes, which also appear as "blue unbelieving eyes," proclaim his perpetual distrust of his fellow-man. "This goggle-eyed imbecile understands nothing." They are the eyes of a man who remorselessly ferrets out the secrets of "subversive minds"; of a man whose "existence has been built on fidelity" to the threatened institutions of autocracy. Councillor of State Mikulin, as befits his gentler methods and more subtle insinuations, has a "mild, expectant glance" "not curious, not inquisitive—certainly not suspicious—almost without expression."[120] Peter Ivanovitch, on the other hand, wears "spectacles with smoked glasses" and because of this, and his beard, he is "a mere appearance of flesh and hair with not a single feature having any sort of character. His eyes being hidden by the dark glasses there was an utter absence of all expression."[121] The glasses are the mask he assumes before the world; behind them he plays his role of "heroic fugitive" on the stage of secret revolutionary activity that is Geneva. Himself "masked by the dark blue glasses," he suggests to the betrayer of Victor Haldin a "good open-hearted talk in one of the shady alleys behind the house"[122]—a scene, at least, of dubious suggestibility hardly calculated to inspire an "open-hearted talk." That only the whites of Ziemianitch's eyes are seen indicates a total loss of his rational faculties and a descent into an animal state of consciousness. Of that "bright Russian soul" Razumov notes that "his eyeballs blinked all white in the light once, twice—then the gleam went out."[123]

---

[119] Conrad, *Under Western Eyes*, p. 346.

[120] *Ibid.*, p. 86.   [121] *Ibid.*, p. 120.   [122] *Ibid.*, p. 173.   [123] *Ibid.*, p. 30.

But if eyes are chosen to recall the personality of the actor—if indeed they are the "mirror of the soul"—they are also the means by which the soul of a man may be influenced by another and may reveal the possession of that second soul. In effect, drunkenness, causing Ziemianitch to forget that he is created in the "image of God"—reasonable—makes him susceptible to the influence of the devil who, he believes, beats him. Once Haldin possesses Razumov's soul, then the latter's eyes no longer function simply as organs to perceive the phenomena of the world of objects. Rather, he begins to have visions or hallucinations which mirror his internal chaos. That Haldin is eternally present becomes clear in Razumov's "extraordinary hallucined, anguished, and absent expression"; he "looked worse than if he had seen the dead." He does not see the narrator as he wanders sightlessly past him before going to admit his crime to Natalia, but the Englishman comments upon his having "the expression of a somnambulist struggling with the very dream which drives him forth to wander in dangerous places."[124] Eleanora, Madame de S——, in her death-like rigidity, seems an "ancient, painted mummy with unfathomable eyes." Her witch-like quality derives sanction both from her reputed ability to "see your very soul" and from Razumov's heightened imagination by which he believes she is "looking at something which was visible to her behind him." Hers is the literary version of the traditional evil-eye that countless societies assign to the purveyor of black magic or to the person born with some visible abnormality of the eye—whether wall-eyes, cross-eyes, or double pupils.

In Razumov's moment of revelation, he relates Victor's claim that Natalia has "trustful eyes"—that is, that she has " 'no guile, no deception, no falsehood, no suspicion—nothing in your heart that could give you a conception of a living, acting, speaking lie, if ever it came in your way.' "[125] When his letter to her finally explains everything, he again speaks of her defenselessness. " 'I remembered the shadow of your eyelashes over your grey trustful eyes.' "[126] He juxtaposes in his discourse both her trustful eyes and his intention to steal her soul. Indeed, he purports to remember

---

[124] *Ibid.*, p. 317.   [125] *Ibid.*, p. 349.   [126] *Ibid.*, p. 361.

Haldin's belief that she will immortalize "his visionary soul" when he looks into the sister's eyes.

Yet Razumov does not consciously exert the destructive influence over Natalia's soul that he defined in his letter. Rather, Conrad emphasizes the same image in its conventional usage—as a reference to human comprehension, to the dominances of rational processes in experience—at the same time that he has Razumov proclaim the possibility of demonic possession. The narrator points out that, though Razumov's face is full of "unexplained suffering," the "look in his eye of dull, absent obstinacy . . . began to pass away."[127] "He seemed to me to be watching himself inwardly, as though he were trying to count his own heartbeats, while his eyes never for a moment left the face of the girl."[128] So too the torture which the struggle of a divided self causes becomes apparent. "It was as though he had stabbed himself outside and had come in there to show it; and more than that—as though he were turning the knife in the wound and watching the effect."[129] Razumov's confession, his final recognition of his guilt, and his acceptance of his irrational action partially free him from the influence of his victim and make him accept the responsibility of his deed. He rushes out to his symbolic death.

But neither the girl nor the narrator, to whom the Russian couple "seemed brought out from the confused immensity of the Eastern borders to be exposed cruelly to the observation of my Western eyes,"[130] can accept Razumov's "appalling expressionless tranquillity." At first Natalia shivers before Razumov's stare, asserting her own frankness and her need "to see clearly in myself"; the narrator remarks, however, that "she was unable to see the truth struggling to his lips."[131] When she perceives the truth, she is unable to comprehend the double-edged effect of her brother's quoted words " '. . . that [it] does not matter if a man always serves something greater than himself—the idea.' "[132] Rather, she loses her soul not to her brother's murderer but to those dark demonic forces which have pursued her from the immensity of Russia and which are represented on Swiss soil by Château Borel.

---

127 *Ibid.*, p. 342.   128 *Ibid.*, p. 349.   129 *Ibid.*, p. 351.
130 *Ibid.*, p. 346.   131 *Ibid.*, p. 354.   132 *Ibid.*, p. 353.

The narrator's shifting presentation of the same image pattern is the reader's clue to his own gradual awareness of truth. His first encounters with Natalia Haldin imbue him with the dark curse of autocratic action which pursues the sister of the man anticipating the future "dawn of concord": "I saw then the shadow of autocracy lying upon Russian lives in their submission or their revolt. I saw it touch her handsome open face nestled in a fur collar and darken her clear eyes that shone upon me brilliantly grey in the murky light of a beclouded, inclement afternoon."[133] For the narrator, as for Razumov, these eyes are frank, innocent, without guile. But as long-haunted, brooding Razumov stands before Natalia, claiming that he is "clear-eyed," the old teacher of languages begins to realize that both are trapped by their origin, the Russian experience itself, whether autocratic or revolutionary.

> To me, the silent spectator, they looked like two people becoming conscious of a spell which had been lying on them ever since they first set eyes on each other. Had either of them cast a glance then in my direction, I would have opened the door quietly and gone out. But neither did; and I remained, every fear of indiscretion lost in the sense of my enormous remoteness from their captivity within the sombre horizon of Russian problems, the boundary of their eyes, of their feelings—the prison of their souls.[134]

Here are mingled in an image cluster that the entire book evidences the two words suggesting that man's abstractions—whether the self-soul desiring some personal immortality or the mind possessing the eternal idea of unity and concord—have their seat in the human eye. The "spell," that staple motif from the fairy tale world, functions here to show that man cannot escape the potentiality of evil which entraps, paradoxically, by means of those very organs of sight by which two people first become acquainted. But the forces which entice and compel are dark, are "somber," or seem "shadows"—images from which one may infer certain truths both about the external world and about the individual soul. When Razumov rushes off with Natalia's veil, having illuminated the world of falsehood by the facts and, symbolically, having given her new insight,

---

[133] Ibid., p. 109.   [134] Ibid., pp. 344–45.

the slamming of the door restores the narrator's "sight" and he perceives not only Razumov's departure but also Natalia's complete lack of understanding. Free from guile, she becomes a prisoner of "the falsehood-breeding spectre" of social revolution. Victor's soul goes on "warring in her."

> She raised her grey eyes slowly. Shadows seemed to come and go in them as if the steady flame of her soul had been made to vacillate at last in the cross-currents of poisoned air from the corrupted dark immensity claiming her for its own, where virtues themselves fester into crimes in the cynicism of oppression and revolt.[135]

Ironically, it is her presence, soon to be consumed by shadows, Razumov asserts in his letter, that has saved him: 'It was as if your pure brow bore a light which fell on me, searched my heart and saved me from ignominy, from ultimate undoing' ";[136] that "light" has freed him " 'from the blindness of anger and hate—the truth shining in you drew the truth out of me.' "[137] But if Razumov's self-awareness results from Natalia's presence, her eventual blindness stems from the concrete knowledge of her brother's death. She is destroyed as a sympathetic and unified human being by the truth, the light of which she symbolically represents. Her "overshadowed eyes" become the mirror of her soul. The Natalia Haldin of the end of the novel becomes very like the Razumov of the beginning, having only a public life, repressing all personal emotion, all feeling, all identity. "There was no longer any Natalia Haldin, because she had completely ceased to think of herself. It was a great victory, a characteristically Russian exploit in self-suppression."[138] Although she believes that her " 'eyes are open at last and . . . [her] hands are free now,' "[139] she returns to Russia to continue her brother's work without realizing the mental contagions of the world that has taken her for its own. She rejects Razumov's suffering—the possibility of individual human companionship—for a vision of the future, an abstract community of mankind.

The man who ends by intuitively understanding the events he records claims to be the "silent spectator" of their Russian world—

---

[135] *Ibid.*, p. 356.   [136] *Ibid.*, p. 361.   [137] *Ibid.*

[138] *Ibid.*, p. 375.   [139] *Ibid.*, p. 376.

whether it be the immense parent to whom Razumov clings in his journal or the disorder of the expatriots of Château Borel. He makes the equation between the journal and the glass into which a man looks to know the nature of his interior self. As the act of reading his own words reveals Razumov to himself, so the journal is constantly "under Western eyes." When the English teacher of languages responds to the inability of the revolutionaries to understand Tekla and her personal loyalty, his answer, "There is not much perspicacity in the world," might be taken as a blanket admission of the failure of personal integration and individual community, the dominance of irrationality and unrest. So earlier Razumov has told Sophia Antonovna, who claims to understand him, that her "perspicacity is at fault." That the old Englishman persists to the end, however, in stressing his role as a "mute witness of things Russian, unrolling their Eastern logic under my Western eyes,"[140] simply reiterates his ultimate inability to see that Razumov's journal is his mirror too, and that a timeless document makes Western eyes project their visions into the immensity of space until they subsume the visions of all eyes. Without the introspective and brooding sensibility that characterizes Razumov during his quest, the narrator has further been conditioned to regard words as "foes of reality." Unlike Razumov, he has never seen "haunting shapes" that cannot be "exorcised"; unlike Razumov his reserve has never been shattered by the emergence of an "apparition" like Haldin to challenge his secret life. But if he fails to admit the intimacy between his own and Razumov's situation, he yet performs a most significant communal service: he judiciously tells the final tale, making a unity of Razumov's "document," his spectator's experience, and the information derived from Natalia and Sophia Antonovna. He bridges the student Razumov's vision which begins with Conrad and ends with us. And he survives as at once the partial, static, and parodic hero, the man who, in a world without hope, watches, rather than the man who acts.

---

[140] *Ibid.*, p. 381.

New Myths for a
Profane Civilization

The hero of myth or of the literature of a "mythologically-charged" society mirrored the collective needs of the group. His traditional quest was undertaken not to enhance his personal prestige but to destroy the forces of darkness threatening to swallow or annihilate his people. Never did he forget his communal responsibility in the gigantic heroism of his actions or in the magnitude of his suffering. Nor was his ritual death a cause for sorrow. Instead, his descent into the underworld was simply a manifestation of his selflessness, his destruction of ego. For within the ambiguous realms of the dead, he found the means for revitalizing his society—the elixir of eternal life. And his ritual rebirth was also a promise to his people of the existence of an eternal order beyond the constant flux of time and the bodily decline to death. In identifying itself with him, the community might recognize the timeless components within themselves. Redeemed by him, they also shared in his heroism and his divinity. Society and hero were one.

But the novel is the genre of a society predicated upon the recognition that every man is equal to every other man in opportunity if not in birth, that every man is a self-determining unit, that each human being is independent "both from other individuals and from that multifarious allegiance to past modes of thought and action denoted by the word 'tradition'—a force that is always social, not individual."[1] Cut off from the past, obsessed by the physical fact of time rather than comforted by the recognition of traditional values that are timeless, today's man lives in a secularized world which has lost its sense of community and identity. The growing desire for the analysis of experience, the emphasis on accumulation of wealth, the gradual diminution of the hierarchical structure of society—all these have augmented the oppressive senses of personal isolation. Even intense loneliness can no longer be shared. The hell described by religion has, indeed, become a hell within, a private inferno of titanic discontent.

What the contemporary novel does is to manifest openly and honestly the genuine despair, the impotence, the frustration and failure, the social and self-estrangement which is the burden of the twentieth-century hero. The heroes of our fiction cannot resolve collective problems, for they inhabit a world which is a particular vision of the world we know. And the world we know is an individually oriented society that promises man at once infinite choice and infinite frustration by baffling his every move, by confusing his senses, by causing him to meditate so tortuously that he cannot act, or by destroying his material or spiritual resources.

Having for years embezzled the trust funds of a young man for whom he is responsible (a characteristic modern crime to be compared with the earlier rape of kingdoms), the impotent narrator of Conrad's and Ford's *The Nature of a Crime* finally writes to the woman he has long silently loved. He claims that he is a man of his time, a time "not of great deeds but of colossal speculations."[2] The word "speculations" assumes an added irony in the consideration of the theme of the story. This defender and defiler of the established order is what Guerard has called an "anti-hero, one of the introspective and self-destructive neurotic[s] of much modern fiction, from Dostoevsky to the present."[3] But, as Guerard recognizes, these anti-

---

[1] Watt, *The Rise of the Novel*, p. 60.

[2] Joseph Conrad and Ford Madox Hueffer, *The Nature of a Crime* (London, 1924), p. 24.

[3] Albert J. Guerard, "The Vanishing Hero of the Modern Novel" (unpublished lecture). Some of the types of anti-hero that I discuss are taken from this lecture.

heroes are heroes—defeated, anxious, pessimistic, more often than not inhabitants of our nightmares instead of products of our day dreams—but heroes nevertheless. These include the "guilty repudiator of self,"[4] such as the self-destructive "mouse" of Dostoevsky's *Notes from Underground;* the impotent, apathetic narrators of Ford, or of Hemingway's *The Sun Also Rises,* whose inertia or physical wounds reflect the malaise of society; the dehumanized products of mechanistic urban mediocrity found in Kafka; the flabby, disintegrating humanity of *The Secret Agent* or of Graham Greene's *The Power and the Glory.* At the extreme end of the social, mental, and moral continuum are the idiots, the Benjys, the Stevies—and the Jim Bonds—who we hope will not inherit the world. All have one thing in common: by their meditations or meaningless actions or neuroses or contradictory impulses they reassert the irrational nature of man and of human life in general. In the final moments of his life, Joseph K., that epitome of rational urban man, reluctantly recognizes the truth of his past insignificant life and of his equally meaningless arrest and condemnation: "Logic is doubtless unshakable, but it cannot withstand a man who wants to go on living."[5] The whole heritage of Aristotelian order cannot sustain him.

The use of myth in modern fiction attempts to recognize the irrational found in society and to channel that irrational into artistic visions. It proposes to re-establish the validity of past values based upon belief rather than upon sense data. By using motifs which are traditional—and, therefore, social—the individual author endows the apparently asocial hero with universal significance. We, as readers who are unwilling to admit the Joe Christmas within ourselves, may let the imperfect use of motifs derived from the story of Christ's life work upon the undifferentiated sections of our consciousness until unconscious identification does evoke sympathy.

Archetypal patterns in the novel may, on the other hand, indicate the real despair and misery which must be the lot of the present-day hero and modern man. Our writers do not exult at the awareness

---

[4] *Ibid.*

[5] Franz Kafka, *The Trial,* trans. Willa and Edwin Muir, rev. E. M. Butler (New York, 1959), p. 286.

that all life is "sacred repetition," that "there is nothing new under the sun," that the hero may die but will surely be reborn either individually or as another manifestation of a particular type. Rather, traditional forms make more ironic the unidealized pictures of modern fiction, show us how very great is the disparity between the homogeneous societies of the past or of present primitive cultures and our own spiritually sick, morally void, emotionally damned world without belief. The contemporary hero's inactive deeds or active thoughts only parody the violent actions of the earlier hero who defended his fellows against nature, or against hostile deities— against forces larger than himself. Our hero's chief antagonist is very simply (and very complexly) another part of himself which must be conquered (and often cannot be) before he can achieve identity and become reintegrated into the social unit.

All this does not mean to imply that the novel is a decadent art form and that the use of myth, by reiterating society's and, consequently, the novel's loss of eternal values, further devaluates the genre. It is society which has become the gross parody of that earlier world where the moral and the desirable tended to fuse inextricably; it is the society of urban mechanization, of nuclear arms, and of international tensions that promises inhuman life and threatens annihilation. And the novel skillfully reveals this decadence, using allusions, images, and typical motifs derived from a stable and socially oriented past as a device for irony.

Where earlier genres employing myth reveled in the heroism of noble actions, the novel has gradually shifted its emphasis. Intensity of despair, the internalized anguish which, as in Decoud's case, may cause the cessation of all action, provide the genuine heroism of much modern fiction. The night-sea journey of older oral narratives furnishes the novelist with a form for the internal quest, a form that appeals at once to our childlike love of story and to our more mature recognition of our own personal involvement. For most of the twentieth-century fiction of despair and absurdity dramatizes our personal night-sea journeys. Its authors give our colossal nightmares ritual form by their narratives, the "myths" of a profane civilization.

Bibliography

I. Works by Joseph Conrad

Conrad, Joseph. *Complete Works*. Kent Edition. 25 vols. Garden City, N.Y.: Doubleday, Page & Co., 1926. The Concord and Canterbury editions, also published by Doubleday, and the British editions of J. M. Dent & Sons follow the same pagination. Volumes V and VII were written by Conrad and Ford Madox Ford (then Hueffer).

————. *Nostromo*. New York: Modern Library, 1951. This is included in the *Complete Works* but is based upon an edition published by Doubleday & Co. in 1904 and differs slightly from Vol. IX of the Kent Edition.

————. *The Secret Agent: A Drama in Three Acts*. London: T. Werner Laurie Ltd., 1923.

————. *The Sisters*. Intro. Ford Madox Ford. New York: Crosby Gaige, 1928.

Conrad, Joseph, and Hueffer, Ford Madox. *The Nature of a Crime*. London: Duckworth, [1924].

II. Works about Joseph Conrad

Allen, Jerry. *The Sea Years of Joseph Conrad*. Garden City, N.Y.: Doubleday & Co., Inc., 1965.

————. *The Thunder and the Sunshine: A Biography of Joseph Conrad*. New York: G. P. Putnam's Sons, 1958.

Baines, Jocelyn. *Joseph Conrad: A Critical Biography*. London: Weidenfeld & Nicolson, 1960.

177

Baines, Jocelyn. "The Affair in Marseilles," *The London Magazine*, IV (November, 1957), 41–46.

Bradbrook, M. C. *Joseph Conrad: Poland's English Genius.* Cambridge: At the University Press, 1941.

Conrad, Jessie. *Joseph Conrad and His Circle.* London: Jarrolds Publishers, 1935.

———. *Joseph Conrad as I Knew Him.* Garden City, N.Y.: Doubleday, Page & Co., 1927.

Curle, Richard (ed.). *Letters: Joseph Conrad to Richard Curle.* New York: Crosby Gaige, 1928.

Ford, Ford Madox. *Joseph Conrad: A Personal Remembrance.* Boston: Little, Brown & Co., 1924.

Gordan, John Dozier. *Joseph Conrad: The Making of a Novelist.* Cambridge, Mass.: Harvard University Press, 1940.

Guerard, Albert J. *Conrad the Novelist.* Cambridge, Mass.: Harvard University Press, 1958.

———. *Joseph Conrad.* New York: New Directions, 1947.

Hay, Eloise Knapp. *The Political Novels of Joseph Conrad.* Chicago & London: University of Chicago Press, 1963.

Hewitt, Douglas. *Conrad: A Reassessment.* Cambridge: Bowes & Bowes, 1952.

Howe, Irving. "Conrad: Order and Anarchy," *Politics and the Novel.* New York: Horizon Press, 1957.

Hueffer, Ford Madox. See Ford, Ford Madox.

Jean-Aubry, G. *Joseph Conrad in the Congo.* London: "The Bookman's Journal" Office, 1926.

———. *Joseph Conrad: Life and Letters.* 2 vols. Garden City, N.Y.: Doubleday, Page & Co., 1927.

———. *The Sea Dreamer: Joseph Conrad.* Trans. Helen Sebba. Garden City, N.Y.: Doubleday, Page & Co., 1957.

Leavis, F. R. "Joseph Conrad," *The Great Tradition.* Garden City, N.Y.: Doubleday Anchor Books, 1954.

Morf, Gustav. *The Polish Heritage of Joseph Conrad.* London: Sampson, Low, Marston & Co., Ltd., [1930].

Moser, Thomas. *Joseph Conrad: Achievement and Decline.* Cambridge, Mass.: Harvard University Press, 1957.

Van Ghent, Dorothy. "On Lord Jim," *The English Novel: Form and Function.* New York: Rinehart & Co., 1953. Pp. 229–44.

Visiak, E. H. *The Mirror of Conrad.* London: Werner Laurie, 1955.

Walpole, Hugh. *Joseph Conrad.* London: Nisbet & Co. Ltd., 1940.

Warren, Robert Penn. Introduction to *Nostromo*. New York: Modern Library, 1951. Pp. vii–xxxix.

Wiley, Paul L. *Conrad's Measure of Man*. Madison: University of Wisconsin Press, 1954.

Wright, Walter F. *Romance and Tragedy in Joseph Conrad*. Lincoln: University of Nebraska Press, 1949.

Zabel, Morton Dauwen. Introduction to *The Portable Conrad*. New York: Viking Press, 1947. Pp. 1–47.

——. Introduction to *Under Western Eyes*, by Joseph Conrad. Garden City, N.Y.: Doubleday Anchor Books, 1963.

III. Works on Myth and Literature

Abraham, Karl. *Dreams and Myths*. Trans. William A. White. Nervous and Mental Disease Monograph Series, No. 15. New York: Journal of Nervous and Mental Disease Publishing Co., 1913.

Auden, W. H. *The Enchafèd Flood or The Romantic Iconography of the Sea*. London: Faber & Faber Ltd., 1951.

Bodkin, Maud. *Archetypal Patterns in Poetry*. London: Oxford University Press, 1934.

——. *Studies of Type-Images in Poetry, Religion and Philosophy*. London: Oxford University Press, 1951.

Burke, Kenneth. *The Philosophy of Literary Form: Studies in Symbolic Action*. New York: Vintage Books, 1957.

Campbell, Joseph. *The Hero with a Thousand Faces*. New York: Meridian Books, 1956.

——. *The Masks of God: Primitive Mythology*. New York: Viking Press, 1959.

Cassirer, Ernst. *Language and Myth*. Trans. Susanne K. Langer. New York: Dover, 1946.

——. "Myth and Religion," *An Essay on Man*. Garden City, N.Y.: Doubleday Anchor Books, 1954.

Dorson, Richard M. *American Folklore*. Chicago: University of Chicago Press, 1959.

Durkheim, Emile. *The Elementary Forms of the Religious Life*. Trans. Joseph Ward Swain. Glencoe, Ill.: Free Press, [1954].

Erikson, Erik. *Childhood and Society*. New York: Norton, 1950.

Fiedler, Leslie. *Love and Death in the American Novel*. New York: Criterion Books, 1960.

Fletcher, Angus. *Allegory: The Theory of a Symbolic Mode*. Ithaca, N.Y.: Cornell University Press, 1964.

Fontenrose, Joseph. *Python: A Study of Delphic Myth and Its Origins.* Berkeley and Los Angeles: University of California Press, 1959.

Frazer, Sir James George. *The Golden Bough* (1-vol. ed.). New York: Macmillan Co., 1948.

Freud, Sigmund. "A Neurosis of Demoniacal Possession in the Seventeenth Century," *Collected Papers.* Vol. IV, ed. Joan Riviere. New York: Basic Books, Inc., 1959. Pp. 436–72.

———. "Dostoevsky and Parricide," *Collected Papers.* Vol. V, ed. James Strachey. New York: Basic Books, Inc., 1959. Pp. 222–42.

———. *Moses and Monotheism.* Trans. Katherine Jones. New York: Vintage Books, 1955.

———. *New Introductory Lectures on Psycho-Analysis.* Trans. W. J. H. Sprott. New York: W. W. Norton & Co., Inc., 1933.

———. *The Interpretation of Dreams.* Trans. and ed. James Strachey. New York: Basic Books, Inc., [1955].

———. *Totem and Taboo.* Ed. James Strachey. New York: W. W. Norton & Co., Inc., 1950.

Fromm, Erich. *The Forgotten Language: An Introduction to the Understanding of Dreams, Fairy Tales and Myths.* New York: Grove Press, 1951.

Frye, Northrop. *Anatomy of Criticism.* Princeton, N.J.: Princeton University Press, 1957.

Glover, Edward. *Freud or Jung?* New York: Meridian Books, Inc., 1956. Pp. 11–51, 107–64.

Gombrich, E. H. *Meditations on a Hobby Horse and Other Essays on the Theory of Art.* London: Phaidon Press Ltd., 1963.

Guthrie, W. K. C. *The Greeks and Their Gods.* Boston: Beacon Press, 1955.

Harrison, Jane Ellen. *Ancient Art and Ritual.* London: Williams & Norgate, 1913.

———. *Themis: A Study of the Social Origins of Greek Religion.* Cambridge, England: University Press, 1912.

———. *Prolegomena to the Study of Greek Religion.* New York: Meridian Books, 1957.

Honig, Edwin. *Dark Conceit: The Making of Allegory.* Evanston, Ill.: Northwestern University Press, 1959.

Huizinga, Johan. *Homo Ludens: A Study of the Play-Element in Culture.* Boston: Beacon Press, 1955.

Hyman, Stanley Edgar. "Constance Rourke and Folk Criticism" and "Maud Bodkin and Psychological Criticism," *The Armed Vision.* New York: Alfred A. Knopf, Inc., 1948. Pp. 127–67.

James, William. *The Principles of Psychology*. 2 vols. New York: Henry Holt & Co., 1890. I, 605, 642.

Jung, C. G. *Aion: Researches into the Phenomenology of the Self*. Trans. R. F. C. Hull. Bollingen XX. New York: Pantheon Books, Inc., 1959. (Vol. 9, II of *The Collected Works of C. G. Jung*.)

———. *The Archetypes and the Collective Unconscious*. Trans. R. F. C. Hull. Bollingen XX. New York: Pantheon Books, Inc., 1959. (Vol. 9, I of *The Collected Works of C. G. Jung*.)

———. *Symbols of Transformation*. Trans. R. F. C. Hull. Bollingen XX. New York: Pantheon Books, Inc., 1956. (Vol. 5 of *The Collected Works of C. G. Jung*.)

———. *Two Essays on Analytical Psychology*. Trans. R. F. C. Hull. New York: Meridian Books, Inc., 1956.

Kahler, Erich. "The Persistence of Myth," *Chimera*, IV (Spring, 1946), 2–11.

Kluckhohn, Clyde. "Myths and Rituals: A General Theory," *The Harvard Theological Review*, XXXV (January 1942), 45–79.

Knight, W. F. Jackson. "Maze Symbolism and the Trojan Game," *Antiquity*, VI (December, 1932), 445–58.

Langer, Susanne K. *Philosophy in a New Key*. Cambridge, Mass.: Harvard University Press, 1942.

Lévi-Strauss, Claude. *La pensée sauvage*. Paris: Librairie Plon, 1962.

———. *Totemism*. Trans. Rodney Needham. Boston: Beacon Press, 1962.

Lévy-Bruhl, Lucien. *How Natives Think*. London: Allen & Unwin, 1926.

———. *L'âme primitive*. Paris: Alcan, 1927.

MacCaffrey, Isabel Gamble. *Paradise Lost as "Myth."* Cambridge, Mass.: Harvard University Press, 1959. Pp. 1–91.

Malinowski, Bronislaw. "Myth in Primitive Psychology," *Magic, Science and Religion*. Garden City, N.Y.: Doubleday Anchor Books, 1948. Pp. 93–148.

Mann, Thomas. "Freud and the Future," *Essays by Thomas Mann*. Trans. H. T. Lowe-Porter. New York: Vintage Books, 1957. Pp. 303–24.

———. "The Making of *The Magic Mountain*," *Atlantic Monthly*, January, 1953, pp. 41–45.

Manuel, Frank E. *The Eighteenth Century Confronts the Gods*. Cambridge, Mass.: Harvard University Press, 1959.

Meyerhoff, Hans. *Time in Literature*. Berkeley and Los Angeles: University of California Press, 1955.

Murray, Gilbert. *Five Stages of Greek Religion*. 3d ed. Garden City, N.Y.: Doubleday Anchor Books.

Murray, Henry. Introduction to *Pierre*, by Herman Melville. New York: Hendricks House, 1949.

"Myth and Myth-making." *Daedalus: Journal of the American Academy of Arts and Sciences*, Spring, 1959. This volume contains essays by Joseph Campbell, Clyde Kluckhohn, Northrop Frye, and Jerome Bruner that are particularly relevant to my study.

Pickard-Cambridge, A. W. "Professor Murray's Theory," *Dithyramb Tragedy and Comedy*. Oxford: Clarendon Press, 1927. Pp. 185–207.

Poulet, Georges. *Studies in Human Time*. Trans. Elliott Coleman. New York: Harper Torchbooks, 1959. Pp. 1–38.

Praz, Mario. *The Romantic Agony*. Trans. Angus Davidson. 2d ed. London: Oxford University Press, 1954.

Radcliffe-Brown, A. R. *Structure and Function in Primitive Society*. Glencoe, Ill.: Free Press, 1952. Pp. 1–31, 133–77.

Raglan, Fitzroy Richard Somerset, Fourth Baron. *The Hero*. New York: Vintage Books, 1956.

Rank, Otto. *Beyond Psychology*. New York: Dover Publications, 1958.

————. *Psychology and the Soul*. Trans. William D. Turner. New York: A. S. Barnes & Co., Inc., 1961.

————. "The Myth of the Birth of the Hero," *The Myth of the Birth of the Hero and Other Writings*. Ed. Philip Freund and trans. F. Robbins and Smith Ely Jelliffe. New York: Vintage Books, 1959. Pp. 3–96.

Seznec, Jean. *The Survival of the Pagan Gods*. Trans. Barbara F. Sessions. New York: Pantheon Books, Inc., 1953.

Van Gennep, Arnold. *The Rites of Passage*. Trans. Monika B. Vizadom and Gabrielle L. Caffee. London: Routledge & Kegan Paul, 1960.

Watt, Ian. *The Rise of the Novel*. London: Chatto & Windus, 1957.

Weber, Max. *The Protestant Ethic and the Spirit of Capitalism*. Trans. Talcott Parsons. London: George Allen & Unwin Ltd., 1956.

Weston, Jessie L. *From Ritual to Romance*. Garden City, N.Y.: Doubleday Anchor Books, 1957.

Whitehead, Alfred North. *Religion in the Making*. New York: Meridian Books, Inc., 1960.

Wimsatt, W. K., Jr., and Beardsley, Monroe. "The Intentional Fallacy," *The Verbal Icon*. New York: Noonday Press, 1958. Pp. 3–20.

Wimsatt, William K., Jr., and Brooks, Cleanth. "Myth and Archetype," *Literary Criticism: A Short History*. New York: Alfred A. Knopf, 1962. Pp. 699–720.

Zimmer, Heinrich. *The King and the Corpse: Tales of the Soul's Conquest of Evil*. Ed. and trans. Joseph Campbell. Bollingen XI. New York: Pantheon Books, Inc., 1956.

Index